HADRAT OTHMAN GHANI (R.A.)

Professor Masudul Hasan

KITAB BHAVAN
NEW DELHI-110002

KITAB BHAVAN
Publishers, Distributors, Exporters & Importers
1784, Kalan Mahal, Darya Ganj
New Delhi-110002 [India]

Phones : (91-11) 3274686, 3277392, 3277393
3258006, 3258007, 3258008
Website : http://www.kitabbhavan.com
E-Mail : nasri@nda.vsnl.net.in
Fax : (91-11) 3263383

Ist Published in India 1999

ISBN 81-7151-256-9

Book Code H00273

Fonts: Helv 10 pt.

Laser Typesetting at:
Laser Track
1784, Kalan Mahal, Darya Ganj
New Delhi-110002 [India]

Printed & Published in India by:
Nusrat Ali Nasri for Kitab Bhavan
1784, Kalan Mahal, Darya Ganj
New Delhi-110002 [India]

CONTENTS

PREFACE

I have the pleasure to present to my readers this book projecting the life story of Hadrat Othman, the third Caliph Islam. I have already produced books on Hadrat Abu Bakr Siddiq and Hadrat Umar Farooq. These books have been popular and I hope this third book in the series will also command favour with the readers.

In writing this book I had to encounter considerable difficulties. While in the case of Hadrat Abu Bakr Siddiq and Hadrat Umar Farooq the sources are plentiful and considerable material is available for research, such is not the case with reference to Hadrat Othman. The source material which has come down to us with regard to Hadrat Othman is very fragmentary and distorted. History has not done justice to Hadrat Othman. Very extensive conquests were made during the time of Hadrat Othman but full accounts of such conquests are not available. It appears that under some conspiracy, such accounts about the achievements of Hadrat Othman were purposely suppressed.

Very few biographies of Hadrat Othman have appeared so far. I have not come across any biography of Hadrat Othman in English. Two books on the biography of Hadrat Othman in Urdu are available. One of these books is by Raza Misri, while the other is by Taha Hussain who also belonged to Egypt. Both these books are Urdu versions of the works in Arabic. This means that no original work on the biography of Hadrat Othman has appeared so far either in English or in Urdu. That brings into bold relief the necessity of a suitable and sizable biography of Hadrat Othman in English and Urdu. That is the genesis of this work.

In Raza Misri's book on Hadrat Othman a few stray facts about the life of Hadrat Othman have been given. There is, however, no coherent account. Taha Hussain's book is more of an impeachment than a biography. In this book no biographical details are given. Taha Hussain's concept of a biography appears to be to project the weak points of the hero and suppress his achievements. Taha Hussain's book is more of condemnation than appreciation of Hadrat Othman.

It appears that Hadrat Othman has fallen a victim to partisan considerations and prejudices. Shia writers regard the first three Caliphs as usurpers. They condemn the caliphate of Hadrat Othman in particular. Syed Ameer Ali, a Shia writer but otherwise an eminent scholar, has assessed the caliphate of Hadrat Othman in very unfavorable terms. Even the Sunni writers have failed to do justice to Hadrat Othman. Most of the early histories were written by Sunni writers during the Abbasid period and the Approach of these writers was anti-Umayyad. As Hadrat Othman was an Umayyad, even the Sunni writers under the influence of the Abbasids suppressed the achievements of Hadrat Othman. Thus while the Shia writers have condemned the caliphate of Hadrat Othman, the Sunni writers have suppressed the facts about his achievements. Hadrat Othman has thus suffered injustice both at the hands of the Shia as well the Sunni writers.

Under the circumstances my task to write the biography of Hadrat Othman became doubly difficult. I could not accept all the facts that are available in the source books as the gospel truth. All these facts had to be tested in the first instance through objective scrutiny with a view to discovering the truth. As a result of my research I have rejected most of the accounts that are available in the source books. This book is accordingly not a mere exercise in narrating the main events in the life story of Hadrat Othman. It is primarily an attempt to rediscover Hadrat Othman. From most of the accounts that have come down to us, the general impression that is created is that Hadrat Othman was a fickle old man who was led by others and had no will of his own. This is quite incorrect. Hadrat Othman was very shrewd and intelligent and he exercised his own judgement in all important matters. He consulted men around him but he was not led by the opinion of others. He took decisions according to his own best judgement.

This book is no apology for Hadrat Othman. My purpose is not to offer a defence for Hadrat Othman for his sins of omission or commission. I do not regard Hadrat Othman as perfect man immune to mistakes. Apart from the Holy Prophet, no other person could be perfect. Hadrat Othman as such could make mistakes and he may have made mistakes but such mistakes, if any, were bonafide and these have been dilated upon in an exaggerated way by those who were for some reason or the other opposed to Hadrat Othman. I do not say that Hadrat Othman was successful as Caliph. My point is that the failure of Hadrat Othman was not due to any fault on his part, it was due to causes beyond his control. Hadrat Othman died as a martyr in the cause of truth. His memory deserves to be honoured. This book will afford help in paying due honour to the memory of Hadrat Othman.

I have divided this book into seven main chapters. Each Chapter deals with an important aspect of the life of Hadrat Othman. The first Chapter deals with the pre-caliphate period. This period covers 68 years of the life of Hadrat Othman from 576 to 644 C.E. The material for this Chapter has been obtained from the well-known biographies of the Holy Prophet, Hadrat Abu Bakr Siddiq and Hadrat Umar Farooq. I have already written biographies of Hadrat Abu Bakr Siddiq and Hadrat Umar Farooq and in writing the first Chapter of the book on Hadrat Othman, I have largely drawn on my books about Hadrat Abu Bakr Siddiq and Hadrat Umar Farooq. During this period we notice some of the main distinctions of Hadrat Othman. He was one of the earliest converts to Islam. He had unflinching faith in Islam and he successfully resisted all pressure on the part of his family members to recant from Islam. He had the unique distinction of marrying two daughters of the Holy Prophet, one after the other. He was the first to migrate to Abyssinia. On the occasion of the Hudaibiya pact, "Baiy'at ul Ridwan" was taken on his account. He was a rich man and he undertook beneficent activities in the cause of Islam on a large scale. He met a greater part of the expenditure for the financing of the expedition to Tabuk.

In the second Chapter I have given an account of the election of Hadrat Othman as the Caliph and some of the measures introduced by him as the Caliph. In some of the accounts that have come down to us an impression is tried to be created that the election of Hadrat Othman was manoeuvred by Abdur Rahman b Auf who was related to Hadrat Othman. The truth of the matter is that Abdur Rahman b Auf took pains to ascertain public opinion in the matter and a predominantly large majority of the people favoured the election of Hadrat Othman. On assuming office, Hadrat Othman had to try the case of Ubaidullah b Umar. Hadrat Othman acquitted Ubaidullah and paid the blood money. In some quarters, Hadrat Othman is criticised for this decision. According to my assessment that was a just and fair decision. As Caliph, Hadrat Othman standardised the text of the Holy Qur'ãn. In some quarters this was made the subject of criticism. Those who criticise Hadrat Othman for this measure do him and Islam a great injustice. In fact what

Hadrat Othman did was a great service to Islam. Hadrat Othman is also criticised that in the prayer at Mina on the occasion of the pilgrimage he offered full four "rakaats" of prayer and did not avail of the concession of the shortening of the prayers in accordance with the precedent set up by the Holy Prophet and followed by Hadrat Abu Bakr Siddiq and Hadrat Umar Farooq. I have shown that Hadrat Othman did the right thing and no criticism against him on this account is justified. In this Chapter I have tried to give an account of political administration, economic administration, military administration and other administrative measures of Hadrat Othman. Here we meet a dilemma. Hadrat Umar was a hard task master and he kept the people under control. On the other hand Hadrat Othman was liberal and kind-hearted. These kind and liberal policies of Hadrat Othman led to the opposite result. Instead of appreciating the liberal policies of Hadrat Othman, the people began to agitate against him and such agitation culminated in his martyrdom. Hadrat Othman failed not because there was anything wrong with him personally but because he was too good. In the course of history men do not suffer always for their vices; they sometimes suffer for their virtues as well. Hadrat Othman's case in one of the most conspicuous cases of a man suffering because of his virtues.

In the third Chapter I have referred to the Governors of the time of Hadrat Othman. In this connection the usual criticism is that he deposed other persons and appointed his relatives. I have objectively examined all the cases of depositions and my conclusion is that all such depositions were made because of just cause. I have also examined the charge of nepotism that has been levelled against Hadrat Othman. According to my assessment there is no force in this charge. Hadrat Othman did not make there appointments because he wanted to provide jobs for his relatives; he appointed such persons who could in his opinion best deliver the goods. All the persons appointed as Governors by Hadrat Othman produced the best results. Abdullah b Saad in Egypt increased the revenues of the State manifold. He conquered the whole of North Africa and even conquered parts of Spain. He also won naval battles against the Byzantines. Amir Muawiyah, the Governor of Syria, was a man of outstanding personality. He was most popular among the people. He conquered the islands of Cypress and Rhodes. He conducted many successful expeditions against the Byzantines. The Governors that Hadrat Othman appointed in the case of Kufa were capable and efficient persons, who made extensive conquests. These Governors came to grief not because there was anything wrong with them but because of the vagaries of the people of Kufa who were given to agitation. Abdullah b Aamir who was appointed by Hadrat Othman as the Governor of Basra produced the best results. The conquests made by him surpassed the conquests made by any Governor in history.

In the fourth Chapter I have given an account of the conquests made during the caliphate of Hadrat Othman. The conquests made during the caliphate of Hadrat Othman were more extensive than the conquests made during the previous regimes. On the death of Hadrat Umar, the whole of Persia rose in revolt. The Byzantines attacked Alexandria in their bid to recapture Egypt. Hadrat Othman did not merely suppress these revolts; he extended the conquests further. In the west, not only were the Byzantines repulsed from Egypt, the Muslims conquered the whole of North Africa and even landed in Spain. On the Syrian front, the Muslims conquered the islands of Cypress and Rhodes and made extensive conquests in Asia Minor. On the Kufa front extensive conquests were made in Armenia and Azarbaijan. On the Basra front revolts were suppressed in Faris, Kirman, Seestan and Khurasan. Thereafter the Muslims crossed the Oxus and made extensive conquests in Transoxiana. In the east the Muslims conquered Kabul and Ghazni and reached the borders of India. It is unfortunate that full details about the conquests made during the caliphate of Hadrat Othman are not available. I have tried to give some idea about the conquests made during the time of Hadrat Othman. This is a matter on which further research is called for. I hope some research scholar of tomorrow will supply this want.

In the fifth Chapter I have given an account of the agitation against Hadrat Othman. There were many strands in the agitation complex. The causes were religious, political, social, as well as personal. Ibn Saba's movement was primarily a religious movement intended to subvert Islam from within. Extensive conquests were made during the time of Hadrat Othman. There were many persons who were not happy at the passing away of the old order. They, therefore, joined the agitation against Hadrat Othman for political ends. There are also grounds to believe that such agitation against Hadrat Othman was supported by foreign powers. Their aim was to incite the Muslim to civil war among themselves. When Hadrat

Othman came to power, a generation had passed to the death of the Holy Prophet. During this period the people became prosperous and the hold of Islam on them was not as firm as it was during the days of the Holy Prophet. With the loosening of the hold of Islam, many of the pre-Islamic Arab traditions which Islam had suppressed were revived. There were some persons against whom Hadrat Othman took action in public interest. Such persons made their personal grievances a ground for agitation against him. In the course of such agitation some vague allegation were levied against Hadrat Othman. Hadrat Othman took pains to refute all these allegations but in spite of such explanation, the agitation persisted.

In the sixth Chapter I have given an account of the martyrdom of Hadrat Othman. Unfortunately all the accounts that have come down to us in this behalf are distorted. In most of these accounts the burden is that though Hadrat Othman undertook to follow the advice of Hadrat Ali, he could not keep up the undertaking as he played into the hands of Marwan b. Hakkam. It is also alleged that while Hadrat Othman agreed to depose Abdullah b Saad from the governorship of Egypt, he sent another letter countermanding the earlier orders and instructing him to put the rioters to death. Hadrat Othman is thus accused of breach of faith. My research has shown that all these accounts are not based on facts. As a matter of fact Muhammad b Abu Hudhaifa had by that time captured power in Egypt, who was hostile to Hadrat Othman and there could be no question of Hadrat Othman writing to him to put the rioters to death.

In the seventh Chapter I have given my assessment of Hadrat Othman. Hadrat Othman was a man of many distinctions and I have tried to project some of his distinctions. I have also advanced my reasons why in spite of being a good and virtuous man, Hadrat Othman did not succeed as a Caliph. I have described Hadrat Othman as I judge him. I have also made an attempt to discuss Hadrat Othman's place in history.

This is an original research work and much that is contained in this book has been expressed for the first time. Because of the lack of source material I regret that I could not make this work as exhaustive as I wished it to be. I have, however, the consolation that I have set the ball rolling. It will be for others to carry the ball forward.

Prof. Masudul Hasan

1

THE PRE-CALIPHATE PERIOD

EARLY LIFE

Date of Birth of Hadrat Othman[1]

The exact date of birth of Hadrat Othman is not known with any degree of certainty. There is also some controversy about the exact age attained by Hadrat Othman. When he died in 656 C.E. some said that he was eighty-five, while others said that he was eighty. There were some persons who held that he was only sixty-three.

The Holy Prophet died at the age of sixty-three. Hadrat Abu Bakr died at the same age. The age of Hadrat Umar at the time of his martyrdom was also around sixty-three. The age of sixty-three thus acquired a particular sanctity among the Muslims and this age was attributed by some persons to Hadrat Othman merely as a mark of sanctity.

The weight of available evidence is to the effect that Hadrat Othman was eighty years old at the time of his martyrdom. On this basis it can be computed that Hadrat Othman was born around 576 C.E. That was six years after the "Year of the Elephant", the year when Abraha, the Christian Viceroy of Yemen, invaded Makkah and had to withdraw having failed in his object. Hadrat Othman was younger than the Holy Prophet of Islam by five or six years.

Although the family of Hadrat Othman belonged to Makkah they had some property in Taif as well and Hadrat Othman was born in Taif and not in Makkah. As Taif is a hill station, the presumption is

1. *Othman b Affan*: Raza Misri.

that Hadrat Othman was born during the summer months of the year 576 C.E.

The Family of Hadrat Othman[1]

Hadrat Othman belonged to the Umayyad section of the Quraish. He was the son of Affan, who was the son of Abi Al A'as, who was the son of Umayyah, who was the son of Abd Shams, who was the son of Abd Manaf.

The Holy Prophet was the son of Abdullah, who was the son of Abdul Muttalib, who was the son of Hashim, who was the son of Abd Manaf.

Abd Manaf was the common ancestor of the Holy Prophet as well as Hadrat Othman. Abd Shams and Hashim were the two sons of Abd Manaf. The Holy Prophet was descended from Hashim, while Hadrat Othman was a descendant of Abd Shams. The Holy Prophet was fourth in descent from Abd Manaf, while Hadrat Othman was fifth in descent from Abd Manaf. Affan, the father of Hadrat Othman, was thus a second cousin of the Holy Prophet and Hadrat Othman was a nephew of the Holy Prophet.

On the mother's side Hadrat Othman's relationship with the Holy Prophet was still closer. His mother was Urwa. She was the daughter of Kariz, who was the son of Rabeah, who was the son of Habib who was the son of Abd Shams.

Urwa's mother was Umm Hakim who was a sister of the Holy Prophet's father. Urwa was thus a first cousin of the Holy Prophet. On this basis, Hadrat Othman was a nephew of the Holy Prophet both on the side of the father as well as the mother.

Early Life of Hadrat Othman[2]

No account has been preserved about the early life of Hadrat Othman. Only a few stray facts can be gleaned from here and there and on the basis of this meagre information we can have some glimpses of the early life of Hadrat Othman.

Hadrat Othman was born with the proverbial silver spoon in his mouth. His father Affan was a merchant and was counted as one of the richest men among the Quraish. Hadrat Othman was one of the few young men in Makkah who could read and write. This shows that

1. Ibid.
2. Ibid.

as a child, Hadrat Othman received formal education.

Hadrat Othman spent the days of his childhood like other Arab children. One of the games played by the Arab children was to uncover themselves and carry stones in their shirts. One day when as a child Hadrat Othman had uncovered himself he heard a voice "Cover yourself". Hadrat Othman hastened to cover himself. Thereafter he never uncovered himself. Thus at an early age, Hadrat Othman developed the habit of modesty and that remained his lifelong attribute.

It is related that while young, Hadrat Othman once travelled with his father to Yemen. They were accompanied by Abdul Rahman b Auf and his father. When they returned they carried the money of a man of Banu Jadhima Amir who had died in Yemen, to his heirs. One man Khalid b Hisham met them in the Jadhima territory before they could get to the family of the dead man who demanded the money. They refused to pay the money to Khalid b Hisham. That led to fighting in which Auf, the father of Abdul Rahman and Al Fakih b Al Mughira were killed. Hadrat Othman and his father succeeded in escaping from the Banu Jadhima territory. The Quraish of Makkah thereupon planned to attack the Banu Jadhima but the Banu Jadhima paid the compensation and the blood money and the dispute was settled.

Affan, the father of Hadrat Othman, died young when travelling abroad. Hadrat Othman was hardly twenty years old at the time of the death of his father. His father, however, left much wealth for him to inherit. Hadrat Othman followed the same profession as his father. His business flourished and after a few years he became a millionaire, one of the richest men among the Quraish. For his wealth, Hadrat Othman came to be called "Othman Ghani".

After the death of Affan, Urwa, the mother of Hadrat Othman, married Uqba bin Muheet. From the accounts that have come down to us it appears that Urwa had only two children from Affan, namely: Hadrat Othman and his sister Amna. She bore Uqba three sons and one daughter, namely: Walid, Khalid, 'Amr and Umm Kulthum.

It appears that during the age of ignorance, Hadrat Othman had two wives, namely Umm 'Amr bint Jandab and Fatimah bint Al Walid. Bint 'Amr was the mother of 'Amr, Khalid, Aban, Umar and Maryam. Fatimah was the mother of Walid, Said and Umm Said.

'Amr was the eldest son of Hadrat Othman and during the pre-Islamic period, Hadrat Othman was known by the surname of Abu 'Amr.

Physical Appearance of Hadrat Othman[1]

Hadrat Othman enjoyed fame as one of the most beautiful men in Makkah.

In his book *History of the Caliphs*, Jalaluddin Suyuti records on the authority of Ibn Asakir that Hadrat Othman was of medium stature, neither short, nor tall. He was of a comely aspect. His complexion was white with a yellowish tinge. There were faint marks of small pox on his face, which instead of disfiguring the comeliness of his appearance, added to his beauty. He was full bearded and the beard looked well on his face. The locks of the hair of his head fell below his ears. He was large of limbs, broad between the shoulders; fleshy in the thighs and long in the forearms. His teeth were most beautiful and were bound with wires of gold.

Abdullah b Hazm Al Mazini said about him that he had never seen a man of more beautiful face than that of Hadrat Othman.

Musa b Talha is reported to have said that Hadrat Othman was the most comely of men.

Personal Character of Hadrat Othman[2]

Hadrat Othman was conspicuous for his strong moral character. He was handsome and wealthy and many women were attracted to him but he never touched a woman beyond wedlock. In the immoral society of Makkah in the age of ignorance, he led a chaste life. He never touched wine. He did not gamble and took no part in the frivolities which formed the pastime of the youth of Makkah.

He was a good trader and made ample money out of trade but he never resorted to unfair practices in trade. He was scrupulously honest and believed in fair deal. He amassed considerable wealth through honest means. On account of his wealth he came to be known as "Ghani". In spite of being a millionaire, his way of life was not that of a capitalist. He was a man of simple habits and did not indulge in a luxurious way of life. He used a greater part of his wealth in helping those in distress. He had a flair for social work. He

1. *History of the Caliphs*: Suyuti.
2. This account is based on my own assessment.

supported many poor families. He awarded liberal stipends to widows and orphans who had none to support them. He was soft spoken and kind hearted. He had a kind word for every one who came across him. He patronised his relatives and gave liberal aid to such relatives who were in straitened circumstances.

He enjoyed the friendship of Hadrat Abu Bakr. Even in the pre-Islamic period he profited from the company of the Holy Prophet. He was much impressed with the personality of the Holy Prophet and always sought his counsel and guidance. He did not worship the idols in the Ka'aba. He had little faith in the superstitious practices in which the people of Makkah indulged. He felt that those who worshipped the idols merely groped in the dark. In his heart of hearts he felt that these lifeless idols could not be expected to control the destinies of mankind. He felt that the centre of power lay elsewhere. He had the inner conviction that some day the Truth would dawn in some manifest form.

He was an embodiment of modesty. In spite of his wealth there was no sense of pride in him. He never boasted of anything. He never tried to thrust his opinion on others. He believed in action rather than talk. There was a particular decorum and dignity about him. He was very particular that by his behaviour he did not offend anybody. On account of his endearing qualities of head and heart, he enjoyed great popularity among the people of Makkah.

CONVERSION TO ISLAM AND AFTER

Travels Abroad[1]

As a trader, Hadrat Othman travelled frequently to Yemen, Syria, Abyssinia and elsewhere. In the year 610, Hadrat Othman went as usual with a trading caravan to Syria. This year the business of Hadrat Othman had been particularly brisk and he had earned a huge profit. On the return journey the caravan halted for the night at a way-side station between Zarqa and Ma'an in Syria. As Hadrat Othman lay on his bed beneath the star studded sky, he felt impressed with the vastness and dimensions of space. He thought that the universe with such vast dimensions could not be without a master. In his heart of hearts he felt that some transcendent Being

---

1. *Othman b Affan*: Raza Misri.

would surely be the master of the universe complex. While he was thus lost in thoughts and was half awake and half asleep, he heard a voice, "O you who are asleep, wake up, for in Makkah the Prophet Ahmád has appeared". Hadrat Othman looked around but there was nobody to be seen. The voice that Hadrat Othman had heard was not a human voice: it appeared to come from outer space.

Conversion to Islam[1]

When Hadrat Othman came to Makkah, he came to know that Hadrat Muhammad (peace be upon him) had declared his Prophetic mission. Hadrat Othman called on Hadrat Abu Bakr and they talked long about Hadrat Muhammad (peace be upon him). Hadrat Othman told Hadrat Abu Bakr of the voice that he had heard while travelling in Syria. Hadrat Abu Bakr told Hadrat Othman that he had taken the oath of allegiance to the Prophet Muhammad (peace be upon him) and he advised Hadrat Othman to do likewise, for verily Muhammad (peace be upon him) was the Apostle of Truth. Hadrat Abu Bakr took Hadrat Othman to the Holy Prophet. The Holy Prophet welcomed Hadrat Othman and told him of his experience in Mt. Hira, the visitation of the angel Gabriel and the call to prophethood. Hadrat Othman felt thrilled on hearing this account. He told the Holy Prophet of the voice that he had heard in the course of his journey in Syria telling of the advent of a Prophet at Makkah. Hadrat Othman said that he had full faith in the Holy Prophet and believed in his mission. The Holy Prophet stretched his hand. Hadrat Othman grasped it in reverence and declared "There is no God but Allah and Muhammad is His Prophet". After Hadrat Abu Bakr, Hadrat Othman was the second person to be converted to Islam.

Reaction to the Conversion of Hadrat Othman[2]

The conversion of Hadrat Othman to Islam led to a violent reaction. There was already outstanding rivalry between the Umayyah and the Hashimite sections of the Quraish and the Umayyads could not tolerate that a young man of the house of the Umayyah should owe allegiance to the prophethood of a scion of the house of Hashim. Affan, the father of Hadrat Othman, was dead by this time and Hakam b Al A'as, an uncle of Hadrat Othman, was the head of the

---

1. Ibid.
2. *Early Heroes of Islam*: G.A. Salik.

family. Hakam was a neighbour of the Holy Prophet and when he came to know that his nephew had been converted to Islam he was infuriated and he took Hadrat Othman to task. He bound Hadrat Othman with a cord and wanted him to repudiate his allegiance to the Holy Prophet. When Urwa, the mother of Hadrat Othman, came to know of his conversion to Islam, she was very bitter and exhorted Hadrat Othman to recant and return to the faith of his forefathers. The stepfather of Hadrat Othman, Uqba b Abi Muheet whom Urwa had married after the death of Affan was in the forefront in the opposition to Islam. Hadrat Othman was warned that unless he recanted from his faith in Islam, he would have to suffer serious consequences. Hadrat Othman remained firm in his resolve. He told all concerned that he was prepared to face the consequences but he could not abandon Islam which was the way of Truth.

Triumph of Hadrat Othman[1]

In this ordeal, Hadrat Othman remained steadfast and firm. He did not waver for a moment in his faith in Islam. On the other hand, the greater the pressure on him, the greater became his faith in Islam. Seeing that nothing could deter Hadrat Othman from his faith his uncle left him to himself. His mother gave expression to her annoyance by enforcing a boycott against him. In this ordeal two persons in the family supported the cause of Hadrat Othman. Out of these one was Saadi, a maternal aunt of Hadrat Othman and a sister of Urwa. The other was Umm Kulsum, a step sister of Hadrat Othman, a daughter of Urwa from Uqba bin Abi Muheet.

Saadi was a poetess and she composed some verses praising the stand of Hadrat Othman. She said:

"Allah called the noble souled Othman to the right way,
And he swore allegiance to Muhammad, the Prophet of Allah.
Verily, Allah guides those whom He likes to the Truth".

Umm Kulsum, in spite of the strong opposition of her parents, accepted Islam. The Holy Prophet married her to his adopted son Zaid b Harith. She thus became a daughter-in-law of the Holy Prophet.

---

1. Ibid.

Marriage with Hadrat Ruqayya[1]

Because of his conversion to Islam, Hadrat Othman had to face another crisis. His wives refused to accept Islam and Hadrat Othman separated himself from his wives. That was a matter of great grief for Hadrat Othman but so great was his love for Islam that he felt no sacrifice too great in the cause of Islam. He felt distressed at the break up of his family life but Islam was certainly more valuable for him.

The Holy Prophet of Islam was much impressed with the sacrifice that Hadrat Othman had made in the cause of Islam and he married his second daughter Ruqayya to Hadrat Othman. In the days of ignorance Ruqayya had been engaged to her cousin Utba, son of Abu Lahb, an uncle of the Holy Prophet. When the Holy Prophet declared his mission Abu Lahb became hostile to him and under his instructions Utba repudiated his engagement to the daughter of the Holy Prophet. Hadrat Othman and Ruqayya made a unique pair. Hadrat Othman was the most beautiful person among men and Hadrat Ruqayya was the most beautiful person among the women of Makkah.

On the marriage of Hadrat Othman and Hadrat Ruqayya, Saadi, the maternal aunt of Hadrat Othman, composed verses. She said:

"Othman the noble souled became a Muslim;
And Muhammad the Prophet of Islam married him
to his daughter;
Thus, the moon and the sun were united;
O son of Banu Hashim, to you I pay my tribute;
You are undoubtedly the Messenger of Allah,
Sent for the guidance of mankind".

In his book *History of the Caliphs*, Jalaluddin Suyuti tells an anecdote highlighting the comeliness of the Othman-Ruqayya pair. It is related that one day the Apostle of Allah sent Usama b Zaid to the house of Hadrat Othman with a dish of meat. Usama was then a child of six or seven years. He says that sometime he looked at Hadrat Ruqayya and sometime at Hadrat Othman and wondered at their beauty. Usama relates that on return from the house of Hadrat Othman, the Holy Prophet asked him, "Have you ever seen a more

---

1. History of the Caliphs: Suyuti.

comely pair than Othman and Ruqayya"? Usama said "Never, O Apostle of Allah".

Migration to Abyssinia[1]

After marriage with Hadrat Ruqayya, Hadrat Othman felt most happy. It was a happy union and Hadrat Othman and Hadrat Ruqayya were lost in the love of each other. That led to jealousies. The wives of Hadrat Othman felt very bitter at their separation from Hadrat Othman. The mother of Hadrat Othman and his other relatives felt unhappy at his marriage to a daughter of the Holy Prophet of Islam. Hadrat Othman and Hadrat Ruqayya felt that the atmosphere in Makkah was not congenial. Hadrat Othman had already some business contacts in Abyssinia and after a good deal of deliberation and consultation with the Holy Prophet, Hadrat Othman and Hadrat Ruqayya decided to migrate to Abyssinia. On their departure the Holy Prophet prayed for their safety and protection. He said that after the Prophet Lot, Othman was the first to migrate with his family in the way of Allah. After Hadrat Othman and his wife had left for Abyssinia, some other Muslims also left for Abyssinia. The Negus of Abyssinia welcomed the emigrants and provided them with all necessary facilities for their stay in his dominions. The Quraish sent a delegation to Abyssinia to prevail upon the Negus to expel the Muslims from his State. The Negus heard the Quraish as well as the Muslims and refused to oblige the Quraish by expelling the Muslims. The Quraish delegation saw Hadrat Othman and prevailed upon him to return to Makkah but they failed in their object.

For long the Holy Prophet got no news about Hadrat Othman and Hadrat Ruqayya and he got worried about their welfare. A Quraish woman came from Abyssinia to Makkah. The Holy Prophet enquired from her about the welfare of Hadrat Othman and Hadrat Ruqayya. She said that she had seen Hadrat Ruqayya riding a pony and Hadrat Othman walking by her side. She added that Hadrat Othman and Hadrat Ruqayya were doing well in Abyssinia.

In Abyssinia, Hadrat Othman followed the profession of a trader. He worked hard and although there were some difficulties at the outset, these were soon overcome and the business of Hadrat Othman flourished. A son was born to Hadrat Othman and Hadrat Ruqayya in Abyssinia. They named him Abdullah. Henceforward

---

1. *Othman b Affan*: Raza Misri.

Hadrat Othman came to be known by the surname of Abu Abdullah. A colony of the Muslims had sprung up in Abyssinia. Hadrat Othman was most popular with the Muslims and he provided liberal aid to such Muslims who were poor or in distressed circumstances.

Return to Makkah[1]

After two years, a news spread among the Muslims in Abyssinia that the Quraish of Makkah had accepted Islam. That made Hadrat Othman, Hadrat Ruqayya and some other Muslims return to Makkah. When these Muslims reached Makkah it transpired that the news about the Quraish having accepted Islam was false. Some of the Muslims who had come from Abyssinia returned there but Hadrat Othman and Hadrat Ruqayya decided to stay in Makkah.

In Makkah, Hadrat Othman had to start his business afresh. The contacts that he had established in Abyssinia stood in good stead and the business of Hadrat Othman prospered. Although the number of the Muslims steadily grew, there was no relaxation in the persecution of the Muslims by the Quraish. The family of Hadrat Othman continued their pressure but Hadrat Othman's faith in Islam was too firm to know of any wavering. In the persecution of the Muslims, Uqba b Abi Muheet, the step father of Hadrat Othman (the man his mother had married) was in the forefront. One day Uqba put his sheet round the neck of the Holy Prophet, while he was praying in the Ka'aba and tried to strangle him. Hadrat Abu Bakr and Hadrat Othman rushed to the aid of the Holy Prophet and frustrated the evil design of Uqba.

In Makkah, Hadrat Othman spent most of his time in the company of the Holy Prophet. He liberally helped such Muslims who were poor. He liberated some Muslim slaves.

When the Holy Prophet and the members of the Banu Hashim were shut up in the valley outside Makkah as a consequence of social boycott by the Quraish, Hadrat Othman took steps to ensure that there was no break in the supply of provisions to the besieged persons. Hadrat Othman exercised his influence on the youth among the Quraish to create an opinion in favour of the lifting of the boycott.

---

1. Ibid.

When after the lifting of the boycott, the Holy Prophet had his experience of the "Miraj" (ascension), there were some persons who were sceptical about it. Hadrat Abu Bakr and Hadrat Othman, however, believed in letter as well as in spirit what the Holy Prophet said.

When in 622 C.E. the Holy Prophet advised the Muslims to migrate to Yathrib, Hadrat Othman migrated to Yathrib with his wife Hadrat Ruqayya. Hadrat Othman was among the few Muslims who undertook two migrations in the cause of Allah—once to Abyssinia and for the second time to Yathrib.

DHUN-NURAIN

To Hadrat Othman belongs the unique honour of having married two daughters of the Holy Prophet, one after the other. For this rare distinction he was called "Dhun-Nurain", the possessor of two lights.

Hadrat Ruqayya[1]

After his conversion to Islam, Hadrat Othman was married by the Holy Prophet to his second daughter Hadrat Ruqayya. Hadrat Othman migrated with Hadrat Ruqayya to Abyssinia. He returned from Abyssinia and then migrated with his wife to Yathrib in 622. In Yathrib (renamed Madinah) Hadrat Othman carried on his business as a merchant. His business flourished and Hadrat Othman and Hadrat Ruqayya lived on happily for sometime in Madinah. Such happiness was, however, shortlived. In 624 C.E. Hadrat Ruqayya fell ill and died when the Holy Prophet and the Muslims were fighting with the Quraish at the battlefield of Badr. The news of the Muslim victory of Badr was received at Madinah when the good lady was being buried. The Holy Prophet could not attend the funeral of Hadrat Ruqayya.

Hadrat Hafsa[2]

Hadrat Hafsa was the daughter of Hadrat Umar. She was married to Khunays. Khunays was wounded in the battle of Uhud. The wounds proved fatal and he died soon after. Hadrat Hafsa became a widow at a young age and Hadrat Umar felt much worried about her marriage.

---

1. Ibid.
2. *Hadrat Umar Farooq*: Prof. Masudul Hasan.

After the death of Hadrat Ruqayya, Hadrat Othman felt much distressed and disconsolate. Hadrat Umar saw Hadrat Othman and dropped hints for offering Hadrat Hafsa to him in marriage. Hadrat Othman did not respond favourably to the proposal. He said that after the death of Hadrat Ruqayya he was too upset to think of another marriage.

Hadrat Umar saw the Holy Prophet and complained against the conduct of Hadrat Othman. The Holy Prophet consoled Hadrat Umar and said, "Umar, do not worry. Hafsa would get a better husband than Othman and Othman would get a better wife than Hafsa".

Umm Kulthum[1]

Towards the close of the year 625, the Holy Prophet married Hafsa and Hadrat Othman was married to Umm Kulthum, the third daughter of the Holy Prophet. While still a child she was engaged to Utaibah, a son of Abu Lahb, an uncle of the Holy Prophet. When the Holy Prophet declared his mission, Abu Lahb opposed him and under his instructions his son Utaibah repudiated his engagement to Hadrat Umm Kulthum.

When the Holy Prophet married Umm Kulthum to Hadrat Othman, he said to her, "Verily, your husband resembles most among men your forefather Abraham and your father Muhammad". Ibn Asakir has recorded on the authority of Ibn Umar that the Holy Prophet said, "I find a resemblance in Othman to my forefather Abraham".

Hadrat Othman's union with Hadrat Umm Kulthum was as happy as that of the union between Hadrat Othman and Hadrat Ruqayya. Unfortunately such happiness was shortlived and Hadrat Umm Kulthum died in 630 barely six years after her marriage. Hadrat Umm Kulthum bore no child. Hadrat Ruqayya left a son Abdullah but he died two years after the death of his mother.

Other Marriages of Hadrat Othman[2]

After the death of Hadrat Umm Kulthum, Hadrat Othman once again became a victim of despair and disconsolation. Touched by the sadness of Hadrat Othman, the Holy Prophet asked the people:

---

1. *Othman b Affan*: Raza Misri.
2. Ibid.

> "Give your daughters in marriage to Othman. If I had a third daughter, I would assuredly give her in marriage to him. I have never wedded any daughter to him save under inspiration".

Ibn Asakir records on the authority of Hadrat Ali that the Holy Prophet said to Othman:

> "If I had forty daughters, I would have wedded them with you one after the other, until no one of them was left".

Thereafter Hadrat Othman married a number of wives but the memories of his union with Hadrat Ruqayya and Hadrat Umm Kulthum always remained fresh in his mind. He felt sorry that he could not enjoy the company of the daughters of the Holy Prophet for long and he had been deprived of the honour of being the son-in-law of the Holy Prophet.

LIFE IN MADINAH

Migration to Madinah[1]

In 622 C.E. Hadrat Othman migrated with his wife Hadrat Ruqayya to Madinah. They were in the third batch of the Muslims who migrated to Madinah. Their companions on the migration included Akasha bin Muhsin, Zainab b Jahsh and her sisters Hamna and Umm Habiba. On arrival in Madinah Hadrat Othman stayed with Hadrat Aus b Thabit Ansari of the Najjar tribe. After sometime Hadrat Othman purchased a house of his own and shifted there.

The World of Madinah[2]

The world of Madinah was quite different from the world of Makkah. At Makkah the Muslims were a persecuted people, at Madinah they were the masters of their destiny. The life at Madinah was a great break with the past. The days of trials, tribulations and tortures were now over; in the new life at Madinah the Muslims were set on the path of fulfilment. To rehabilitate the immigrants from Makkah in the society of Madinah the Holy Prophet established a fraternity among the Muslims from Makkah and the Muslims of Madinah, whereunder each immigrant was paired with an Ansar of corresponding status. The brotherhood thus established was unique in the annals of mankind. So strong and cordial were these bonds

---

1. Ibid.
2. Ibid.

that they even surpassed the relationship of blood. The Ansars helped their immigrant brothers liberally. Hadrat Othman did not stand in need of any financial help from his Ansar brother. He was one of the richest merchants of Makkah and had amassed considerable fortune. He brought all such fortune with him to Madinah. In Madinah the Muslims were generally agriculturists and were not very much interested in trade. The trade of the town was in the hands of the Jews. There was thus considerable scope for the Muslims in promoting trade. Hadrat Othman took advantage of this position and established himself as a trader in Madinah. He worked hard and honestly and his business flourished. Soon he became one of the richest man in Madinah as he had been one of the richest merchants in Makkah.

Generosity of Hadrat Othman[2]

Hadrat Othman already well known for his generosity stepped up his beneficent activities. He financed the project for the construction of the Prophet's mosque in Madinah.

In Madinah, the Muslims faced the problem of water supply. Most of the wells in Madinah had brackish water supply. There was only one well of sweet water in the town namely Beer Rauma. It belonged to a Jew and he did not allow free access to the Muslims. One day in the Prophet's mosque at Madinah the Muslims brought their difficulty to the notice of the Holy Prophet. Thereupon addressing the congregation the Holy Prophet said, "O ye Muslims, who among you would like to purchase the Beer Rauma for the Muslims in return for a home in paradise. Hadrat Othman purchased the well for ten thousand dirhams and dedicated it to the free use of the Muslims. Pleased with this beneficent act of Hadrat Othman, the Holy Prophet gave him the tiding of paradise in the world to come.

Death of Hadrat Ruqayya[1]

Hadrat Othman, Hadrat Ruqayya and their son Abdullah adjusted themselves to the new surroundings. Hadrat Othman devoted most of his time to his business and whatever time he could spare, he spent it in the company of the Holy Prophet. The Holy Prophet called frequently at their house to enquire about their welfare. The Holy Prophet had great liking for the young Abdullah and often played with him.

1. Ibid.

The happiness of the family was, however, shortlived. The climate of Makkah was dry but the climate of Madinah was damp. That adversely affected the health of the immigrants. During the first year of their migration many Muslims from Makkah suffered from fever. In the second year of the migration small pox broke out in Madinah. In 624 C.E., Hadrat Ruqayya suffered from malaria and then caught small pox. No remedy availed her and her malady grew worse day by day.

On the occasion of the battle of Badr, Hadrat Ruqayya lay on the sick bed. Hadrat Othman offered to join the battle. The Holy Prophet made him stay at Madinah as his vicegerent and also to look after the ailing Hadrat Ruqayya. The Holy Prophet assured him that he would have the reward of participating in the battle and would have his share in the booty captured from the enemy.

Hadrat Ruqayya died while the Holy Prophet was still at Badr. When the news of the victory of Badr was brought to Madinah, the good lady Hadrat Ruqayya was being buried. The Holy Prophet could not attend her funeral.

In the battle of Badr the Quraish suffered a serious defeat. Seventy men of the Quraish were killed and about seventy of them were taken as prisoners. Among those taken captive was Uqba b Abi Muheet, the man Hadrat Othman's mother had married. Uqba had been in the forefront in his hostility to the Holy Prophet and Islam. While most of the other captives were released on ransom, Uqba on account of his crimes, was ordered by the Holy Prophet to be killed. Uqba wanted Hadrat Othman to intercede in his behalf but Hadrat Othman refused to interfere on the ground that his crimes were too heinous to be forgiven. When Uqba was being led to execution, he asked the Holy Prophet, "Who will take care of my children"? The Holy Prophet said, "Hell would take care of you and your children who die in disbelief".

The Battle of Uhud[1]

The battle of Uhud was fought in 625 C.E. It was really an extension of the battle of Badr. This time the Quraish of Makkah came with a force of 3,000 men to avenge their defeat at Badr. To meet them the Muslims could raise a force of 1,000 persons only and even out of these three hundred persons under Abdullah b Ubayy,

1. *Digest of the Holy Qur'ān*: Prof. Masudul Hasan.

a hypocrite withdrew at the last moment thus leaving seven hundred persons only to face the hostile Quraish.

The Holy Prophet arranged his force in battle array and posted a contingent of archers to guard a vulnerable passage in the rear. The archers were instructed that they were not to leave their positions without further orders.

The Quraish charged with full force but the Muslims held fast. Then in a counter attack the Muslims broke the enemy's line and the Quraish fell back. At this stage the contingent of the Muslim archers left their positions in order to plunder the camp of the retreating Quraish. Khalid b Walid who was a non-Muslim at the time and was fighting on the side of the Quraish rushed forward with his contingent and occupied the positions vacated by the Muslim archers. That turned the tide of the battle. The Quraish rallied and launched an attack on the Muslims both from the front as well as the rear. In the confusion that followed many Muslims were martyred. Even the Holy Prophet was wounded and he fell in a pit where many of his followers lay dead. That led to the rumour that the Holy Prophet was dead. At this critical stage some of the Muslims left the battlefield thinking that if the Holy Prophet was dead, everything was lost and nothing was left to fight about. Hadrat Othman was one of the persons who left the battlefield.

This conduct of the Muslims who had left the battlefield was not approved by Allah. Allah, however, forgave them as their lapse was not deliberate and was based on misunderstanding. A revelation to the Holy Prophet said:

> "Behold you were climbing up the high ground, without even casting a single glance at any one and the Apostle in your rear was calling you back. There did Allah give you one distress after another by way of requittal, to teach you not to grieve for the booty that had escaped you and for the ill that had befallen you. For Allah is well aware of what you do".[1]

> The revelation continued:

> "Those who turned back on the day the two hosts met, it was Satan who caused them to fail but Allah has blotted out their fault, for Allah is oft-forgiving, most forbearing".[2]

---

1. III. 153.
2. III. 155.

Hadrat Othman felt sorry that at that crucial stage, he had lost the equilibrium of his mind and his conduct had not been approved by Allah. He, however, felt consoled that Allah in His Mercy had forgiven him and blotted out his lapse. When Hadrat Othman saw the Holy Prophet later and expressed his regrets the Holy Prophet asked him to cheer up for Allah had forgiven him for his lapse. That made Hadrat Othman make the resolve that in other expeditions he would not lag behind.

Post-Uhud Period[1]

In the post-Uhud period, Hadrat Othman felt very sad and disconsolate. Hadrat Othman felt disconsolate at the passing away of Hadrat Ruqayya. He also felt remorseful at his lapse on the occasion of the battle of Uhud. The Holy Prophet felt for Hadrat Othman and married his daughter Umm Kulthum to him. Hadrat Othman felt happy at this honour. Umm Kulthum filled the vacuum that had been created due to the death of Hadrat Ruqayya. Hadrat Ruqayya had left a son Abdullah and Umm Kulsum showered the affection of a mother on him. The Holy Prophet visited the house of Hadrat Othman frequently. That was a source of great satisfaction for Hadrat Othman.

A year after the battle of Uhud, Abdullah died. Hadrat Othman had great love for him and he was intensely grieved at his death. The Holy Prophet led the funeral prayer. He consoled Hadrat Othman and advised him that as a true Muslim he should resign himself to the will of Allah.

In the battle of the Ditch, Hadrat Othman was in charge of a sector. The enemy made several attempts to cross the Ditch in this sector. The vigilance of Hadrat Othman and his contingent frustrated the designs of the enemy.

After the battle of the Ditch when a campaign was undertaken against the Jews of Banu Qainuqa, Hadrat Othman was in the forefront of the action. When the Jews were taken captive and the question of the disposal of the slaves became a problem, Hadrat Othman resolved the issue by purchasing all the slaves and depositing their price in the Baitul Mal. Such of these slaves who accepted Islam were liberated by Hadrat Othman in the name of Allah. It is reliably reported that Hadrat Othman used to liberate a slave every Friday.

1. *Othman b Affan*: Raza Misri.

TREATY OF HUDAIBIYAH

Performance of the Pilgrimage[1]

Early in 628 C.E., the Holy Prophet decided to proceed to Makkah to perform the pilgrimage. He was accompanied by 1,400 companions including Hadrat Othman. When the Quraish of Makkah came to know that the Muslims were coming to Makkah, they sent Khalid and Ikramah bin Abu Jahl with two hundred horsemen to intercept the Muslims and prevent their advance to Makkah. Finding the main route to Makkah barred, the Muslims turned aside and took an alternative unfrequented route to Makkah. The way led through rough rocks and ravines. After a weary march, the Muslims reached Hudaibiyah on the lower side of Makkah within the sacred precincts.

Urwah b Masud[2]

The Muslims encamped at Hudaibiyah and here Urwah b Masud came to see the Holy Prophet on behalf of the Quraish. He talked in diplomatic terms and tried to create the impression that the Quraish were strong and would not permit the Muslims to visit Makkah except by agreement. He insinuated that at the time of the crisis, the companions of the Holy Prophet were likely to leave him. Thereupon the companions of the Holy Prophet said, "May Allah curse you; how dare you think that we will abandon the Holy Prophet. Rest assured we will sacrifice our lives for him". The discussions with Urwa proved inconclusive but when he returned to the Quraish, he reported about the Holy Prophet and the Muslims in the following terms:

> "O people of the Quraish, I have seen kings but by Allah, I have never seen a king as I have seen Muhammad amongst his followers. If he makes his ablution they would not let the water fall on the ground; if a hair of his body falls they pick it up. They will not surrender him for anything in any case, do what you may".

Khirash b Umayyah[3]

On the departure of Urwa, the Holy Prophet sent Khirash b Umayyah as an emissary to the Quraish. When he arrived in Makkah

---

1. *Life of Muhammad*: Hafiz G. Sarwar.
2. Ibid.
3. Ibid.

he was maltreated by the Quraish and the camel on which he rode was hamstrung. In turn the Quraish sent a detachment with the object of killing the Holy Prophet. These persons were taken captive by the Muslims. The companions wanted to kill them but the Holy Prophet forbade the shedding of blood within the precincts of the sacred territory.

Hadrat Othman b Affan[1]

Thereafter the Holy Prophet decided to send another emissary to the Quraish to negotiate terms of agreement with them. For such mission, a person had to be chosen who commanded influence with the Quraish. The choice fell on Hadrat Othman b Affan. Hadrat Othman b Affan accompanied by ten companions left for Makkah. Hadrat Othman went to Aban b Saeed b 'Aas, an old friend. He welcomed Hadrat Othman and gave him the necessary protection. Thereafter Hadrat Othman saw the principal Quraish leaders and explained to them that the Muslims were on a mission of peace; their object was merely to perform the pilgrimage and they wanted to extend the hand of friendship to the Quraish. The Quraish leaders said that if he wanted to perform the pilgrimage he was free to do so but they could not allow the Muslims an entry in Makkah until an agreement was reached with them. Hadrat Othman said that he could not perform the pilgrimage unless the Holy Prophet performed the pilgrimage first. They said that they would send another emissary to the Muslim camp to arrive at some agreement with the Muslims. The Quraish took sometime in nominating their emissary and during this period they detained Hadrat Othman at Makkah.

Baiy'at-ur-Ridwan[2]

When there was a delay in returning of Hadrat Othman from Makkah, a rumour spread in the Muslim camp that Hadrat Othman had been killed by the Quraish of Makkah. That considerably upset the Muslims. At this juncture the Holy Prophet asked his followers to make a pledge with him to fight in the way of Allah to the bitter end. All the Muslims responded enthusiastically to the call. The Holy Prophet sat under a tree and all the Muslims in the camp took the pledge one by one. After everybody had taken the pledge, the Holy Prophet placed his own right hand on his left hand and took the

---

1. Ibid.
2. Ibid.

pledge on behalf of Hadrat Othman. Hadrat Othman thus secured the unique honour that the Holy Prophet himself took the pledge on his behalf.

About his ceremony of oath taking at Hudaibiyah, it was revealed in the Holy Qur'ān:

> "Surely, Allah was pleased with the believers when they took the pledge under the tree. Allah knew what was in their hearts. He sent down tranquillity upon them and rewarded them with near victory" (XLVIII: 18-19).

In view of Allah's pleasure at the pledge taking, the pledge came to be known as "Baiy'at-ur-Ridwan".

Hadrat Othman returned from Makkah in the company of an emissary from the Quraish. On coming to know that in his absence the Muslims in the camp had taken the pledge and the Holy Prophet had taken the pledge on his behalf, he took the pledge in person as well.

The Treaty of Hudaibiyah[1]

The Quraish sent Suhail b Amr as their emissary. After considerable discussion an agreement was arrived at and this came to be known as the Hudaibiyah pact. According to the pact there was to be truce between the Quraish and the Muslims for a period of ten years. Each party was free to make its own alliances but they were not to resort to war. Any person who deserted the Muslims and sought refuge with the Quraish was not to be returned but any person who escaped from the Quraish to the Muslims was to be returned to the Quraish. It was stipulated that the Muslims were to return to Madinah that year without performing the pilgrimage but they could come to Makkah the following year for performing the pilgrimage when the Quraish would vacate the city for them for three days.

After the pact had been signed, the Muslims sacrificed the animals they had brought with them; broke the camp and started on the return journey to Madinah.

Reaction to the Hudaibiyah Pact[2]

On the fact of it the Hudaibiyah pact appeared to be loaded in favour of the Quraish. Some of the Muslims, particularly Hadrat

---

1. Ibid.
2. *Hadrat Abu Bakr Siddiq*: Prof. Masudul Hasan.

Umar, felt dissatisfied with the terms of the pact and gave expression to their dissatisfaction. Hadrat Othman, however, felt satisfied with the terms of the agreement. He was confident that the pact though apparently in favour of the Quraish would ultimately turn out to be against them. He said that the Quraish were fast losing their will to resist Islam and when in pursuance of the pact the Muslims and the Quraish would come in contact, most of the Quraish were likely to accept Islam.

While on the way to Madinah, Allah revealed to the Holy Prophet that the Hudaibiyah pact was indeed a victory for the Muslims, as it would work to their advantage and the disadvantage of the Quraish. When the Holy Prophet told of these tidings to Hadrat Umar and his other followers, all of them felt happy.

The assessment of Hadrat Othman also proved correct, for, in the period following the Hudaibiyah pact, many Quraish including such stalwarts as Khalid b Walied and Amr b Al 'Aas accepted Islam.

CONQUEST OF MAKKAH

Extension of the Prophet's Mosque[1]

One of the consequences of the treaty of Hudaibiyah was that the Arab tribes had to ally themselves with the Quraish of Makkah or the Muslims of Madinah. The Arab tribes who were not favourably inclined to the Quraish sought alliance with the Muslims. Most of these tribes accepted Islam. In view of large scale conversions that took place in the post-Hudaibiyah period, the Prophet's mosque at Madinah became too small to accommodate all the Muslims who came there to pray and the need for extension came to be felt. The Holy Prophet appealed to his followers to finance the project for the extension of the mosque. Hadrat Othman financed the entire project and it was no longer necessary for the other Muslims to make any contribution. Immensely pleased with the conduct of Hadrat Othman, the Holy Prophet gave him the tidings of paradise in the next world. On this occasion, Hadrat Ali is said to have composed the following verses in the honour of Hadrat Othman:

There's one that labours night and day,
To build us mosques of brick and clay,

1. *Othman b Affan*: Raza Misri.

And one who turns from dust away.
There's no life but life of next world
O Allah have mercy on the Muhajreen and the Ansar".

Battle of Khyber[1]

After their expulsion from Madinah most of the Jews settled at Khyber. They were a cunning and crafty people and were notorious for their intrigues. The Hudaibiyah pact provided for peace between the Muslims and the Quraish for a period of ten years. This meant that the Quraish could no longer openly aid the Jews against the Muslims. In spite of this change in the situation, there was no diminution in the hostility of the Jews against the Muslims and they conspired to form another coalition against the Muslims.

To forestall the evil designs of the Jews, the Holy Prophet marched to Khyber in 629 C.E. with a force of 1,400 Muslims. The Jews shut themselves in their forts. These forts were formed of frowning walls built of the living rock and were considered invulnerable. The Jews thought that in these forts they would be able to defy the Muslims. The Jews had ample provisions and there was no shortage of arms with them. The battle waged for some days with no tangible result. The Muslims attack became more violent and they succeeded in capturing one of the Jewish forts named 'Naam'. Hadrat Othman was the first to climb the walls of this fort. The second person to climb the walls was Mahmud b Salma. The Jews stoned from above. Mahmud b Salma was martyred but Hadrat Othman remained unhurt. He was the hero of the day and the Holy Prophet appreciated his feat of bravery. The Jews surrendered and peace was concluded on the Jews agreeing to pay a tribute equivalent to one half of the land produce.

The battle of Khyber had far reaching consequences. It established the paramountcy of the Muslims in the Arabian peninsula. The Jews now became the subject of the Muslims. The Quraish thus lost the support of the Jews and as such the battle of Khyber paved the way for the conquest of Makkah.

At Khyber, a Jewish lady served poisoned meat to the Muslims. Bishr b Bra, one of the companions who ate a good deal of the meat, died on the spot. Hadrat Othman did not taste the meat and thus escaped from the effects of the poison.

1. Ibid.

Makkah Revisited[1]

A year after the Hudaibiyah pact the Holy Prophet at the head of 2,000 Muslims proceeded to Makkah to perform the Hajj in accordance with the terms stipulated in the pact. As the Muslims reached Makkah, most of the Quraish left their houses and took to the neighbouring hills. In view of the Hudaibiyah pact, the Quraish had no option but to permit the Muslims visit Makkah and perform the pilgrimage but they were loath to offer any welcome to the Muslims. The general view among the Quraish was that if their young men and women came in contact with the Muslims they were apt to be attracted by the new faith and as such any contacts with the Muslims were to be avoided. The permission to the Muslims to visit Makkah extended to three days only.

In contrast the Muslims were happy to visit the city of their birth. The Muslims were no longer a small group of helpless persons exposed to the persecutions of the Quraish; they were now a power in Arabia. That was a positive proof of the truth of Islam. On their visit to Makkah the Muslims offered their prayers in the Ka'aba. The Adhan, the Muslim call to prayer, resounded in the hills and dales of Makkah and as the Quraish heard the call they felt much perturbed. They felt that they had made a mistake in making the treaty of Hudaibiyah and allowing the Muslims to visit the Ka'aba.

Some of the Muslims suggested to the Holy Prophet that as the city was deserted, it should be occupied. The Holy Prophet vetoed the suggestion and held that the pledge once made could not be violated. The Holy Prophet assured his followers that the day was not far when they would return to Makkah as victors and that might be sooner than what they could think of.

On the occasion of the visit to Makkah, Hadrat Othman met his mother and family members. He felt that they were now not so hostile to Islam as they had been previously. Hadrat Othman hoped that erelong his friends and family members would accept the faith of Islam.

End of the Hudaibiyah Pact[2]

According to the Hudaibiyah pact the Arab tribes had the option to be allied with the Quraish or the Muslims. In pursuance of

---

1. Ibid.
2. *Hadrat Abu Bakr Siddiq*: Prof. Masudul Hasan.

these terms the Arabs of the Banu Bakr allied themselves with the Quraish, while the tribe of the Banu Khuza'ah allied themselves with the Muslims.

In disregard of the terms of the treaty of Hudaibiyah, the Banu Bakr attacked the Banu Khuza'ah and even when the Banu Khuza'ah sought the sanctuary of the Ka'aba, many of them were killed. The Banu Khuza'ah thereupon appealed to the Holy Prophet to come to their aid. The Holy Prophet assured them that in pursuance of the terms of the Hudaibiyah pact, the Muslims would come to their assistance.

The Holy Prophet thereupon took up the matter with the Quraish and offered them three alternatives. They were required in the first instance to pay the blood money for the victims of the high handedness of the Banu Bakr. In the alternative they should terminate their alliance with Banu Bakr. If either of these alternatives was not agreed to, then as the last resort the Hudaibiyah pact should be considered to be abrogated.

The Quraish who were already feeling unhappy at the visit of the Muslims to Makkah decided to abrogate the treat of Hudaibiyah. The Holy Prophet welcomed this move on the part of the Quraish and declared that the Quraish would have to bear the consequences of the breach of faith.

The Quraish soon realised that they had made a mistake in abrogating the treaty of Hudaibiyah. Abu Sufyan, the leader of the Quraish, visited Madinah to make amends. He sought an interview with the Holy Prophet to discuss the issue. The Holy Prophet refused to see him because of the Quraish breach of faith. One of the daughters of Abu Sufyan was a wife of the Holy Prophet. Abu Sufyan wanted her to plead his case with the Holy Prophet but she refused. Abu Sufyan was related to Hadrat Othman. He wanted Hadrat Othman to intercede with the Holy Prophet on his behalf. Hadrat Othman politely refused to oblige him. Abu Sufyan returned disappointed from Madinah.

Conquest of Makkah[1]

In 630 C.E. the Holy Prophet mustered a force ten thousand strong and marched to Makkah. The Quraish of Makkah were no

1. Ibid.

longer capable of offering any resistance to the Muslims. Abu Sufyan, the leader of the Quraish, waited on the Holy Prophet, offered submission and became a convert to Islam. The city of Makkah was occupied by the Muslims without any battle. The Muslims who had been driven away from the city only eight years earlier were now the masters of the city. Thus Allah fulfilled the promise that He had made to His Prophet. It was a veritable vindication of the truth of Islam.

The Holy Prophet visited the Ka'aba and one by one all the idols therein were broken and destroyed. That marked the coming of the Truth and the vanishing of falsehood. Thereafter the Holy Prophet addressed the people assembled in the Ka'aba in the following terms:

> "There is no God but Allah. He has no associate. He is omniscient and omnipotent. He has made good the promise that He had held to His Messenger. He had helped him in overcoming his enemies. With the triumph of Truth a new era has dawned characterised by the vanishing of falsehood. Henceforward there will be no faith other than Islam, the faith ordained by Allah.
>
> I give you the tidings of an era of justice and peace. Bear in mind that every claim of privilege whether that of blood or property is abolished, except that the custody of the Ka'aba and of supplying water to the pilgrims. Let it be known that for any one who is slain the bloodwit is hundred camels. O people of the Quraish, surely Allah has abolished from you all pride of the time of ignorance and all pride in your ancestry because all men are descended from Adam".

Then turning to the people of Makkah, the Holy Prophet posed the question:

> "O you Quraish, what do you think of the treatment that should accord you"?
>
> The people said with one voice:
>
> "Mercy O Prophet of Allah; we expect nothing but good from you".

In the hour of triumph the Holy Prophet was most forgiving. He said:

> "O the people of Makkah, I speak to you in the same words as the prophet Joseph spoke to his brothers. This day there is no reproof against you. Go your way, for you are free".

The announcement was received with great joy and applause. Although general immunity was granted to the people of Makkah, an exception was made in the case of half a dozen persons whose crimes had been too heinous to be forgiven. These persons included Abdullah b Saad, a foster brother of Hadrat Othman. Abdullah b Saad had accept Islam and the Holy Prophet availed of his services as a scribe for noting down the revelations. Abdullah b Saad was found guilty of interpolation and falsifying the revelations. When taken to task Abdullah b Saad apostatised and escaped to Makkah. The Holy Prophet was too much annoyed with him and his orders were that he was to be executed for his sacrilegeous conduct. Abdullah b Saad sought the protection of Hadrat Othman and prevailed upon him to intercede with the Holy Prophet on his behalf. Hadrat Othman was not inclined to undertake the hazardous mission but when his foster mother, the mother of Abdullah b Saad, appealed to him Hadrat Othman promised to do whatever he could do to save the life of Abdullah b Saad.

When the Holy Prophet granted general amnesty to the people of Makkah Hadrat Othman waited on the Holy Prophet and said, "On this day of triumph I seek a favour from you O Prophet of Allah". The Holy Prophet said, "Yes, Othman, you may ask whatever you wish". Hadrat Othman said, "I crave the life of Abdullah b Saad. I know of his crimes but he is repentant and Allah is Forgiving. He is my foster brother and my foster mother has put great pressure on me to intercede in his behalf". The Holy Prophet remained silent. After sometime Hadrat Othman repeated his request. The Holy Prophet still gave no reply. When Hadrat Othman repeated his request for the third time, the Holy Prophet said: "Alright; let him be free. May Allah forgive him".

Thereafter all the Quraish of Makkah were converted to Islam and they took the oath of allegiance to the Holy Prophet. These included the mother of Hadrat Othman, his step brothers and sisters and other members of his family. The family which had remained apart on account of difference in faith was now reunited and this reunion was a matter of great joy for Hadrat Othman. After conversion to Islam, the people of Makkah began a new life. Heretofore they had been the inveterate enemies of Islam, henceforward they were to be the dedicated servants of Islam.

Battle of Autas[1]

After the fall of Makkah, the neighbouring tribes of Hawazin and Thaqueef had to choose between peace by conversion to Islam or war with the Muslims. These tribes considered that the Quraish had been guilty of cowardice by submitting to Islam. They accordingly chose the way of war with the Muslims.

From Makkah the Holy Prophet marched to Autas at the head of an army twelve thousand strong. Out of these ten thousand warriors belonged to the army that had come from Madinah. The other two thousand persons were the warriors from the Quraish of Makkah who had volunteered to fight in the way of Allah. As this army was mustered, the Muslims felt proud of it and considered that it was invincible.

As the Muslim army passed through the valley of Hunain, some eleven miles north-east of Makkah, a rain of arrows fell on it let loose by a group of archers of the hostile tribes that lay hidden in the mountain pass. The surprise attack caused a great confusion among the ranks of the Muslim force. In utter confusion, the men ran in all directions to seek cover. The Holy Prophet stood firm at his place and he called the Muslims to his side. In the first instance only nine persons stood by the side of the Holy Prophet. These included Hadrat Othman. After sometime the Muslims gathered round the Holy Prophet and under his direction made a violent charge on the enemy. After sometime the pass was captured. The Holy Prophet posted a guard at the pass and the main army marched to Autas.

In the confrontation at Autas, the hostile tribes were soon defeated. Large booty fell into the hands of the Muslims which was distributed among the warriors.

Siege of Taif[2]

From Autas the Muslim force marched to Taif. The people of Taif chose to oppose the Muslims. They, however, shut themselves in the fort and refused to come into the open. The Muslims tried the testudo device whereunder a group of soldiers shielded by a cover of cow hide advanced to set fire to the gate. The enemy threw red hot scraps of iron on the testudo which made it ineffective. Taif was a hill station and the fort was situated at a height while the besiegers had to camp

1. Ibid.
2. Ibid.

at a lower plane. It was not possible to take the fort by assault. The only way to overcome the resistance of the enemy was to tighten the blockade and drag on the siege till the provisions in the fort were exhausted. That meant that the siege had to be continued for a long time. The Holy Prophet had other pressing business to undertake and he could not afford to spend so much time in besieging Taif. The Holy Prophet held a council of war as to the course of action. The council included Hadrat Othman. After consulting his companions the Holy Prophet raised the siege of Taif and retired to Makkah.

A few days later, Malik b Auf, the chief of Taif, came to Makkah. As Hadrat Othman had property at Taif, Malik b Auf saw Hadrat Othman. Hadrat Othman stressed on him the advisability of accepting Islam. Malik b Auf asked a few questions and being satisfied asked Hadrat Othman to take him to the Holy Prophet. Malik b Auf declared the article of faith and became a Muslim. Thus the Muslims gained by raising the siege of Taif what they could not secure by carrying on the war.

From Makkah the Holy Prophet and his companions returned to Madinah. Some eight years ago the Holy Prophet and his companions had come to Madinah as refugees. Now they came to Madinah as victors, the masters of Makkah and Arabia.

PASSING AWAY OF THE HOLY PROPHET

Back to Madinah[1]

After the conquest of Makkah, Madinah rose in importance. Heretofore it was a city of the Muslims whose sphere of influence was limited. After the conquest of Makkah, Madinah became the capital of Arabia. Delegations started pouring in into Madinah from all parts of Arabia and the pace of conversion to Islam received a tremendous acceleration.

To Hadrat Othman the conquest of Makkah and Taif were of particular significance. He had considerable property at Makkah and Taif and he could now profitably develop it. He was also able to set up sub-offices of his business concern at Makkah and Taif.

---

1. Ibid.

The joy of Hadrat Othman at the conquest of Makkah and Taif was overshadowed by his grief at the death of his wife Umm Kulthum, the third daughter of the Holy Prophet. Umm Kulthum died soon after the conquest of Makkah. The Holy Prophet led the funeral prayer. The Holy Prophet asked the Muslims to marry their daughters to Othman. He said that if he had forty daughters, he would have married them to Othman one after the other.

Expedition to Tabuk[1]

In 630 C.E. the Holy Prophet decided to lead an expedition to Tabuk on the Syrian border. After the victory of the Byzantines over the Persians there was the danger of the Byzantine penetration into Arabia and the Holy Prophet wanted to forestall such a move on the part of the Byzantines, by consolidating the Muslim position on the borders.

The call to arms was given at a time when the weather was burning hot. Crops were ripe and the people were not inclined to leave their homes before harvesting the crops. The journey was long and tedious and many persons were averse to undertake the journey. In spite of these difficulties and setbacks, an army of thirty thousand persons was raised.

In order to finance the expedition the Holy Prophet invited contributions from his followers. Hadrat Othman made the largest contribution. He contributed one thousand dinars in cash, besides a thousand camels for transport. The Holy Prophet greatly appreciated the services of Hadrat Othman. He gave him the tidings of paradise. He also declared that in view of this great service, Othman was not to be judged hereafter.

The Muslim army including Hadrat Othman marched to Tabuk under the leadership of the Holy Prophet. They reached Tabuk after a weary march. There was no Byzantine army to meet the Muslims. On learning of the approach of the Muslim army, the Byzantine army had withdrawn into the interior of Syria. The Byzantine threat to invade Arabia was thus averted by the timely action on the part of the Holy Prophet. The border tribes who owed allegiance to the Byzantines transferred their allegiance to the Muslims. That made the borders safe for the Muslims.

---

1. Ibid.

At Tabuk, the Holy Prophet delivered an historic address. He said:

"Verily the most veracious discourse is the Book of Allah.
The most trusty stronghold is the word of piety.
The best of religions is the religion of Islam.
The best of precedents is the precedent of Muhammad.
The noblest speech is the invocation of Allah.
The finest of the narratives is the Qur'ān.

The best of the affairs is that which has been firmly resolved upon.

The worst in religion are those things which are created without sanction.

The best of the ways is the one trodden by the prophets.
The noblest death is the death of a martyr.
The most miserable blindness is waywardness after guidance.
The best of the actions is that which is beneficent.
The best guidance is that which is put into practice
The worst blindness is the blindness of the heart".

Proclamation about the Banning of Polytheism[1]

In 631 C.E. the Muslims from Madinah proceeded to Makkah to perform the Hajj. The Holy Prophet stayed at Madinah and the pilgrims were led by Hadrat Abu Bakr as "Amir ul Hajj". Hadrat Othman accompanied the caravan.

On the occasion of the Hajj, a proclamation was made to the effect that henceforward non-Muslims were not to be allowed to visit the Ka'aba or perform the pilgrimage. No one was to circumambulate the Ka'aba naked. Polytheism was banned. Where the Muslims had any agreements with the polytheists such agreements were to be honoured. Where there was no agreement, the polytheists were allowed a grace period of four months after which polytheism was not to be tolerated. That made Arabia the land of Islam.

After the Hajj, Hadrat Othman stayed at Makkah for sometime. He married at Makkah Umm Saeed Fatima b Al Walid b Abd Shams, a Quraish lady. Thereafter Hadrat Othman returned to Madinah with his bride.

---

1. *Life of Muhammad*: Hafiz G. Sarwar.

The Farewell Pilgrimage[1]

In 632 C.E. the Holy Prophet decided to proceed to Makkah to perform the pilgrimage. This time the pilgrimage was planned on a large scale. After the necessary arrangements had been made, a caravan of one lakh persons started for Makkah. The Holy Prophet rode at the head of the caravan. He was accompanied by all his wives. Hadrat Othman, accompanied by his wife, also travelled with the caravan.

At Dhul Hulaifa the Muslims put on the 'Ihram', the pilgrim's garb. The Holy Prophet gave the signal call "Labbayk, Allahhumma Labbayk" "Here I am at Your service O Lord!". The party reached Makkah on the 4th of Dhul Hajj after a journey of 19 days. After a stay of four days in Makkah the party left for Mina and passed the night there. The following day the pilgrims proceeded to Arafat. After midday prayer on the 9th of Dhul Hajj at Arafat, the Holy Prophet delivered his historic address:

After praising Allah, the Holy Prophet said:

"O people, listen carefully to my words for I may not be among you next year, nor ever address you again from this spot.

O people, just as you regard this month as sacred, so regard the life and property of every Muslim as sacred.

Return the goods entrusted to you for custody to their rightful owners.

Hurt no one that none may hurt you.

Usury is forbidden.

Satan has despaired in leading you astray in big things; so beware of obeying him in small things.

Women have rights over you and you have rights over them. Be good to them.

You may soon have to appear before Allah and answer for your deeds. So beware.

Do not go astray after I am gone. O people, no prophet will come after me and no new faith will be born.

Worship your Allah, say your prayers, fast during the month of Ramadhan and give of your wealth in charity.

1. Ibid.

All Muslims, free or slave, have the same rights and the same responsibilities. None is higher than the other unless he is higher in virtue.

Feed your slaves as you feed yourself. Do not oppress them, nor usurp their rights".

Turning to the heavens, the Holy Prophet said:

"Be my witness that I have conveyed the message I was commissioned to deliver".

Then the entire congregation with one voice said: "Yes, O Prophet of Allah, you have delivered the message".

Thereafter, Allah revealed:

"This day I have perfected for you your faith,
And completed My blessing upon you,
And have chosen for you Islam as your religion".

Passing away of the Holy Prophet[1]

On return to Madinah, the Holy Prophet fell sick. From this sickness he did not recover and ultimately passed away to the great grief and distress of the Muslims. When it was reported that the Holy Prophet had died, most of the Muslims did not believe in such news. Even men like Hadrat Umar said, "Who says that the Holy Prophet is dead? Moses-like he has gone to have an interview with Allah and would soon return to us". Hadrat Othman also shared this view. It was Hadrat Abu Bakr who broke this spell. Addressing the people gathered in the mosque he said, "Listen to me, O men! know that Muhammad being mortal is dead but the Allah of Muhammad is alive and will live forever".

On hearing the sad news of the passing away of the Holy Prophet, Hadrat Othman sat stunned in a corner of the mosque lost in thoughts. Hadrat Umar passed by him and offered him salutation but Hadrat Othman did not notice him. Later both Hadrat Abu Bakr and Hadrat Umar came to Hadrat Othman. Hadrat Abu Bakr enquired of Hadrat Othman as to why he had not responded to the salutation of Hadrat Umar. Hadrat Othman said that he had not noticed him as he was lost in thought. Hadrat Abu Bakr enquired as to what was the thought wherein he had been lost. Hadrat Othman said that he felt worried that the Holy Prophet had passed away and

1. *Hadrat Abu Bakr Siddiq*: Prof. Masudul Hasan.

yet they had not asked him as to how they could be safe from the snares of the world and the devil? Hadrat Abu Bakr said, "Do not worry, I made the necessary enquiry from the Holy Prophet. He had declared that if one has complete faith that there is no God but Allah and Muhammad is His Prophet, he will remain safe from the snares of the world and the devil".

Throughout his life Hadrat Othman had complete faith that there is no God but Allah and that Muhammad is His Prophet and as such although he was a rich man he remained free from the snares of the world and the devil.

THE CALIPHATE OF HADRAT ABU BAKR AND HADRAT UMAR

Hadrat Abu Bakr[1]

Hadrat Othman had very close and intimate friendly relations with Hadrat Abu Bakr. It was, as a matter of fact, at the instance of Hadrat Abu Bakr that Hadrat Othman had accepted Islam. Accordingly when Hadrat Abu Bakr was elected as the Caliph, Hadrat Othman was the first person after Hadrat Umar to offer allegiance to Hadrat Abu Bakr. Hadrat Othman served in the contingent that was sent by Hadrat Abu Bakr to Syria under the command of Usama. During the apostasy wars, Hadrat Othman remained at Madinah to act as Hadrat Abu Bakr's Adviser.

On his death-bed Hadrat Abu Bakr dictated his will about his successor to Hadrat Othman. Hadrat Abu Bakr dictated in order to avoid the conflict among the Muslims in the matter of his successor, he proposed to make the nomination himself. Thereafter Hadrat Abu Bakr fell into a swoon and Hadrat Othman wrote of his own accord that the person to be nominated as his successor was to be Hadrat Umar. When Hadrat Abu Bakr recovered from the swoon he wanted Hadrat Othman to read what he had written. Hadrat Othman read the passage including the nomination of Hadrat Umar. Hadrat Abu Bakr praised Hadrat Othman for his foresight in reading what was in the mind of Hadrat Abu Bakr. Hadrat Abu Bakr held that fearing that he (Abu Bakr) might not recover from the swoon, Hadrat Othman did the right thing in inserting the name of Hadrat Umar for that was

---

1. Ibid.

indeed his intention. After the death of Hadrat Abu Bakr, Hadrat Othman was the first person to offer allegiance to Hadrat Umar.

Hadrat Umar[1]

During the caliphate of Hadrat Umar, Hadrat Othman remained at Madinah as his Adviser. Hadrat Umar did not allow the Companions including Hadrat Othman to leave Madinah, nor did he employ them for the purposes of the State. Hadrat Umar is reported to have said that he did not employ such eminent persons to high offices because of their virtues. He said that he did not appoint them to high offices lest for any lapse they might lose the eminence that they enjoyed.

During the time of Hadrat Umar considerable wealth flowed into the public treasury. Heretofore the practice was that all that was received in the treasury was immediately distributed among the people. Hadrat Othman advised that instead of such distribution, some amount should be kept in the treasury as reserve for future needs. This advice was accepted by Hadrat Umar.

In the time of Hadrat Umar, a controversy arose about the land in conquered lands. The army was of the view that all lands in conquered territories should be distributed among the soldiers of the conquering army. Another view was that lands should remain with the original owners and the lands whereof the owners left the country should be declared state property. Hadrat Othman supported the latter view and this view was ultimately accepted.

At the time of the conquest of Jerusalem the Christians desired that Hadrat Umar should himself come to Jerusalem to accept the surrender of the city. Hadrat Othman was of the view that it was not necessary for the Caliph of the Muslims to go to Jerusalem and that the enemy when defeated would of its own accord surrender the city. There was much force in the view point of Hadrat Othman but in order to win the goodwill of the Christians, Hadrat Umar decided to go to Jerusalem to accept the surrender of the city.

In the time of Hadrat Umar, a severe famine broke out in the country and there was acute shortage of food supply. At that time a large caravan belonging to Hadrat Othman, carrying large supplies of food grains arrived in Madinah. Traders rushed to the house of Hadrat Othman and tried to prevail upon him to sell the grain to them

---

1. *Hadrat Umar Farooq*: Prof. Masudul Hasan.

at profit. Hadrat Othman wanted them to indicate the profit they would allow him. The highest bid they could offer was cent per cent profit. Hadrat Othman said that he would not sell his goods at a profit less than ten times the original price. The traders said that they could not afford him profit to that extent and that nobody could do that. Hadrat Othman said that he had already an offer for ten times profit. "Who had made such offer", enquired the traders. Hadrat Othman said that Allah had assured him of ten times profit. Thereafter Hadrat Othman distributed the entire stock of food grains among the poor free of cost and expected ten times profit from Allah.

When Hadrat Umar died, looking at the dead face of Hadrat Umar, Hadrat Othman said, "Out of us who can equal Umar". That was a great tribute to Hadrat Umar.

2

THE CALIPHATE OF HADRAT OTHMAN

The Dilemma of Hadrat Umar[1]

When Hadrat Umar lay on his death-bed, the question that vexed him was whether he should or should not nominate his successor. If he did not nominate a successor he would be following the precedent set by the Holy Prophet. On the other hand if he nominated a successor he would be following the precedent of Hadrat Abu Bakr.

As he weighed the claims of various persons around him he could not make up his mind to nominate any of them as his successor. He sighed and said whom should he nominate as his successor. He thought that if Abu Ubaidah had been alive, he could have nominated him as his successor, for the Holy Prophet had regarded him as the trustee of the Muslim community. In the alternative if Salam, the liberated slave of Abu Hudhaifa, had been alive he would have appointed him as his successor, for according to the assessment of the Holy Prophet, among the Muslims he loved Allah most.

Nomination of His Son Abdullah[2]

Someone suggested to Hadrat Umar that he should nominate his son Abdullah as his successor. That evoked a violent reaction from Hadrat Umar. He said:

---

1. *Hadrat Umar Farooq*: Prof. Masudul Hasan.
2. Ibid.

"May Allah curse you for tempting me to nepotism by nominating my son, when I am going to meet my Creator. The caliphate is an affair affecting the entire Muslim community and I would not like to make it an hereditary affair in my family. I swear by Allah that I never coveted the caliphate for myself. Therefore what I never coveted for myself, I would not like to pass on to my family. If the caliphate is something good, then by holding the office for the last ten years I have had the blessing for my family. If the caliphate is bad, then why should I pass on this bad thing to my family? Allah is my witness that during my caliphate I showed no favour to my family members. On the other hand, I was more hard with them than with the other Muslims. I have always tried to fulfil the obligation of the office under the shadow of the fear lest I may at any stage falter in the performance of my duties. I do not know whether I have succeeded in my purpose but I will be happy if my achievements and failures just balance so that I am neither rewarded nor punished for holding the office of the caliphate. Remember ye men that if I nominate a successor, a better man than me, namely Hadrat Abu Bakr also nominated a successor. And again if I do not nominate a successor, remember that the best of men, namely the Holy Prophet of Islam did not nominate a successor. Whatever the case Allah Himself would protect the interests of Islam and the Muslim community".

Hadrat Umar's Dream[1]

As Hadrat Umar lay thinking about the issue of nominating a successor he fell asleep. In the dream he saw that a man who had laid out the garden was plucking all the ripe and unripe fruit and gathering it on the ground. He interpreted this dream to mean that he should name the eligible candidates and then leave them to choose one of themselves as the Caliph. Hadrat Umar accordingly constituted a Committee of six persons to choose the next Caliph out of themselves.

This Committee comprised:

(1) Hadrat Ali b Abu Talib,
(2) Hadrat Othman b Affan,
(3) Abdur Rahman b Auf,
(4) Saad b Abi Waqas,

1. Ibid.

(5) Zubair b Awwam and
(6) Talha b Ubaidullah.

All these persons were among the most eminent companions of the Holy Prophet, whom he had given the tidings of paradise in their lifetime.

The Committee in Session[1]

When the Committee was constituted, Talha was out of Madinah. The remaining five members met immediately. It was soon found that there were strong differences among the members over the question of choosing a leader and loud voices were raised projecting the differences. When the dying Caliph heard of these voices he ordered that the Committee should adjourn and meet after his death. He directed that after his death the Committee should reach the final decision within three days and the next Caliph should take the oath of office on the fourth day. Hadrat Umar's son Abdullah was to sit with the Committee as Adviser or Moderator but he was not to have a vote, nor was he to be eligible for election as the Caliph. If Talha joined the Committee within this period, he was to take part in the deliberations but if he did not return to Madinah within this period, the other members of the Committee could proceed to take the decision. If there was a tie among the members, Abdul Rahman b Auf was to have the casting vote. Pending the election of the Caliph, Suhaib was to lead the prayers. When the Caliph was elected, the prayers were to be led by him.

Testament for His Successor[2]

Thereafter, Hadrat Umar dictated a testament for his successor. It provided:

> "I enjoin upon you to have trust and faith in Allah, He Who has no peer.
>
> Be kind and generous to the Muhajreen and the Ansar. Those out of them who are good, be good to them. Those who are bad overlook their lapses.
>
> Be good to the people of the conquered lands. They are the outer line of our defence and they are the target of the anger and distress of the enemies. They contribute to our revenues. They should be taxed only on their surplus wealth.

1. Ibid.
2. Ibid

Be gracious to the Bedouins as they are the backbone of the Arab nation.

I instruct you to be good to the Dhimmis, for they are your responsibility. Do not tax them beyond their capacity. Ensure that they pay "Jizya" without undue inconvenience.

Fear Allah and in all that you do, keep His pleasure in view. In the matter of people fear Allah and in the matter of Allah do not be afraid of the people.

With regard to the people, I enjoin upon you to administer justice with an even hand. See that all the legitimate requirements of people are met. Be concerned for their welfare. Ensure the safety of their person and property.

See that the frontiers of our dominions are not violated. Take steps to guard the frontiers.

In the matter of administration do not prefer the rich to the poor. Be hard against those who violate the law. Show them no mercy. Do not rest content until you have brought the miscreants to book.

Treat all the people as equal. Be a pillar of strength for those who are weak and oppressed. Those who are strong but do wrong, make them pay for their wrong doings.

In the distribution of booty and other matters, be above nepotism. Let not considerations of relationship or selfish interest weigh with you.

The Satan is at large; it will tempt you. Rise above all temptations and perform your duties in accordance with the injunctions of Islam.

Get guidance from the Holy Qur'ãn and Sunnah. Freely consult the wise men around you. Apply your own mind to difficult cases and seek light from Allah.

Be simple in your living and your habits. Lead life as a model Muslim. As you are the leader of the Muslims, justify your leadership by being the best among them. May Allah bless you".

Death of Hadrat Umar and After[1]

When Hadrat Umar died, both Hadrat Ali and Hadrat Othman wanted to lead the funeral prayer. Abdul Rahman b Auf, however,

1. *Ashab-e- Rasul Ke Karname*: Nabi Ahmad Suha.

advised that as both of them were candidates for the office of the Caliph they should not lead such prayer. The funeral prayers were accordingly led by Suhaib, the man who had been authorised by Hadrat Umar to lead the ordinary prayers. Hadrat Umar was put in the grave by all the five members of the Selection Committee constituted by him.

Immediately after the burial of Hadrat Umar, the Selection Committee constituted by him to nominate his successor met in session. As Talha b Ubaidullah was still out of Madinah, the meeting of the Committee was attended by five persons only. The Committee had a long session for two days but it was unable to arrive at any decision. The differences among the parties were acute and no reconciliation appeared to be in sight.

Dream of Abdul Rahman b Auf[1]

The instructions of Hadrat Umar were that the Selection Committee should choose the successor within three days and he should assume office on the fourth day. As two days passed away without arriving at a decision, the members felt anxious that the time was running fast and still no solution to the problem appeared to be in sight.

On the night after the second day, Abdul Rahman b Auf had a dream. He saw that in a wilderness a strong and handsome camel appeared and the wilderness was converted into a rich green pasture on which it fell and then moved away. Thereafter another camel came. It tarried in the pasture for a short time and then following in the footsteps of the first camel moved away. Then the third camel came. It tarried in the pasture for sometime and then thereafter looking right and left, it also moved away following the footsteps of the first two camels. Then came the fourth camel. It limped and could walk with difficulty. Then a strong hot wind began to blow from the desert and the pasture became parched. The camel was unable to feed itself and then limping it moved away in the same direction which the previous three camels had left.

Abdul Rahman b Auf interpreted this dream to signify that the first camel represented the Holy Prophet who gave mankind the message of Islam and thereby spearheaded a great revolution. The second camel represented Hadrat Abu Bakr who followed in the

1. Ibid.

footsteps of the Master but whose rule was short. The third camel represented Hadrat Umar whose rule was comparatively longer. The fourth camel represented the successor of Hadrat Umar. The dream signified that the rule of such successor was to end in some disaster.

That made Abdul Rahman b Auf feel that he should not covet the office for himself. On the third day addressing the members of the Selection Committee, Abdul Rahman b Auf observed that if they went on debating and wrangling in that way, differences among them would grow in dimensions and they would fail in the objective set for them. He suggested that in order to narrow down the choice, some of them should withdraw from the contest voluntarily. Thereupon he declared that in the interests of the Muslim community, he withdrew from the contest on his free-will. The choice now came to be restricted to the remaining four members but still no headway was made. There were some further deliberations and thereafter it was decided that as Abdul Rahman b Auf had retired voluntarily from the contest and had given proof on his selflessness, he might choose the Caliph out of the remaining four members. Abdul Rahman accepted the onerous task and undertook that in arriving at his decision he would be just and impartial and would be guided solely by the interests of the Muslim community. He added that he would try to ascertain public opinion and his choice would be in accord with such opinion.

Choice of Abdul Rahman b Auf[1]

Commissioned to make the selection Abdul Rahman b Auf began his task by interviewing each member of the Committee separately. Interviewing Hadrat Ali he asked him, "Suppose I do not choose you, in that case whom would you like me to choose?" Hadrat Ali said, "In that case you may choose Hadrat Othman". Hadrat Othman was interviewed next and he was asked the question, "If you are not selected who should be the next choice?" Hadrat Othman said, "In that case the obvious choice would be Hadrat Ali". When Zubair b Awamm was put the same question he said, "Ali or Othman". When Saad b Abi Waqas was interviewed he said that he would like Abdul Rahman b Auf to be the Caliph. Abdul Rahman said that as he had withdrawn from the contest his choice should be from among the other four members. Saad b Abi Waqas said that in that

1. *Othman b. Affan*: Raza Misri.

case, Hadrat Othman would be his choice. Analysing these answers, Abdul Rahman b Auf came to the conclusion that Hadrat Othman commanded the majority of votes among the members of the Selection Committee.

Thereafter Abdul Rahman b Auf proceeded to consult the other leaders of public opinion in Madinah. Some Bedouin chiefs had arrived in Madinah to participate in the funeral ceremonies of Hadrat Umar. Abdul Rahman b Auf consulted these men as well. Obviously the choice lay between Hadrat Ali and Hadrat Othman. Out of these Hadrat Ali was still young being less than fifty, while Hadrat Othman was old being nearly seventy. According to the Arab traditions of respect for old age, the common men expressed themselves in favour of Hadrat Othman, the older among the two candidates.

Hadrat Umar had been a hard task master. He was not only harsh with the people, he was harsh even with himself and his family members. The people now wanted a change and they favoured Hadrat Othman who was well-known for his mildness, kindness and generosity. The people could not forget that Hadrat Othman was a rich man and he had used a greater part of his wealth for public welfare. He had purchased the Beer Rauma well from the Jews for the purpose of supplying water to the Muslims. He had financed the project for the extension of the Prophet's mosque. He had financed a greater part of the expedition to Tabuk. In the time of famine he had donated large stocks of grain for public distribution. He used to liberate a slave every Friday.

After meeting the public, Abdul Rahman b Auf arrived at the conclusion that an overwhelming majority of the people favoured the election of Hadrat Othman. Thereafter Abdul Rahman had another round of meeting with Hadrat Ali and Hadrat Othman. Addressing Hadrat Ali he asked, "If you are elected as the Caliph do you undertake to follow the Qur'ãn and the Sunnah and the traditions set by your predecessors?" Hadrat Ali said that he would follow the Qur'ãn and the Sunnah but in the matter of the traditions of his predecessors he would follow them as far as possible and would execute his own judgement in each case. When the same question was put to Hadrat Othman, he gave an unconditional undertaking. That made Abdul Rahman b Auf give his verdict in favour of Hadrat Othman.

ELECTION OF HADRAT OTHMAN[1]

On the fourth day after the death of Hadrat Umar, the Muslims gathered in the Prophet's mosque at Madinah. Abdul Rahman b Auf took the stage and recounted the efforts that he had made in arriving at a decision with regard to the successor to Hadrat Umar. He observed that the choice lay between two candidates namely Hadrat Ali and Hadrat Othman. He dwelt at length on the merits of both the candidates and observed that after consulting the people at large he had arrived at the conclusion that the majority of the people favoured the succession of Hadrat Othman. He declared on solemn oath that in arriving at the decision he had not been moved by any extraneous consideration. He had taken the decision in the sole interest of the Muslim community. Addressing Hadrat Ali he said that he should not feel annoyed at the decision. He was still young and there would be further opportunities for him to come to power. He appealed to him to accept the decision in the interests of Muslim solidarity. Thereafter Abdul Rahman b Auf said to Hadrat Othman, "Stretch forth your hand so that I may take the oath of allegiance to you". Hadrat Othman stretched his hand and Abdul Rahman b Auf took the oath of allegiance to him as the Caliph. Thereafter all the Muslims gathered in the mosque, took the oath of allegiance to Hadrat Othman. Hadrat Ali felt dissatisfied but he too took the oath of allegiance to Hadrat Othman. Thus Hadrat Othman was elected as the third Caliph. That was the first day of the year 24 A.H.

Inaugural Address of Hadrat Othman[2]

After election, Hadrat Othman took his stand on the pulpit and addressed the congregation. He glorified Allah and His Prophet and then talked the transitoriness of the world. He wanted the people to do good deeds which might stand them in good stead in the next world. He said that he was conscious of his limitations but he would do his best to serve Islam and the people. Then overwhelmed by emotions, Hadrat Othman broke down and could not complete his address. He said:

> "O people, it is not easy to manage a new horse. If Allah willing I live, there will be several other occasions to talk to you. Right now I cannot address you. You know that I am not good at making public speeches".

1. Ibid.
2. *Suyuti's History of the Caliphs*: Major H.S. Jarrett.

Reaction to the Election of Hadrat Othman[1]

The reaction to the election of Hadrat Othman as the Caliph was on the whole favourable. After the stern rule of Hadrat Umar, the people welcomed the mild rule of Hadrat Othman.

In his book *History of the Caliphs*, Suyuti observes that Ibn Sa'ad and Al Hakim record on the authority of Ibn Mas'ud that he said:

> "When Othman was sworn allegiance, we placed the best among us in authority and we were not remiss".

It is recorded that addressing Abdul Rahman b Auf, Mughira b Sha'aba said, "O Abdul Rahman, by offering allegiance to Othman you have taken the correct decision. We would not have agreed to any other decision".

Farzuq, the poet composed the following verses to mark the occasion:

> "Suhaib led the prayers for three days,
> And then handed over the custody of the Muslim community to Othman b Affan;
> It's the caliphate which Abu Bakr had entrusted to Umar;
> And which has now been passed on to Othman.
> Verily, all of them were rightly guided persons,
> Who were very dear to the Prophet of Islam".

THE TRIAL OF UBAIDULLAH BIN UMAR

Assassination of Hadrat Umar Whether the Result of a Conspiracy[2]

When Hadrat Umar was stabbed by a Persian slave Firoz, a question arose whether this was the act of a single disgruntled person or whether it was the result of a conspiracy. Abdur Rahman b Abu Bakr reported that the previous day, he had seen Firoz, Jafina and Hurmuzan conferring together. Seeing him the three men were confused and a double edged dagger fell from the hands of one of them. It was alleged that that was the dagger with which Hadrat Umar had been stabbed.

---

1. *Othman b. Affan*: Raza Misri.
2. Ibid.

Ubaidullah's Orgy of Murder[1]

When Ubaidullah, a son of Hadrat Umar, heard the report of Abdur Rahman, he took his sword and rushed out of his house to take the revenge for the assassination of his father. After stabbing Hadrat Umar, Firoz had killed himself. Ubaidullah first went to the house of Firoz and killed his wife and daughter. He then sought Jafina. He was a Christian of Hirah, who had been brought to Madinah after the conquest of Iraq. He was employed in teaching the art of writing to the Arab students. Ubaidullah killed Jafina. Thereafter Ubaidullah went to Hurmuzan and killed him likewise. Hurmrzan was a Persian General who had been taken captive in one of the Persian campaigns. He accepted Islam and settled in Madinah. Hadrat Umar had sanctioned a stipend for him. When the Muslims came to know that in a fit of frenzy Ubaidullah had killed four persons, they apprehended him and confined him to his house.

The Trial of Ubaidullah[2]

After assuming office as the Caliph, the first case that Hadrat Othman was to try was the case of Ubaidullah. Apart from Abdur Rahman b Abu Bakr no other person supported the theory of any conspiracy. Adequate evidence was thus not forthcoming to support the theory of the involvement of Jafina and Hurmuzan in the alleged conspiracy. Again, even if it was established that these persons had entered into a conspiracy, there was no justification for the killing of the wife and daughter of Firoz. Even if there were strong *prima faciè* grounds for holding that the assassination was the result of a conspiracy, the State alone could have tried the accused and condemned them only when they had offered their defence and the case was established against them. Ubaidullah had no right or justification to take the law in his own hand and murder four persons without affording them an opportunity for defence. That was the Arab practice of the days of ignorance which was in violation of the injunctions of Islam.

The Verdict of Hadrat Othman[3]

The case was tried by Hadrat Othman with the help of a jury. The jury included Hadrat Ali, Amr b Al A'as and some prominent

---

1. Ibid.
2. Ibid.
3. Ibid.

Companions. Hadrat Ali was of the opinion that the dictates of justice demanded that Ubaidullah should be executed for taking the law in his hand and murdering four citizens without cause. Hadrat Ali was emphatically of the view that in Islam law was no respector of persons and Ubaidullah could not be saved from the penalty of law merely on the ground that he was the son of the late Caliph.

Amr b Al A'as and other companions were of the view that they lost Hadrat Umar only yesterday and it could not be that today his son should be killed. They said that they owed to the memory of Hadrat Umar that his son should be protected.

Hadrat Othman pondered over the matter. He said that as the murdered person had left no heir, he was their heir and in this capacity it was open to him to accept blood money for the murdered persons. His verdict was that Ubaidullah should pay a thousand dinars as blood money for each murdered person.

Ubaidullah was not in a position to pay the blood money. Hadrat Othman paid the blood money out of his own pocket and credited it into the Baitul Mal.

Reaction to the Verdict of Hadrat Othman[1]

On the whole the people were satisfied with the verdict of Hadrat Othman and they praised him for his generosity in paying the blood money out of his own pocket. There were, however, a few persons who found fault with his judgement and insisted that Ubaidullah should have been executed. In a poem the poet Ziyad b Labid said:

> "O Othman, there is no doubt that after the assassination of Hurmuzan, Ubaidullah had no right to live.
>
> You have unjustly pardoned him although you had no right to do so."

Hadrat Othman summoned Ziyad and explained to him the justification for his verdict. Thereafter Ziyad composed some verses praising Hadrat Othman for his verdict and for his generosity in paying the blood money out of his pocket.

Tabari's Version[2]

In Tabari's *History*, a somewhat different version of the incident is given. It is stated that Qamazban, the son of Hurmuzan, appeared

1. Ibid.
2. Tabari's *History*.

as a witness before the Caliph. He stated that a day previous to the assassination of Hadrat Umar his father came across Firoz. A double edged dagger fell from the hands of Firoz. Hurmuzan had asked Firoz why he had that dagger with him. Firoz had given an evasive reply but Hurmuzan warned him not to use the dagger as that would involve them all in trouble.

In view of the evidence of Qamazban it was established that the assassination of Hadrat Umar was the sole act of Firoz and neither Hurmuzan nor Jafina were involved in the conspiracy in any way. Thereupon the Caliph decided that Qamazban could deal with Ubaidullah in any way he liked. Qamazban was originally of the view to murder Ubaidullah but later he changed his view and pardoned him for the sake of Allah. Thereupon Hadrat Othman paid the blood money out of his pocket.

DIRECTIVES OF HADRAT OTHMAN

On assuming office, Hadrat Othman issued a number of directives. These directives provided the guidelines for the functionaries of the state and set out the policies of Hadrat Othman in specific terms. All concerned were required to implement such directives in letter as well as in spirit.

Directive to the Administrators[1]

Hadrat Othman issued the following directive to the persons responsible for administration in various parts of the dominions:

> "After glorifying and offering all praise to Allah Almighty, it may be stated that Allah requires the administrators to be the well-wishers and protectors of the people. The administrators have not been vested with power merely to collect taxes from the people. In Islam the position of an administrator is that of a protector and not a mere tax collector. A time will come when the administrators will concentrate on the exercise of power and would overlook their obligations to the people. That will be the age of tyranny. Bear in mind that your main obligation is to study the problems of the people and help them in the solution of such problems. See that a proper equation is maintained between the rights and duties of the people. Everybody should perform his

1. *Othman b. Affan*: Raza Misri.

duty and at the same time he should be assured that he would have what is due to him. Also keep an eye on the enemies. See that such subversive activities, if any, are suppressed but whatever promises are made, even with the enemy, should be respected".

Directive to the Defence Forces[1]

Hadrat Othman issued the following directive to the defence forces:

"Keep in mind that you are to guard the frontiers of the Muslim dominions. You are to protect the life and property of the Muslims. I am aware of the laws that Hadrat Umar formulated for your guidance. Indeed such laws were made with my consultation and the consultation of other Muslims. Be wary that I do not receive any complaint that you are violating or thwarting such laws. If you do so, Allah will place other persons in your stead. I am under obligation to protect your rights and privileges but you should always weigh how far you deserve such rights and privileges."

Directive to the Tax Collectors[2]

Hadrat Othman issued the following directive to the tax collectors:

"Know you all that all glory and praise is for Allah. Allah enjoins justice and He would not approve any act of administration which is not based on justice. Be just and fair to all concerned. Do not realise from anybody what is not due from him. Be honest. See that the trust reposed in you is not betrayed. Do not oppress or harass the people. Pay particular regard to the orphans and the poor. See that they are not made to bear a burden which is beyond their capacity."

Directive for the General Public[3]

Hadrat Othman issued the following directive for the general public:

"Know that whatever you have attained is due to Islam and following the injunctions of the Holy Prophet. If you are lost in the world you will betray the objective of your life. Follow Islam

---

1. *Hadrat Othman ne Farmaya*: Abdul Jalil Quraishi.
2. Ibid.
3. *Othman b. Affan*: Raza Misri.

faithfully and do not introduce any innovations. See that the abundance of wealth does not divert you from the ideals of Islam. The extension of your dominions has brought various peoples within your fold. See that this does not lead to any differences among you. Remain united. Hold fast to the rope of Allah. May Allah bless you."

SERMONS OF HADRAT OTHMAN

Sermons of Hadrat Othman[1]

Some sermons of Hadrat Othman have been preserved in history. We refer to some of these sermons with a view to illustrating the beliefs of Hadrat Othman. These sermons speak of Hadrat Othman's unshakable faith in Islam.

His Role

In one of the sermons, Hadrat Othman defined his role as Caliph. He said:

"My role is to follow what has already been laid down. I do not intend to be an innovator. I declare that I will faithfully follow the Qur'ãn and the Sunnah. In matters not covered by the Qur'ãn and the Sunnah, I promise that I will follow all such things which command concensus before my caliphate. If in any matter no concensus has been reached already, I will follow the way of the good with your consultation. I assure you that I will restrain my hand from you till that is the dictate of law."

The World is a Tarrying Place[2]

In another sermon Hadrat Othman said:

"O people, this world is merely a tarrying place. You are marching towards your goal. Do as many good deeds as you can, so that when death overtakes you, there is much of good in your account. Learn from the lives of those who are dead. O people, you consider yourself to be safe within your houses. Beware that you are in the latter part of your life. Therefore do good deeds during whatever life is left for you. Nobody knows when the call of death may come. You should spend your life in

1. Ibid.
2. Ibid.

such a way that when you die, you die as a true Muslim. Take lesson from death and be constantly engaged in good works. It is a matter of wonder that man believes in death and yet laughs. O men, instead of running after the world run for the hereafter. In the Holy Qur'ān Allah asked the Holy Prophet to explain to the people the simile of the world. The life is like water which descends from the heavens. In the hereafter there will be punishment as well as reward. Worry for the world darkens the soul and anxiety for the hereafter brightens the soul. Know that the world is not everlasting; the hereafter is everlasting. Therefore prefer the hereafter to this world. If your eyes can have true vision then everyday is doomsday."

Unity[1]

Exhorting the people to maintain unity, Hadrat Othman said:

"Remain united. Let there be no dissension in your ranks. You were the enemies of one another. Allah blessed you with Islam and you began to love one another and became brothers. Maintain your unity. Do not break up into sections. Allah is happy with your unity and exhorts you to refrain from disunity."

The People of Madinah[2]

Stressing the importance of the people of Madinah in the Islamic community, Hadrat Othman said:

"O the people of Madinah, you are the backbone of Islam. If you stray from the right path, the other Muslims will also stray. Therefore maintain the highest standards of integrity. Beware that if I come to know of any dereliction on your part I will exile you. In this respect no excuse will be entertained. You know that in the previous regimes those who strayed were put to death. I will overlook your petty lapses but such conduct which is violative of Islam will not be tolerated. Things are happening which I do not approve either for you or for myself. I will have to be very cautious. You should also be careful. Reform your tongue. When the tongue is restrained the heart is purified. When Allah sees His men making efforts to reform He gets pleased. He becomes wroth when He sees the people bent on mischief. Man should therefore try to reform himself."

---

1. Ibid.
2. Ibid.

The Last Sermon[1]

According to Tabari, the last sermon of Hadrat Othman was as follows:

> "The truth of the matter is that you are in this world merely to prepare for the next world. Allah never intended that you should be attracted by the world. This world will not last; the hereafter alone will be eternal. Therefore you should not be proud of anything in this world. Beware that you do not become forgetful of the next world. Prefer the hereafter to this world, for you have to ultimately return to Allah. Always fear Allah. This fear will serve you as a shield against His punishment. Be afraid of the punishment of Allah. Remain united and be not divided into sections. Remember that you were the enemies of one another and under Islam, Allah made you like brothers. See that this unity is maintained at all costs."

RELIGIOUS MEASURES OF HADRAT OTHMAN

Promotion of the Purposes of Islam

Hadrat Othman was a great Muslim. He followed the injunctions of Islam rigorously in letter as well as in spirit. He spent a greater part of the night in prayers. He knew the Holy Qur'ãn by heart and would complete the recitation of the whole of the Holy Qur'ãn during a night. He held that the primary and basic responsibility of the Caliph was to protect and safeguard Islam and take steps to promote its purposes and values. During his caliphate Hadrat Othman took several measures with a view to promoting the purposes of Islam.

Recension of the Holy Qur'ãn[2]

To Hadrat Othman belongs the honour of undertaking the measure of the recension of the Holy Qur'ãn and uniting the Muslim community on a standard text of the Holy Qur'ãn for all times.

The Holy Qur'ãn was revealed to the Holy Prophet in parts extending over a period of twenty-three years. Whenever the Holy Prophet received a revelation, he would dictate it to some person

---

1. Tabari: *History of Islam*.
2. *Early Heroes of Islam*: G.A. Salik.

who would record it on some piece of leather, date skin or even bones and stones. The principal scribe of the Holy Prophet was Zaid b Thabit. Hadrat Othman also served as the scribe occasionally. Many companions committed the Holy Qur'ãn to heart and Hadrat Othman was one of them.

Many *Huffaz* (those who had learnt the Holy Qur'ãn by heart) died in the battle of Yamama during the caliphate of Hadrat Abu Bakr. It was felt that it was necessary that the Holy Qur'ãn should be compiled in a book form for the guidance of the people. A compilation was thus prepared and it was called *Mashaf.* In the time of the caliphate of Hadrat Abu Bakr this compilation was kept in the custody of Hadrat Ayesha. In the time of the caliphate of Hadrat Umar this compilation was kept in the custody of Hadrat Hafsa, daughter of Hadrat Umar and a wife of the Holy Prophet.

In the time of Hadrat Othman, Hudhafa who had been to different parts of the Muslim dominions came to Madinah and reported that the people of different regions had different readings of the Holy Qur'ãn. The people of Homs held that their reading of the Holy Qur'ãn was correct as they had learnt it from Hadrat Miqdad, an eminent companion. The men of Basra held that their reading was correct as they had learnt it from Abu Musa Ash'ari. In Kufa, the people claimed superiority for their reading as they had learnt it from Abdullah bin Masud, an authority on the subject. There were thus divergent readings of the Holy Qur'ãn. It was stressed that unless some attempt was made to unify the text, that was likely to be a cause of split among the people.

The question was considered by the Majlis-i-Shura and it was decided that an authoritative standardised text should be compiled and no divergence should be permitted from the standard text. Hadrat Othman appointed a Committee comprising Zaid b Thabit, Abdullah b Zubair, Saeed b Al 'Aas and Abdur Rahman b Al Harith. This Committee was commissioned to prepare an authorised text. Copies of the Holy Qur'ãn in use in various parts of the dominions were collected and compared with the copy in the custody of Hadrat Hafsa which had been compiled in the time of Hadrat Abu Bakr. The Committee worked hard. All the discrepancies were reconciled and an authorised standard edition was prepared. Hadrat Othman checked the compilation himself and finally approved it. Copies of this edition were prepared and supplied to all parts of the dominions.

All previous copies in use in the various parts of the Muslim dominions were collected and burnt.

This was a measure of great importance and significance and thereby Hadrat Othman did a great service to the cause of Islam. The books revealed to all previous prophets had been corrupted by the followers of the respective prophets. But for the measure undertaken by Hadrat Othman, the same fate would have befallen the Holy Qur'ãn. Hadrat Othman deserves the gratitude of the Muslims by this single service in preserving the Holy Qur'ãn in its original form free from any corruption. It is surprising that some of the critics of Hadrat Othman made this measure a matter of criticism against Hadrat Othman. They said that the burning of the copies of the Holy Qur'ãn with a view to introducing a uniform text was a sacrilege. This criticism is entirely misconceived. The burning of the unauthorised texts could by no stretch of imagination be called a sacrilege. It was on the other hand a most pious act inasmuch as it united the Muslim community on an authoritative and standard text for all times.

Zakat on Horses and Slaves[1]

According to the Shariah, the Muslims were enjoined to pay *Zakat* on their capital assets. In the time of the Holy Prophet, Hadrat Abu Bakr and Hadrat Umar, no *Zakat* was levied on horses and slaves. Hadrat Othman reviewed the position and ordered that *Zakat* should be levied on horses and slaves as well. This measure was approved by the people in general but some of the persons hostile to Hadrat Othman made it a subject of criticism. They argued that as *Zakat* had not been levied on horses and slaves by the Holy Prophet, Hadrat Othman had violated the Sunnah by levying such *Zakat*.

During the earlier period there was a great dearth of horses. Most of the horses had been killed in early battles. In the time of Hadrat Othman things had changed. With the expansion of the Muslim dominions the supply of horses had considerably improved and the population of horses had increased. The position regarding slaves was similar. With the expansion of the Muslim dominions the number of slaves had considerably increased and the people owning slaves were deriving much advantage from them. Indeed the

---

1. *Othman*: Taha Hussain.

slaves were great assets for their masters and they played an important role in economy.

As a matter of fact *Zakat* is leviable on all capital assets. In the time of the Holy Prophet horses and slaves had not acquired the dimensions of capital assets and as such these were not assessed to *Zakat*. As in the time of Hadrat Othman these things had become definite capital assets, Hadrat Othman subjected them to the levy of *Zakat*. Such levy was in accord with the spirit of Islam and was in no way repugnant thereto. Where any articles were not subjected to *Zakat* because of special circumstances and these articles were later subjected to the levy as the special circumstances necessitating exemption no longer obtained, such levy was not repugnant to the injunctions of Islam. The levy would have been repugnant if the Holy Prophet had ordered the levy and such levy was withdrawn. The levy of *Zakat* on horses and slaves was based on Hadrat Othman's *Ijtihad* and his *Ijtihad* was correct and in public interest.

In the time of Hadrat Othman, a question arose whether *Zakat* should be assessed by the person concerned or it should be assessed by the State functionaries. Hadrat Othman's view was that *Zakat* was not a tax; it was a species of religious obligation and was a matter between the person concerned and Allah. Hadrat Othman, therefore, held that while the *Zakat* should be assessed by the person concerned himself, it should be collected by the State functionaries.

Prayers on the Occasion of the Hajj[1]

During the first year of his caliphate, Hadrat Othman suffered from blood haemorrhage of the nose. Many other persons suffered likewise and in the Arab annals this year came to be known as the year of the haemorrhage. Hadrat Othman was not able to perform the Hajj during the first year of his office but in subsequent years he performed the Hajj and presided at the Hajj functions.

When offering the prayers on the occasion of the Hajj between Mina and Mt Arafat, the Holy Prophet had shortened the prayers from four rakaats to two rakaats. Thereafter Hadrat Abu Bakr and Hadrat Umar while presiding at the Hajj functions followed the precedent set up by the Holy Prophet and offered only two rakaats

1. *Othman b. Affan*: Raza Misri.

in prayers. In the early years of his caliphate, Hadrat Othman followed the same precedent but in the year 649 C.E. Hadrat Othman offered the full prayers in four rakaats.

Hadrat Othman was criticised by hostile circles for making this departure from the precedent set up by the Holy Prophet. Even such companions like Abdur Rahman b Auf and Hadrat Ali questioned Hadrat Othman about the advisability of such innovation. Hadrat Othman argued that as a matter of fact the prayer comprised four rakaats and it could be shortened to two rakaats under special circumstances. When the Holy Prophet shortened the prayer, he had settled at Madinah and had come to Makkah as a visitor. Hadrat Othman said that his case was different. He had married in Makkah and had a house there. He also had some property at Taif. As such when he came to Makkah his status was not that of a mere visitor. As such he did not feel himself entitled to enjoy the concession of shortening the prayers. He also argued that in case he continued the practice of shortening the prayers, the Bedouins were apt to feel that the prayers comprised two rakaats only. In order to remove such impression it was necessary that the prayer should be offered in full. Hadrat Othman further argued that the shortening of the prayer was a concession. A concession was in principle meant to meet certain exigencies and had to be withdrawn when such exigencies no longer existed. Hadrat Othman held that according to his *Ijtihad,* a stage had reached when the concession was no longer necessary and the prayer should be offered in full. Hadrat Othman also elaborated that the offering of the prayers in full was in no way repugnant to the injunctions of Islam or Sunnah. If Islam had provided for four rakaats and he had offered two rakaats that would have been repugnant to Islam. Where Islam provided for four rakaats and gave the option of shortening the prayer in certain circumstances and he chose to offer the prayer in full and not to avail of the concession, such an act was in furtherance of the purposes of Islam and was in no way repugnant thereto.

Other Measures of Hadrat Othman[1]

Hadrat Othman introduced a few other measures as well to promote the purposes of Islam. On the occasion of the Friday prayers he introduced a second call or Takbir for the convenience

1. Ibid.

of the people. He provided stipends for the first time for the 'Muezzins'. On the occasion of the 'Ramadhan', he increased the daily allowances of the people. He also arranged to supply free meals to all concerned at the time of the breaking of the fast. Hadrat Othman made special arrangement for the upkeep of mosques.

ECONOMIC POLICIES OF HADRAT OTHMAN

Economic Resources of the State[1]

In the time of Hadrat Othman the economic resources of the State were: Zakat, Ushr, Kharaj, Jazya, Fay and Ghanimah. Zakat was a $2\frac{1}{2}$ per cent levy on capital assets. Hadrat Othman levied the Zakat on some of the items which had escaped taxation previously. Ushr was a ten per cent levy on agricultural land as well as merchandise imported from abroad. Kharaj was a levy on land in conquered territories. The rate of Kharaj was higher than the Ushr. Jizya was a poll tax levied on non-Muslims. Fay was the income from State land. Ghanimah was the booty captured on the occasion of war with the enemy. Four-fifth of the booty was distributed among the soldiers taking part in the war while one-fifth was credited to the State fund. During the time of Hadrat Othman the income of the State increased considerably. When 'Amr b Al 'Aas was the Governor of Egypt the complaint against him was that the receipts from Egypt were low. He said that the she-camel could not give more milk. When Abdullah bin Sa'ad was appointed as the Governor, the revenues of the province increased. When confronted with this situation 'Amr b Al 'Aas said, "Yes, the she-camel has given more milk but its young ones have been starved." This shows that under Hadrat Othman the revenues of the State increased. The view of 'Amr b Al 'Aas that the young one of the she-camel had been starved was merely an apologetic way of justifying his own administration.

Stipends of the People[2]

Hadrat Umar had fixed the stipends of the people. On assuming office, Hadrat Othman increased these stipends by 25 per cent. That was an economic measure which contributed to the prosperity of the

---

1. Ibid.
2. Ibid.

people. Writers like Taha Hussain have taken the view that there was no justification for an increase in the stipends so soon after the death of Hadrat Umar. It is very strange that the critics of Hadrat Othman blame him for regarding the public funds as the property of Allah and not that of the people and not distributing all the funds among the people and on the other hand they criticise Hadrat Othman for raising the stipends. This view is uncharitable. Taha Hussain has dropped the hint that this was the means of political publicity to secure popularity. This view is obviously biased. An unbiased writer cannot help but admire the beneficent measure of Hadrat Othman which promoted the material prosperity of the people.

Land Administration[1]

Under Hadrat Umar it had been laid down as a policy that the lands in conquered territories were not to be distributed among the combatants but were to remain the property of the previous owners. The army felt dissatisfied at this decision but Hadrat Umar suppressed the opposition with a strong hand. Hadrat Othman followed the policy devised by Hadrat Umar. In the time of Hadrat Othman there were more conquests and the revenues from land increased considerably. In the time of Hadrat Othman the army once again raised the demand for the distribution of the lands in conquered territories among the fighting soldiers. Hadrat Othman turned down the demand. The army could not agitate openly against Hadrat Othman but in the vilification campaign that was carried against Hadrat Othman, the rebels had the indirect support of the army.

Economic Restraints[2]

Hadrat Umar had placed restraints on the economic activities of the people. He had placed restrictions on the trading activities of the Quraish. Hadrat Umar had placed a ban on the sale of lands in conquered territories. He had also placed a ban on the movements of the Companions and did not permit them to leave Madinah. Hadrat Othman was a shrewd businessman and trader. He knew that trade could not flourish under restraints. He was a democrat by temperament and he therefore withdrew the restrictions that had been imposed by Hadrat Umar with regard to the sale of land or the

---

1. Ibid.
2. *Othman*: Taha Hussain.

movements of the people. Hadrat Othman also permitted the eminent Companions to draw loans from the public treasury. The economic reforms introduced by Hadrat Othman had a far reaching effect. The Quraish, shrewd businessmen as they were, took full advantage of the liberal policies of Hadrat Othman and as a consequence their business flourished and they amassed a good deal of fortune. With this wealth they purchased lands in the conquered territories particularly Sawad in Iraq. In the time of Hadrat Othman, they did not merely enjoy dominance in political power, they came to enjoy monopoly in economic power as well. When the Companions were allowed the right of free movement and they were allowed the facility of drawing loans from the public treasury, most of the Companions purchased lands in conquered areas. Some of the Companions became the owners of large estates. The policy of Hadrat Umar was that whatever the Companions had gained during the time of the Holy Prophet was enough for them and that they should live henceforward a retired life, whereunder neither the world should see them, nor they should see the world. Hadrat Othman had a different view about the role of the Companions. He was of the view that the services of the Companions, the founding fathers of Islam, should be recognised and facilities should be provided to them so that they might live in comfort in their old age. During the time of Hadrat Othman, because of the economic measures most of the Companions grew very rich. Brisk building activity took place in Madinah. Many palatial buildings grew up in the city and the city expanded a good deal. The economic policies of Hadrat Othman though conceived in public interest had serious political repurcussions. Economic power came to be concentrated in the hands of a small group. That led to a gulf between the haves and the havenots. Most of the troubles that Hadrat Othman had to face were directly or indirectly due to the economic measures of Hadrat Othman which led to the creation of a class which monopolised economic power. This led to some imbalance in Islamic society committed to an egalitarian order. We cannot blame Hadrat Othman for these economic measures. His policies aimed at the economic development of the country and no person can be blamed for promoting economic prosperity. Difficulties arose because some of the persons grew rich overnight and no institutions were devised to regulate the proper flow of wealth. That provided an opportunity to some of the Muslims like Abu Dhar Ghaffari who stood for an austere way of life to criticise Hadrat Othman and his administration. If all these facts are assessed objectively the conclusion emerges is that Hadrat Othman was in advance of his age and he devised measures for which instead of being praised and admired he was criticised and even maligned.

PUBLIC WORKS

Public Works Under Hadrat Umar[1]

Hadrat Umar stood for simplicity and austerity. Consequently he did not believe in any large scale programme of public works involving extravagance. Nevertheless as a consequence of the extension of the Muslim rule to distant lands the undertaking of works of public utility became imperative. As Muslim conquests extended east and west and more and more persons embraced Islam it became necessary to construct mosques. During the caliphate of Hadrat Umar, as many as four thousand mosques were constructed. During the caliphate of Hadrat Umar many new cities were founded. These included Kufa, Basra and Fustat. Hadrat Umar issued instructions against the construction of double storeyed houses and palatial buildings. Many buildings were constructed for administrative purposes. Many cantonments were constructed at strategic places. Special stables were provided for cavalry.

Public Works Under Hadrat Othman[2]

Under Hadrat Othman the people became economically more prosperous and they invested their money in the construction of buildings. Many new buildings came to be constructed in Madinah and the city expanded considerably. Hadrat Othman relaxed the restriction on the construction of large houses. Hadrat Othman built a palatial building for himself known as the "Zawar". Many other Companions constructed large buildings. Intensive building activity took place at Kufa, Basra, Damascus, Fustat and other cities.

During the caliphate of Hadrat Othman as many as five thousand new mosques were constructed. Hadrat Othman enlarged, extended and embellished the Prophet's mosque at Madinah. He enlarged and extended the Holy Ka'aba as well. With the expansion in army,

1. *Hadrat Umar Farooq*: Prof. Masudul Hasan.
2. *Othman b. Affan*: Raza Misri.

the cantonments were extended and enlarged. More barracks were constructed for the soldiers. Stables for the cavalry were extended. Hadrat Othman provided separate pastures for State camels. During the caliphate of Hadrat Othman, guest houses were provided in main cities. More and more markets were constructed. Hadrat Othman appointed Market Officers to look after markets.

Hadrat Umar had placed restriction on the purchase of agricultural lands in conquered territories. Hadrat Othman withdrew this restriction. The Arabs purchased lands in conquered territories and exchanged them with lands in Arabia. Big landed estates came to be established in Arabia, Iraq and elsewhere. In Iraq, Egypt and Persia numerous canals were dug which stimulated the process of agricultural development.

In the cities, particular attention was directed towards the provision of water supply. In Madinah, a number of wells were dug to provide drinking water for the people. The water supply in Makkah was also improved. Water was brought to Kufa and Basra by canals.

Heretofore Shuaibia was the port for Makkah. It was inconvenient. Hadrat Othman selected Jeddah as the site of the new sea port. Hadrat Othman bathed in the sea water at Jeddah and said that it was a blessed spot. Other companions also bathed in the sea water at Jeddah. Hadrat Othman prayed for the prosperity of the new sea port.

PUBLIC TREASURY

Public Treasury in the Time of the Holy Prophet[1]

In the time of the Holy Prophet there was no public treasury. Whatever revenues or other amounts were received these were distributed immediately. There were no salaries to be paid and there was no State expenditure. As such the need of a treasury to keep a reserve at public level was not felt.

Public Treasury in the Time of Hadrat Abu Bakr[2]

In the time of Hadrat Abu Bakr as well there was no treasury. A separate building was kept aside as treasury but as all money was

---

1. *Hadrat Umar Farooq*: Prof. Masudul Hasan.
2. Ibid.

distributed immediately on receipt, the treasury generally remained locked up. At the time of the death of Hadrat Abu Bakr, there was only one dirham in the public treasury.

Public Treasury During the Caliphate of Hadrat Umar[1]

In the time of Hadrat Umar things changed. With the extension in conquests, money was received in larger quantities and heavy surplus was left even after distribution among the people. Hadrat Umar also allowed salaries to men fighting in the armed forces. That necessitated the maintenance of a full-fledged treasury to meet the State needs. A public treasury was accordingly established at Madinah. Similarly treasuries were established at the provincial levels. Separate Accounts Departments were set up to maintain accounts.

Public Treasury Under Hadrat Othman[2]

Hadrat Othman maintained the system set up under Hadrat Umar. Hadrat Umar was very strict in the use of money from the public treasury. Apart from the meagre allowance that had been sanctioned in his favour Hadrat Umar took no money from the treasury. He did not receive any gifts, nor did he allow any of his family members to accept any gift from any quarter. It appears that during the time of Hadrat Othman there was some relaxation in such strictness. In Kufa a dispute arose between Sa'ad b Abi Waqas and the treasurer Abdullah b. Mas'ud over a certain amount which Hadrat Sa'ad b. Waqas, as Governor, had taken as a loan from the treasury and which he was not able to repay within the stipulated period. A similar dispute arose between Walid b Uqba, the successor of Sa'ad b Abi Waqas and Abdullah b Mas'ud.

Hadrat Othman did not draw any allowance from the treasury for performing the functions of the caliphate. He was a wealthy man with sufficient resources of his own and he had no need to draw any allowance from the treasury. There were, however, some complaints that Hadrat Othman was not as strict as his predecessor about the use of public funds. It was alleged that out of the public treasury Hadrat Othman made liberal grants to certain favourites. It was also alleged that unlike Hadrat Umar, Hadrat Othman accepted gifts and allowed his family members to accept gifts from certain quarters.

1. Ibid.
2. Ibid.

Abdullah b Arqam was in charge of the treasury at Madinah and according to some accounts that have come down to us, it is alleged that he resigned from his office as a protest against Hadrat Othman's policies with regard to the utilisation of public funds.

The various accounts that have come down to us are prejudiced and biased. Hadrat Othman was a very rich man; he was most religious and pious. We cannot, therefore, imagine that Hadrat Othman was corrupt in any way. He always acted in a *bona fide* way. What appears to have happened is that Hadrat Othman had his own concept about the public funds, while his critics held an entirely different view on the subject.

Companions like Abu Dhar Ghaffari sponsored the theory that the funds in the public treasury were the property of the Muslims and as such had to be distributed equally among the Muslims. Under the circumstances the Caliph had no authority to make any grant to any person at the cost of the Muslims.

Hadrat Othman's view on the other hand was that the amount in the treasury was not the property of the Muslims. After the Muslims had received their due share, all that was in the treasury was the property of Allah and not of the Muslims. As the Caliph was in charge of the affairs of the State, he was a trustee of such property and he could utilise the funds, on his own authority in public interest, according to his best judgement. Hadrat Othman honestly felt that he had the right to utilise the public funds, according to his best judgement and no one had the right to criticise him for that. Hadrat Othman's argument was that if he could not spend the fund at the disposal of the State at his discretion, then what was the fun in being the Caliph?

As all the facts pertaining to the allegations are not available, it is not possible to say with any degree of certainty as to how far Hadrat Othman was right or how far his critics were right. The view of the critics that the funds in the public treasury were the property of the Muslims and not of Allah does not appear to be correct. As in an Islamic State, the State sovereignty vests in Allah, it follows as a matter of basic principle that all property vests in Allah. As the Caliph was the Head of Government he obviously had the authority to disburse funds for such purposes as he thought necessary. A Caliph is, however, not an absolute ruler and if there is anything wrong with his exercise of discretion he can certainly be called in question. Thus while we can hold that the Caliph had the right to spend the money on his own authority it has also to be conceded that the people had the right to criticise the Caliph in case he had not exercised his discretion properly. At that stage of Islamic polity no machinery had been evolved to take cognisance of such criticism and give its verdict which should be binding both on the Caliph as well as the people. Thus my personal view is that whatever difficulties arose during the caliphate of Hadrat Othman about the administration of the public funds were due more to procedural defects than because of any lapse on the part of Hadrat Othman.

MILITARY ADMINISTRATION[1]

Military Administration in the Early Days of Islam

In the early days of Islam there was no standing army. On the occasion of any battle contingents were raised from the various tribes and such contingents were disbanded when the battle was over. No regular salaries were paid to those who fought. Those who took part in a battle were compensated by the distribution of the spoils of war among them.

Organisation of the Army as a State Department

The army was organised as a State Department under Hadrat Umar. A register of male adults who could be called to war was prepared tribewise and a scale of salaries was fixed. All registered men were divided into two categories, those who formed the standing army and those who lived in their homes but were liable to be called to colours whenever necessary.

Military centres called "Jund" were set up at Kufa, Basra, Fustat, Damascus, Jordan and Palestine. Cantonments were established in important cities of strategic importance. Here barracks were constructed for the residence of troops. Big stables were provided for stabling the horses and other animals of the army. A separate commissariat department was set up to attend to the food supply problems of the army units. Pay was paid to the army in the month of Moharrum. The allowances were paid at the harvest time. Every tribal unit was under a tribal leader called '*Areef*. A group of '*Areefs* was in turn placed under the command of an *Ameer-al-Ashar*.

1. The section is based on the account given in my book *Hadrat Umar Farooq*.

Organisation at the Battlefield

On the battlefield the army operated in six wings, namely:

(1) *Qalb,* the centre,
(2) *Maqadamah,* the vanguard,
(3) *Maimanah,* the right wing,
(4) *Maisarah,* the left wing,
(5) *Saqah,* the rear, and
(6) *Rid,* extreme rear.

Other Components

Other components of the army were:

(1) Talayah or patrols who kept watch over the movements of the enemy,
(2) *Ra'id* or foraging parties,
(3) *Rukban* or the camel corps,
(4) *Farsan* or the cavalry,
(5) *Rajil* or the infantry, and
(6) *Ramat* or the archers.

War Weapons

Catapults were used for siege operations.

Dabbabah was a wooden tower which moved on wheels and consisted of several storeys. It was used for siege operations.

Walls were pierced by stone throwers and wall piercers.

Reporting and Espionage

Reporters were attached to every unit who kept the Caliph fully informed about the military operation. There was a separate department for espionage, who procured intelligence about the movements and activities of the enemy.

General Review of Military Operations

In the time of Hadrat Othman, the military organisation set up under Hadrat Umar was duly maintained. The Governor of each province acted as the commander of the forces. The Caliph acted as the Commander-in-Chief and he directed the military activity under Hadrat Umar and extensive conquests were made during the period. During the time of Hadrat Othman, most of Persia, Azarbaijan and Armenia revolted and these areas had to be reconquered.

Further conquests were made. In the north the Oxus was crossed and a greater part of Transoxiana was occupied. In the east the frontiers were pushed upto India. In the west the whole of North Africa was conquered. From North Africa the Muslims crossed over to Spain and occupied a part thereof. In the Mediterranean the islands of Cypress and Rhodes were conquered during the reign of Hadrat Othman. Under Hadrat Othman the Muslims became a naval power for the first time. They undertook some fifty military operations against the Byzantines. In the war against the Byzantines many forts were captured in Asia Minor. A campaign was undertaken against Constantinople itself but it had to be abandoned because of the disturbed state of home politics.

POLITICAL ADMINISTRATION

Pattern of Political Administration

Hadrat Othman maintained the pattern of political administration as it stood under Hadrat Umar. The country was divided into twelve provinces. These were Madinah, Makkah, Yemen, Kufa, Basra, Jazira, Fars, Azarbaijan, Khurasan, Syria, Egypt and North Africa. Under Hadrat Umar Egypt was divided into two provinces, Upper and Lower Egypt. Hadrat Othman made Egypt one province. Hadrat Othman created a new province for North Africa. Under Hadrat Umar Syria was divided into two provinces. Hadrat Othman made Syria one province.

Administrative Organisation

Each province was under the charge of a Governor or Wali. The Governor was in charge of civil as well as military administration. He was assisted by Katib—Chief Secretary; Katib-i-Diwan—Secretary Defence; Sahib-i-Kharaj—Revenue Collector; Sahib-ul-Ahdath—Inspector General of Police; Sahib-i-Baitul Mal—Treasury Officer; and Qadi—Chief Judge.

Every province was divided into districts. There were about 100 districts in the country. Each district was under the charge of an *Aamil*. The Qadi was responsible for judicial administration.

Governors of Hadrat Othman

The Governors were appointed by the Caliph. Every appointment was made in writing. At the time of appointment an instrument of instructions was issued with a view to regulating the conduct of Governors. On assuming office, the Governor was required to assemble the people in the main mosque and read the instrument of instructions before them.

One of the main allegations against Hadrat Othman was that he had appointed his relatives as Governors. Another allegation was that he exercised little check over the Governors.

As the Caliph, Hadrat Othman had the absolute right to appoint the Governors of provinces at his discretion. In theory this discretion could not be questioned. There was no legal bar to the appointment of relatives as Governors. Abdullah b Sa'ad, a foster brother of Hadrat Othman, had been appointed as the Governor of Egypt by Hadrat Umar. Hadrat Othman merely continued him in office. Hadrat Othman consolidated Egypt in one province and placed the enlarged province under the charge of Abdullah b Sa'ad. This was an administrative reform in the right direction and any criticism against the measure was misplaced.

In Syria, Muawiyah was the Governor under Hadrat Umar. Hadrat Othman allowed him to continue in office. Hadrat Othman consolidated Syria into one province. In view of the threat from the Byzantines this reform was necessary and very much in public interest.

In Kufa, Hadrat Othman appointed Sa'ad b Abi Waqas as the Governor in the first instance. Sa'ad was not related to Hadrat Othman and he made the appointment in deference to the will of Hadrat Umar. Later Sa'ad was deposed and Hadrat Othman appointed his step brother Walid b Uqba as the Governor. Sa'ad was not deposed because Hadrat Othman wanted to make room for his step brother. Sa'ad was deposed because of his failure to control the situation and Walid was appointed because Hadrat Othman considered that a young man who enjoyed his confidence could alone deliver the goods in Kufa. Walid justified this selection and during the first five years of his rule he was most popular with the people of Kufa. Later there was agitation in Kufa and Hadrat Othman deposed him in public interest. As a matter of fact the agitation against Walid was not due to the fact that anything had gone wrong with Walid; the reality was that the people of Kufa being fickle by nature were won over by the conspirators and wanted a change. Hadrat Othman accepted their demand even though he was convinced that Walid was not to be blamed in any way and that during the tenure of his office he had served the people of Kufa to the best of his ability.

In Basra, Abu Musa Ash'ari was deposed at the demand of the people of Basra. Hadrat Othman asked the representatives of the people of Basra to suggest a person who could be appointed as their Governor. They said that some young person who enjoyed the confidence of the Caliph should be appointed as the Governor. It was in deference to the wish of the people of Basra that Abdullah b Aamar was appointed as the Governor of Basra. He was a cousin of Hadrat Othman and he justified his selection in every way.

Allegation of Nepotism How Far Justified?

The Shia writers because of partisan considerations condemn the administration of Hadrat Othman in strong terms and hold him guilty of nepotism. Most of the Sunni writers in order to give an impression of their objectivity and fairness impliedly concede that the charge of nepotism was justified against him. If we examine the issue objectively the allegation stands rebutted. There were twelve provinces in the country but Hadrat Othman as Caliph appointed his relatives in four provinces only, namely Egypt, Syria, Kufa and Basra. In the remaining eight provinces persons other than his relatives were appointed. If Hadrat Othman was out to give high offices to his relatives, he could have appointed his family members to high offices in the other provinces as well. As he did not do so, the point that is forced to notice is that he appointed his relatives to four provinces not because he wanted to bestow high offices on his family members but because the strategic importance of these four provinces demanded that in these provinces there should be Governors who were loyal to him and enjoyed his confidence. In the age in which Hadrat Othman lived, blood relationship could be the only guarantee for loyalty. It may be appreciated that even in the modern times when the political systems are highly developed, high offices are bestowed on the members of the parties on the maxim that spoils belong to the victors. In the age of Hadrat Othman when the party system was not developed, only blood relations could serve as the party. As such if Hadrat Othman appointed some of his relatives as Governors no blame rests on him. He acted in public interest. It may be recalled that when Hadrat Ali became the Caliph he also appointed his relatives as Governors. No blame rests on Hadrat Ali for such appointments because what he did was in the best interests of the State. As such we can emphatically state that when Hadrat Othman appointed some of his relatives as Governors there was nothing wrong in that.

Some of the writers find fault with Hadrat Othman that he appointed incapable persons as Governors. This view is incorrect and uncharitable. All the persons appointed by Hadrat Othman were capable persons of great calibre. Muawiyah was a ruler of outstanding capacity and as a ruler and administrator he was second to none. Abdullah b Sa'ad was successful as Governor. Under his rule the revenues increased manifold. He conquered the whole of North Africa and that was a great achievement. In Kufa, Walid enjoyed great popularity for the first five years. He conducted successful campaigns in Azarbaijan and Armenia. In Basra Abdullah bin Aamar proved to be most successful. He reconquered the whole of Fars, Seestan and Khurasan and even penetrate into Transoxiana. None of the Governors appointed by Hadrat Othman proved to be a failure and it is unjust to condemn Hadrat Othman for appointing Governors who made great conquests. Hadrat Othman did not make such appointments arbitrarily. He made the appointments after assessing the merits of the persons concerned. It may be recalled that Hadrat Othman had brought up Muhammad b Huzaifa as his son. When Muhammad b Huzaifa wanted to be appointed as a Governor, Hadrat Othman did not oblige him because he did not consider him fit enough for such office. If nepotism was the sole consideration with Hadrat Othman as alleged by his critics he could have appointed Muhammad b Huzaifa to some high office. Muhammad b Huzaifa later led the agitation against Hadrat Othman. That clearly establishes that there is no substance in the allegation of nepotism against Hadrat Othman.

Autonomy for the Governors

It was also alleged that Hadrat Othman was weak and he did not exercise check on his Governors. In the accounts that have come down to us, only vague allegations have been made and no hard and fast facts have been cited to establish what lapses did the Governors of Hadrat Othman make and how Hadrat Othman failed to check them. It is made out that these Governors acted according to their own caprices and did not carry out the orders of Hadrat Othman. If the orders of Hadrat Othman were not obeyed, Hadrat Othman should have been the first person to complain against his Governors.

We do not come across in history a single complaint in this connection and it is difficult to subscribe to the view that in the time of Hadrat Othman, the administration had become so lax that the Governors did not care for the orders of the Caliph. That appears to be a sheer propaganda motivated by partisan considerations. As a matter of fact Hadrat Othman was as vigilant as a Caliph could be and he issued policy guidelines to his Governors from time to time. The true position is that as these Governors enjoyed the confidence of Hadrat Othman, he allowed them a good deal of autonomy and did not interfere in the day to day administration. Hadrat Umar had imposed some restrictions on his Governors. The Governors had been enjoined not to ride a Turkish horse, not to wear fine clothes, not to eat sifted flour and not to keep a porter at their door. Hadrat Othman did not consider such restrictions necessary and he allowed his Governors greater liberty. This was a step in the right direction and it is unfair to criticise Hadrat Othman on this account.

SOCIAL ORGANISATION UNDER HADRAT OTHMAN[1]

Social Revolution of Islam

Islam revolutionised social life in Arabia. Islam created new social values. The Holy Prophet set the pattern of conduct for the Islamic society. He was the embodiment of all the social values for which Islam stood. The Holy Prophet disciplined the Muslims into a solid community conspicuous for its piety, bravery, unity and high social and moral values. After the Holy Prophet, Hadrat Abu Bakr and Hadrat Umar carried forward the mission of the Master and promoted social values of Islam.

Muslim Society Under Hadrat Othman

Hadrat Othman became the Caliph a generation after the passing away of the Holy Prophet. Hadrat Othman himself was an embodiment of all the Islamic social values but the society around him underwent a change. During this period, most of the old companions passed away and a new generation grew up, whose faith in Islam was not as deep as that of the generation which lived during the lifetime of the Holy Prophet. Islam stood for an egalitarian

1. The section is based on my own assessment and research.

society wherein all were equal politically, socially, as well as economically. During Hadrat Othman's time the State became prosperous and that created a gulf between the rich and the poor. With the lapse of the time there was a recrudence of some of the social practices which characterised the age of ignorance in the pre-Islamic period. In Madinah the flying of pigeons and the shooting of arrows for divining fortune became the pastime of the people during the time of Hadrat Othman. Hadrat Othman took strong note of these social evils. Under his orders the wings of the pigeons were cut and the bows were broken. That made Hadrat Othman unpopular with the younger generation in Madinah.

Social Discipline and Social Solidarity

Islam stood for social discipline and social solidarity. The Muslims were enjoined by Islam to be a disciplined people and obey those in authority among them. The Muslims were required to maintain social solidarity and preserve unity in their ranks. During the caliphate of Hadrat Othman the Muslims lost their sense of discipline and they also lost their strength of solidarity. Certain sections grew among the Muslims who made it a point to carry on propaganda against authority. Hadrat Othman took steps to redress the legitimate grievances of the people but there was no slackening in the virulence of the vilification campaign against Hadrat Othman and his government.

Islam stood for unity in the ranks of the Muslims. During the caliphate of Hadrat Othman the Muslim society fell a prey to disunity and things came to be looked at from the partisan point of view rather than from the point of view of the interests of the Muslim community as a whole.

Disintegration of the Social Values of Islam

Causes for the disintegration of the social values of Islam were political, social as well as economic. Political cause was that political power came to be captured by a particular section and that caused discontentment among the other people. Economically the people came to be motivated by the desire to get rich. That created imbalance in society and the gulf between the haves and the havenots came to be widened. Socially the society lost the homogeneity of the day of the Holy Prophet and came to be dominated by the diversity of social interests. The towns expanded and more and more Beduoins from the desert came to settle in the cities. That created social tensions and some of the social evils of the days of ignorance which had been suppressed under the impact of Islam came to be revived. Instead of looking at things from the Islamic point of view the people began to see things from the personal and parochial points of view. That led to indiscipline among the people. Hadrat Othman as Caliph did his best to arrest this process of social disintegration but for causes beyond his control he could not overcome the social cirsis. He died fighting in the defence of Islamic social values and for this "Jihad", Hadrat Othman deserves great respect and honour.

HADRAT OTHMAN'S CONCEPT OF THE CALIPHATE[1]

Concept of the Caliphate

Most of the difficulties in the time of Hadrat Othman arose because of differences about the concept of the Caliphs. Most of the people regarded the Caliph as an Arab Sheikh on a higher scale amenable to the will of the people and even their idiocynracies. Hadrat Othman was of the view that the analogy of a tribal Sheikh did not apply to the Caliph. He held that there was a divinity about the office of the Caliph, which had to be understood with reference to the Qur'ãn and the traditions and not in accordance with any man made concepts.

The Holy Qur'ãn and the Caliphate

In the Holy Qur'ãn, the term "caliphate" has been used in general terms with reference to communities or people in their collectivity. The word "Caliph" with reference to an individual has been used only once in the Holy Qur'ãn with reference to David. Here the word "Caliph" has been used with reference to a ruler or a vicegerent.

The Traditions

There are, however, numerous traditions on the point. The Holy Prophet said:

> "Whoso obeys me obeys Allah and whoso rebels against me rebels against Allah. Whoso obeys the ruler obeys me and

1. *The Caliphate*: Thomas Arnold.

whoso rebels against the ruler rebels against me."

The Holy Prophet said:

"After me will come rulers; tender them your obedience for the ruler is like a shield wherewith a man protects himself; if they are righteous and rule you well, they shall have their reward but if they do evil then punishment will fall upon them and you will be quit of it, for they are responsible for you and you have no responsibility."

The Holy Prophet said:

"Obey your rulers whatever may happen; if they bid you do anything different from what I have taught you, they shall be punished for it and you will be rewarded for your obedience."
According to another tradition, the Holy Prophet said that on the Day of Judgement, the people will say to Allah: "O Lord, You sent us prophets and we obeyed them by Your permission and You set over us Caliphs and we obeyed them by Your permission. Our rulers gave us orders and we obeyed them for Your sake."

Thereupon Allah will say, "You speak the truth; theirs is the responsibility and you are quit of it."

The Holy Prophet said:

"Obey every ruler; pray behind every Imam and do not insult my Companions."

The Holy Prophet said:

"O men, obey Allah even though He sets over you as your ruler a mutilated Abyssinian slave."

The Holy Prophet said:

"When Allah wishes good for a people He sets over them the forbearing and wise and places their goods in the hands of generous rulers but when Allah wishes evil for a people He sets over them the witless and base and entrusts their goods to avaracious rulers."

The Holy Prophet said:

"When in the days to come you see the caliphate of Allah on earth, attach yourself closely to it even though it may consume your body and rob you of your property."

The Holy Prophet also said:

> "If the Government is just it may expect reward from Allah and the people ought to show their gratitude to it; if it is unjust, it incurs the guilt of sin but the people must give proof of their obedience to it."

Hadrat Othman's Concept of the Caliphate

In view of these traditions the view of Hadrat Othman was that there was a divinity about the office of the Caliph and as such the Caliph was responsible to Allah and not to the people. As such the people had no right to disobey or criticize the Caliph. If the Caliph was just his reward lay with Allah. On the other hand if he was unjust his punishment lay with Allah. Accordingly when a demand for his deposition was made he turned down the demand not because he was fond of power but because he held that an office which he held on behalf of Allah had divinity about it and he was bound to perform his duties to Allah whatever the odds. According to Hadrat Othman his resignation from an office which he held on behalf of Allah would amount to his refusal to serve Allah and that was against the spirit of Islam. He, therefore, welcomed death to deposition and that was certainly most noble and elevating on the part of Hadrat Othman. Some writers have indulged in the view that at the last moment, Hadrat Othman had agreed to be deposed but that the rebels did not allow him time to announce his deposition. There is no truth in such stories. Hadrat Othman stuck to his view to the last and he preferred to die rather than abandon the post which he held on behalf of Allah.

As a matter of principle the view that Hadrat Othman held about the caliphate was correct and in conformity with the traditions of the Holy Prophet. The people had no right to demand his deposition and he had no right to resign. The concepts of the so-called democracy and the sovereignty of the people were developed later in secular context. Unfortunately most of the writers, Muslims as well as non-Muslims, have tried to judge Hadrat Othman in the light of concepts which were developed much later and which are strictly speaking not in consonance with the spirit of Islam. Hadrat Othman acted strictly in accordance with the injunctions of Islam and who rebelled against his authority were rebels against Islam. As a matter of fact all the allegations that had been levelled against Hadrat Othman were frivolous and had no substance. Hadrat Othman duly considered these allegations and he explained his position in sufficient detail. After such explanation the people had no right to agitate and rebel against the authority of the State. That was outright sedition. In his book on Hadrat Othman, Taha Hussain has taken pains to establish that most of the complaints against Hadrat Othman were justified. I am afraid Taha Hussain has missed the point that under the Islamic constitutional law the authority to determine how far these complaints were justified was the Caliph himself and when he took cognisance of these complaints and explained his position publicly that was the end of the matter and it does not lie within the competence of any writer, howsoever eminent, to sit in judgement over the conduct of Hadrat Othman and hold that most of the complaints against him were justified. My submission is that posterity has no right to sit in judgement over the caliphate of Hadrat Othman. Hadrat Othman acted to the best of his judgement and we are precluded from finding any fault with what he did. It may be recalled that on the occasion of the expedition to Tabuk when the Holy Prophet gave the tidings of paradise to Hadrat Othman he also said that Hadrat Othman was not to be judged for anything thereafter. In view of this verdict of the Holy Prophet, it is not open to any Muslim to sit in judgement over what Hadrat Othman did as Caliph and criticise him for any sins of omission or commission. As a matter of fact the revolt against Hadrat Othman was not due to any legitimate grievances of the people; it was due to extraneous cause and was abetted by foreign powers who wanted to subvert Islam from within. The revolt against Hadrat Othman was in fact revolt against Islam. Hadrat Othman met a martyr's death in defence of Islam.

3

GOVERNORS OF HADRAT OTHMAN[1]

'AMR B AL 'AAS

Early Life

'Amr b Al 'Aas belonged to the Sahm section of the Quraish. When the Holy Prophet declared his mission, 'Amr was one of the great opponents of Islam. He even planned the murder of the Holy Prophet. When some of the Muslims migrated to Abyssinia, the Quraish sent a delegation to Abyssinia to prevail upon the Negus to expel the Muslims from his State, 'Amr was one of the members of this delegation. 'Amr was an active member of the delegation but the delegation failed in its object. At the battle of Uhud, 'Amr commanded the Quraish cavalry.

Conversion to Islam

After the Hudaibiya pact, 'Amr b Al 'Aas and Khalid b Walid came to Madinah and were converted to Islam. On conversion, 'Amr b Al 'Aas wanted an assurance that his past sins had been forgiven and the Holy Prophet gave him the necessary assurance. Thereafter he participated in all the battles fought under the Holy Prophet. In the apostasy wars under Hadrat Abu Bakr, he undertook a campaign against the Kalb tribe. When Hadrat Abu Bakr declared Jihad against the Byzantines, 'Amr offered his services and said, "I am one of the arrows of Allah, shoot me where you will."

1. The views expressed in this section are based on my own assessment and research.

Conquest of Egypt

Under Hadrat Umar, 'Amr became the Governor of Palestine in 638 C.E. In 639 C.E. after the death of Ubaidullah b Jarah, 'Amr became the supreme commander of the armed forces in Syria. That provided him an opportunity to conquer Egypt. Hadrat Umar was averse to the extension of Muslim dominions. When 'Amr b Al 'Aas pressed for the conquest of Egypt, Hadrat Umar reluctantly gave his permission to try his luck in Egypt. 'Amr b Al 'Aas invaded Egypt with a small force in the closing months of 639 C.E. Egypt fell before the Muslim arms as if by a miracle.

'Amr b Al 'Aas as the Governor of Egypt

After the conquest of Egypt, 'Amr b Al 'Aas became the first Governor of Egypt. Egypt was the richest province in the Muslim dominions but the revenues that 'Amr b Al 'Aas sent to Madinah from Egypt were not commensurate to the importance of the province. 'Amr b Al 'Aas was a good administrator and a skilful General but he was not an expert in financial affairs. There were complaints that the financial affairs of the province were not managed efficiently.

Later, Hadrat Umar partitioned Egypt into two provinces, namely Upper Egypt with the capital at Fayyum and Lower Egypt with the capital at Fustat. 'Amr b Al 'Aas remained the Governor of Lower Egypt, while Abdullah b Sa'ad b Abi Sarah was appointed as the Governor of Upper Egypt.

The measure of the partition was not popular with the people. 'Amr b Al 'Aas felt dissatisfied that his charge had been curtailed. Hadrat Umar was a stern and hard task master and he suppressed all opposition with a stern hand.

Administration of Egypt under Hadrat Othman

In his testament, Hadrat Umar had instructed his successor not to make any change in the administrative set up for one year after his death. True to these instructions; Hadrat Othman maintained the status quo in the administrative set up of Egypt.

'Amr b Al 'Aas smarted under the loss of power and felt dissatisfied at the partition of the province. Soon after the death of Hadrat Umar, 'Amr b Al 'Aas came to Madinah and apprised Hadrat Othman of the state of affairs in Egypt. He pointed out that Egypt was a unity and its division into two provinces was undesirable politically as well as economically. He pressed Hadrat Othman to rescind the orders of partition, depose Abdullah b Sa'ad and make him ('Amr) the Governor of United Egypt once again.

Hadrat Othman listened to the demands of 'Amr b Al 'Aas patiently. He said that in principle he agreed with him that the provinces of Upper Egypt and Lower Egypt should be reintegrated into one province. He said that because of the testament of Hadrat Umar he was committed not to make any change in the administrative set up for one year. He wanted 'Amr to wait till one year was over and he was free to act according to his own discretion and judgement. He also observed that Abdullah b Sa'ad was his foster brother and he could not despose him without cause.

'Amr b Al 'Aas said that he was the conqueror of Egypt and in order to maintain proper hold on the province it was necessary that all power was concentrated in his hands. 'Amr b Al 'Aas also complained bitterly against Abdullah b Sa'ad. Hadrat Othman pointed out that he was related both to him ('Amr) as well as Abdullah b Sa'ad and he should be given sometime to resolve the dispute to the satisfaction of all concerned. 'Amr b Al 'Aas was married to a step sister of Hadrat Othman while Abdullah was his foster brother. Hadrat Othman wanted to evolve some way whereby 'Amr b Al 'Aas and Abdullah b Sa'ad could be reconciled.

'Amr b Al 'Aas precipitated the crisis by giving the challenge that unless his demand was accepted, he would not return to Egypt. No argument availed with him and in view of his refusal to return to Egypt unless his demand was accepted, Hadrat Othman had no option but to pass the order that 'Amr b Al 'Aas was not willing to carry on his responsibilities under the existing set up, he was deposed and Abdullah b Sa'ad would hold the charge of both the provinces.

'Amr b Al 'Aas made this order of deposition a cause of personal grievance. In a fit of anger he divorced the step sister of Hadrat Othman. He also declared that as his demand had not been accepted and due regard had not been paid to his services as the conqueror of Egypt, he would inflame the people against Hadrat Othman.

Recall and Re-deposition of 'Amr b Al 'Aas

Early in 646 C.E. a large Byzantine force landed at Alexandria and occupied it. From the base at Alexandria, the Byzantines planned to reconquer the whole of Egypt. The Muslims of Egypt sent a delegation to Madinah to prevail on Hadrat Othman to restore 'Amr b Al 'Aas and appealed to him to take over the command of Egypt. He stipulated some terms which were accepted by Hadrat Othman. 'Amr b Al 'Aas was made the Governor of United Egypt and he was also to be the supreme commander of the military forces in Egypt. Abdullah b Sa'ad was to hold a subordinate position under 'Amr b Al 'Aas.

'Amr b Al 'Aas took over the command in Egypt and drove away the Byzantines from the soil of Egypt. After the re-conquest of Egypt another crisis developed. As under Abdullah b Sa'ad the revenues of the province had risen considerably, Hadrat Othman made Abdullah b Sa'ad hold independent charge of the Revenue Department while 'Amr b Al 'Aas was to be the Governor and supreme commander of the military forces. 'Amr b Al 'Aas protested against this arrangement. He said that under such an arrangement he would be holding the cow by the horns while someone else would be milking it. Hadrat Othman desired that 'Amr b Al 'Aas should guarantee that the revenues would not fall below the stipulated level. 'Amr b Al 'Aas was not prepared to give even such guarantee. The dispute could not be resolved and ultimately Hadrat Othman passed orders for the deposition of 'Amr b Al 'Aas.

'Amr b Al 'Aas's Opposition to Hadrat Othman

After deposition 'Amr b Al 'Aas returned to Madinah and spearheaded the movement for agitation against Hadrat Othman in Madinah. 'Amr b Al 'Aas freely indulged in the criticism of Hadrat Othman and lost no opportunity in agitating against Hadrat Othman. Once when Hadrat Othman took him to task for indulging in base talk, 'Amr b Al 'Aas said some unkind words against Affan, the father of Hadrat Othman. Marwan took objection to these insulting remarks but Hadrat Othman chose to remain quiet. Once when Hadrat Othman was addressing the congregation in the mosque and justifying his position, 'Amr b Al 'Aas contradicted him and adopted an insulting stance. 'Amr b Al 'Aas had a strong party in Egypt and his party created a good deal of trouble for Hadrat Othman. When the rioters from Egypt came to Madinah they enjoyed the support of 'Amr b Al 'Aas. When the agitation against Hadrat Othman grew in momentum, 'Amr b Al 'Aas left Madinah for Palestine. While departing from Madinah, 'Amr b Al 'Aas spoke contemptuously about Hadrat Othman and said that he would raise even the shepherds of the desert against Hadrat Othman.

ABDULLAH BIN SA'AD

Abdullah b Sa'ad was a foster brother of Hadrat Othman. Hadrat Othman had drunk milk of the mother of Abdullah b Sa'ad. Under the influence of Hadrat Othman, Abdullah b Sa'ad accepted Islam before the conquest of Makkah. He came to Madinah and the Holy Prophet employed him for recording the revelations. He tampered with some of the revelations and when taken to task he apostatised and returned to Makkah. When the Holy Prophet conquered Makkah he granted general amnestly to the Quraish. An exception was made in the case of ten persons who were to be killed for their heinous crimes. Abdullah b Sa'ad was one of these ten persons who were to be killed. Abdullah b Sa'ad sought the protection of Hadrat Othman and appealed to him to intercede on his behalf with the Holy Prophet. The foster mother of Hadrat Othman appealed to him to save his foster brother. Hadrat Othman was reluctant to intercede because under Islam apostasy was a crime punishable with death. On account of the persistent entreaties his foster mother for whom he had great respect Hadrat Othman agreed that he would do whatever he could. Hadrat Othman took Abdullah b Sa'ad to the Holy Prophet and placed him at the mercy of the Holy Prophet. When the request for forgiveness was made the Holy Prophet made no reply. Hadrat Othman repeated the request for the second time and still the Holy Prophet remained silent. The request was made for the third time and out of regard for Hadrat Othman, the Holy Prophet agreed to spare the life of Abdullah b. Sa'ad. Abdullah repented and craved for forgiveness. He was forgiven and was readmitted to the fold of Islam.

After Reconversion to Islam

After reconversion to Islam, Abdullah b Sa'ad proved to be a good Muslim. He allowed all the injunctions of Islam. He participated in the various battles and gave a good account of himself. He was intelligent and was particularly good in revenue collection. Hadrat Umar was a good judge of men and impressed by Abdullah's abilities, he appointed him as a Governor of Upper Egypt. As Governor

Abdullah b Sa'ad did well and Hadrat Umar was well pleased with him.

Criticism Against Hadrat Othman

When Hadrat Othman appointed Abdullah b Sa'ad as the Governor of Egypt in succession to 'Amr b Al 'Aas he was accused of nepotism and of doing grave injustice to 'Amr b Al 'Aas, the conqueror of Egypt. The charge of nepotism against Hadrat Othman is not correct, because Abdullah had been appointed as Governor by Hadrat Umar. Hadrat Othman merely carried forward the policies that had been laid down by Hadrat Umar. The charge of nepotism falls to the ground because Abdullah b Sa'ad alone was not related to him. 'Amr b Al 'Aas was also related to him. If Abdullah b Sa'ad was the foster brother of Hadrat Othman, 'Amr b Al 'Aas was a brother-in-law of Hadrat Othman as he had married a sister of Hadrat Othman. Hadrat Othman had no intention to depose 'Amr b Al 'Aas. He wanted him to remain the Governor as well as the supreme military commander and he only wanted to give independent charge of revenue department to Abdullah b Sa'ad. Abdullah b Sa'ad was an expert in revenue administration and financial management while 'Amr b Al 'Aas was good as a military commander. The division of functions proposed by Hadrat Othman was sound in principle and was in the best interests of the State. 'Amr b Al 'Aas did not accept the reform because he was interested more in matters of personal prestige than in measures devised in the interests of the State. If in the circumstances 'Amr b Al 'Aas was deposed, the blame did not lie with Hadrat Othman 'Amr b Al 'Aas was himself to be blamed for the crisis.

Achievements of Abdullah b Sa'ad

Abdullah b Sa'ad held the office of the Governor under Hadrat Othman for eleven years. Abdullah b Sa'ad made extensive conquests. He conquered the whole of North Africa. He even conquered a part of Spain. He undertook an expedition to Nubia. He built a strong navy and defeated the Byzantines in numerous naval battles. Under him the revenues increased substantially. Abdullah b Sa'ad was a good ruler but in spite of that Egypt became a hotbed of sedition against the Government of Hadrat Othman. Muhammad b Hudhaifa, Muhammad b Abu Bakr poisoned the political atmosphere in Egypt by carrying a vilification campaign against Hadrat Othman. They were supported by Umar b Yasir, Ibn Saba and the party of

'Amr b Al 'Aas. In 655 C.E. when Abdullah b Sa'ad went to Madinah, power was captured in his absence by Muhammad b Hudhaifa, Abdullah returned to Egypt but he was unable to recapture power. He retired to Ramlah where he died two years later.

MUHAMMAD BIN ABU HUDHAIFA

Family of Muhammad b Abu Hudhaifa[1]

Muhammad bin Abu Hudhaifa belonged to the Ummayyad section of the Quraish. His father's original name was Utba bin Rabea'ah. Utba's daughter was Hind who was the wife of Abu Sufian and the mother of Muawiyah. Muhammad was thus the maternal uncle of Muawiyah. Utba was one of the early converts to Islam. It is to be noted that while Abu Sufian led the Quraish in all wars against the Muslims till the Muslim conquest of Makkah, Abu Sufian's father-in-law accepted Islam at an early stage. One of the daughters of Abu Sufiyan was also converted to Islam at an early stage and she was later married to the Holy Prophet. Abu Hudhaifa migrated with his wife Suhaila to Abyssinia. In Abyssinia Hadrat Othman and Abu Hudhaifa worked in close unison. Muhammad, the son of Abu Hudhaifa, was born in Abyssinia. On return from Abyssinia Abu Hudhaifa migrated to Madinah. In the battle of Badr, Abu Hudhaifa fought against his father who was an infidel. Later he fought in all the battles under the command of the Holy Prophet. He participated in the apostasy wars during the caliphate of Hadrat Abu Bakr. Abu Hudhaifa was martyred in the battle of Yamamma. Muhammad was then a boy, fourteen or fifteen years old.

Hadrat Othman's Guardianship of Muhammad[2]

On the death of Abu Hudhaifa, Hadrat Othman assumed the guardianship of Muhammad b Hudhaifa. Muhammad b Abu Hudhaifa was brought up under the loving care of Hadrat Othman. Hadrat Othman treated him as a son. When Hadrat Othman became the Caliph, Muhammad bin Abu Hudhaifa desired that he should be made the Governor of some province. He wanted him to wait for sometime as he was not yet fit for the high office of the Governor. That annoyed Muhammad b Abu Hudhaifa. He desired that in the circumstances he should be permitted to go somewhere else to

---

1. *Othman*: Taha Hussain.
2. Ibid.

seek his fortune. Hadrat Othman gave him some money and permitted him to go anywhere he liked. Muhammad b Abu Hudhaifa chose to go to Egypt.

Muhammad b Abu Hudhaifa in Egypt[1]

In Egypt Abdullah b Sa'ad, a foster brother of Hadrat Othman, was the Governor. Hadrat Othman had deposed 'Amr b Al 'Aas from the governorship of Egypt and appointed Abdullah as the Governor instead. In Egypt there was a strong party which favoured 'Amr b Al 'Aas, the original conqueror of Egypt. Muhammad b Abu Bakr who had some personal grievances against Hadrat Othman also came to Egypt. The two Muhammads joined hands in carrying on propaganda against Abdullah b Sa'ad and Hadrat Othman. Ibn Saba also came to Egypt and he led a campaign for the subversion of Islam. Hadrat Othman sent an emissary 'Ammar b Yasir to Egypt to report about the state of affairs in Egypt. Those who were opposed to the administration carried on propaganda in favour of the caliphate of Hadrat Ali. 'Ammar b Yasir had his affiliations with Hadrat Ali and he too joined the opposition in Egypt. The opposition movement came to command a good following. Muhammad b Abu Bakr and Muhammad Abu Hudhaifa ingratiated themselves with the army. When Abdullah b Sa'ad won the battle of the Masts, the opposition tried to belittle the achievement by declaring that the real Jihad lay in protesting against Hadrat Othman who had deviated from the path of Islam. Propaganda against the Government was carried to the mosques. Abdullah b Sa'ad reported the matter to Hadrat Othman and wanted his permission to take action against Muhammad b Abu Bakr, Muhammad b Abu Hudhaifa and 'Ammar b Yasir. Hadrat Othman did not approve any action against 'Ammar b Yasir because he was an eminent companion. No action was to be taken against Muhammad bin Abu Bakr, because of the respect for Hadrat Abu Bakr. No action was to be taken against Muhammad b Abu Hudhaifa for he was his adopted son. Want of action on the part of Government emboldened the opposition and the situation in Egypt worsened day by day.

Coup d'etat of Muhammad b Abu Hudhaifa[2]

In 655 C.E. when the agitation against the Government grew in momentum Abdullah b Sa'ad went to Madinah to apprise the Caliph

1. Ibid.
2. Tabari: *History of Islam.*

of the state of affairs in Egypt. In the absence of Abdullah b Sa'ad from Egypt Muhammad b Abu Hudhaifa staged a coup d'etat and captured power. On coming to know of the coup Abdullah b Sa'ad returned to Egypt but he failed to recapture power. He retired to Ramlah where he died two years later. On coming to power in Egypt Muhammad b Hudhaifa sent Muhammad b Abu Bakr and 'Ammar b Yasir to Madinah to prepare the ground in Madinah for revolt against Hadrat Othman. Thereafter he sent a strong contingent from Egypt with the instructions to overthrow the Government of Hadrat Othmar and kill him if he refused to abdicate.

After the assassination of Hadrat Othman, Hadrat Ali becam the Caliph and he appointed Muhammad b Abu Bakr as the Governo of Egypt. Muhammad b Hudhaifa resented his deposition. 'Amr b A 'Aas who was originally opposed to Hadrat Othman turned a somersault and joined Muawiyah against Hadrat Ali. Muhammad b Abu Hudhaifa also joined 'Amr b Al 'Aas. 'Amr b Al 'Aas capture Egypt and Muhammad b Abu Bakr was killed.

In Islamic history, Muhammad b Abu Hudhaifa stands for ar ungrateful person who worked for the murder of the man who wa more than a father to him.

AMIR MUAWIYAH

Early Life

Amir Muawiyah was the son of Abu Sufian. He was the leader of the Quraish. He led the Quraish in the battle of Uhud. He was the inveterate enemy of Islam and he tried his best to overpower the Muslims. All his efforts, however, failed and after the conquest of Makkah he had no option but to accept Islam. Muawiyah's mother was Hindah. She led a contingent of women in the battle of Uhud. At the battle of Uhud she chewed the liver of Hadrat Hamza, an uncle of the Holy Prophet. One of the sisters of Muawiyah Umm Habibah was married to the Holy Prophet. After conversion to Islam, Abu Sufian and his sons worked faithfully in the cause of Islam. Muawiyah was attached to the Holy Prophet. The Holy Prophet had a high opinion about the capacities of Muawiyah.

Amir Muawiyah as Governor of Syria

During the caliphate of Hadrat Umar, Amir Muawiyah was the

ruler of Damascus. Yazid, a brother of Muawiyah, was the ruler of Jordan. When Yazid fled, Hadrat Umar placed Jordan also under the charge of Muawiyah.

During the caliphate of Hadrat Othman when Alqama Kinani, the ruler of Palestine, died Palestine was also entrusted to the charge of Muawiyah. A little later when 'Amir b Sa'ad Ansari, the ruler of Emessa resigned because of ill health, Hadrat Othman added Emessa as well to the charge of Amir Muawiyah. Under Muawiyah, Syria thus came to be consolidated into a single province.

Achievements of Muawiyah

Syria became an important and strategic province because of its proximity to the dominions of the Byzantines. Muawiyah proved to be a Governor of exceptional character. He ruled as Governor for twenty years and thereafter ruled as Caliph for another twenty years. In the history of the world we do not come across an instance of a Governor who was as popular as Muawiyah.

Muawiyah conquered the islands of Cypress and Rhodes. The Byzantines invaded Spain with a large force. Amir Muawiyah defeated the Byzantines. The Byzantines evacuated the border forts in the Tarsus which were occupied by the Muslims. The Muslims under Amir Muawiyah raided the Byzantine territories every year and made extensive conquests.

Muawiyah proved to be the most popular Government. While in other provinces, the Governors had to be deposed every now and then, Amir Muawiyah enjoyed a long spell of rule as Governor for twenty years. While other provinces became the hotbeds of sedition and agitation during the caliphate of Hadrat Othman, Syria remained free from such agitation. The credit for this state of affairs belonged to Muawiyah

Hadrat Othman and Amir Muawiyah

Amir Muawiyah was the second cousin of Hadrat Othman and he supported Hadrat Othman through thick and thin. When the agitation against Hadrat Othman mounted high, Muawiyah made three offers to Hadrat Othman. He requested Hadrat Othman to go with him to Damascus as the people there were very loyal. Hadrat Othman did not accept this offer as he did not want to leave the city of the Holy Prophet. In the alternative Muawiyah offered to send a force from Syria who could act as the guard of the Caliph. Hadrat

Othman did not accept this offer as he was averse to civil war among the Muslims. In the last resort, Muawiyah made the offer that if Hadrat Othman was killed he should be authorised to raise the demand for the avenging of his blood. This alternative was accepted by Hadrat Othman. After the martyrdom of Hadrat Othman, Muawiyah raised the demand for the vengeance for the blood of Hadrat Othman. This culminated in the establishment of the Umayyad rule after the death of Hadrat Ali.

Taha Hussain's Criticism

In his book *Othman*, Taha Hussain has found fault with Hadrat Othman for enlarging the jurisdiction of Amir Muawiyah as Governor. Taha Hussain considers that if Muawiyah had not been made so strong, he would not have aspired to the caliphate later on. The criticism of Taha Hussain is misconceived. Muawiyah was a Governor of exceptional merit and if in recognition of such merit, Hadrat Othman enlarged the jurisdiction of Muawiyah there was nothing wrong therein and he did what was in the best interests of the State.

In the accounts that have come down to us, it is observed that Hadrat Ali criticized Hadrat Othman for allowing too much latitude to Muawiyah. It is alleged that Muawiyah took action on his own account and declared that it was the order of the Caliph. No specific instances in this behalf have been cited and we are not in a position to observe how far the criticism of Hadrat Ali was justified. *Prima facie* this was a matter of personal equation between Hadrat Othman and Muawiyah and if Hadrat Othman had confidence in Muawiyah such confidence cannot be made a ground for criticism.

MUGHEERA BIN SHU'BA

Early Life

Mugheera b Shu'ba belonged to the tribe of Thaqueef of Taif. He became a convert to Islam after the battle of Taif in 628 C.E. On conversion to Islam he took part in all the battles. He was a brave fighter. He lost an eye in the battle of Yammama. During the caliphate of Hadrat Umar, Utba b Ghazwan was the Governor of Basra while Mugheera b Shu'ba was the Deputy Governor. Utba b Ghazwan died in 639 C.E. and Mugheera b Shu'ba became the Governor of Basra.

Deposition of Mugheera b Shu'ba

Mugheera b Shu'ba had a weakness for women. He would marry women and would divorce them after sometime to make room for some more beautiful face. In this way he married no less than eighty women, taking steps to ensure that at a time his wives were not more than four, the limit prescribed by the Shariah. In those days there was a beautiful woman Umm Jamil at Basra who belonged to the same tribe as that of Mugheera. Her husband had died and she had become notorious for her love affairs. Mugheera was attracted by her and she visited him often.

Some Muslims in Basra became critical of the conduct of Mugheera. Among them was Abu Bakra Thaqueefi whose house was across the street facing the house of Mugheera. One day a strong wind blew and the windows of the houses of Abu Bakra and Mugheera got opened through the force of the wind. Abu Bakra saw through his window that in his houses Mugheera was locked up in an uncompromising state with a woman. He suspected that the woman was Umm Jamil. He had some friends with him and they also saw Mugheera involved with a woman.

Abu Bakra wrote to Hadrat Umar accusing Mugheera of adultery. The report was endorsed by four witnesses who had seen Mugheera in an uncompromising state with a woman. Mugheera as well as the complainants were summoned to Madinah. At the trial, Mugheera pleaded not guilty. His defence was that the woman in question was his wife and not Umm Jamil. Out of the four witnesses, one witness stated that he had not seen the face of the woman and as such he did not know who was she. The other witnesses were cross examined and on such examination it was found that there are some weak points in their evidence. They were asked whether that woman had her face or her back towards them. They said that she had her back towards them. They tried to make out that even from her back, she could be identified as Umm Jamil. They said that the scandal of Mugheera and Umm Jamil was very common in Basra and that the lady was none other than Umm Jamil. Mugheera was given the benefit of doubt and acquitted. He was, however, deposed from the governorship of Basra and Abu Musa Ash'ari was appointed as the Governor in his place.

Mugheera as Governor of Kufa

In 643 C.E. Hadrat Umar appointed Mugheera b Shu'ba as the Governor of Kufa. When Hadrat Othman became the Caliph, Mugheera continued in his office for one year and was thereafter deposed to make room for the appointment of Sa'ad b Abi Waqas, according to the testament of Hadrat Umar.

SA'AD BIN ABI WAQAS[1]

Sa'ad b Abi Waqas belonged to the section of the Quraish to which the mother of the Holy Prophet belonged. Sa'ad became a convert to Islam at the age of seventeen. He participated in all the expeditions undertaken by the Holy Prophet. He had the distinction of shooting the first arrow in the cause of Islam. He was the only person to whom the Holy Prophet said, "May my parents be your ransom". He was very close to the Holy Prophet. The Holy Prophet held him in high esteem. He was one of the ten distinguished Muslims whom the Holy Prophet gave the tidings of paradise in their lifetime.

Victor of Qadisiyia[2]

Sa'ad b Abi Waqas rose into prominence when Hadrat Umar appointed him as the Commander of the Muslim forces at the battle of Qadisiyia. The battle was won by the Muslims and Sa'ad b Abi Waqas earned the title of "Victor of Qadisiyia." Thereafter the Muslims under Sa'ad b Abi Waqas captured Al Madain the capital of the Persians in Iraq. Sa'ad b Abi Waqas made Al Madain his headquarter for sometime. When the city of Kufa was built Sa'ad b Abi Waqas was made the Governor of Kufa and he shifted there. Sa'ad b Abi Waqas built a splendid palace for himself at Kufa modelled on the Tak-i-Khusro palace at Al Madain. When this was brought to the notice of Hadrat Umar he administered a rebuke to Sa'ad for his indulgence in luxury. He deputed Muhammad b Musalama to make an enquiry on the spot and report about the way of living of the Governor. Muhammad had the palace built by Sa'ad b Abi Waqas demolished. He reported that Sa'ad b Abi Waqas indulged in a luxurious way of living. Hadrat Umar deposed Sa'ad b Abi Waqas from the governorship of Kufa in 640 C.E.

---

1. *Othman b Affan*: Raza Misri.
2. Ibid.

Hadrat Umar's Instructions About Sa'ad b Abi Waqas to His Successor[1]

On his death-bed Hadrat Umar nominated Sa'ad b Abi Waqas as a member of the Committee who were to choose the next Caliph from among themselves. He also left instructions that in case Sa'ad b Abi Waqas was not chosen as the Caliph, he who was chosen as the Caliph should duly compensate Sa'ad b Abi Waqas for his services to Islam. He declared that in 640 C.E. he had deposed Sa'ad from the governorship of Kufa merely by way of policy and not for any of his faults. After the deposition of Sa'ad, Ammar b Yasir was appointed as the Governor of Kufa. He held the office for a short time and was replaced by Mugheera b Shu'ba as the Governor of Kufa.

Appointment of Sa'ad b Abi Waqas as the Governor of Kufa

Hadrat Umar left instructions for his successor that no change should be made in the Governors appointed by him for one year and that thereafter his successor was free to make whatever changes he deemed necessary in public interest. When Hadrat Othman became the Caliph, Mugheera b Shu'ba was the Governor of Kufa. True to the instructions of Hadrat Umar, Hadrat Othman allowed the Governors appointed by Hadrat Umar to continue in their office. After the expiry of one year, Hadrat Othman deposed Mugheera and appointed Sa'ad b Abi Waqas as the Governor of Kufa.

Sa'ad b Abi Waqas as the Governor of Kufa[2]

Back in office, Sa'ad b Abi Waqas tried to win the hearts of the people by his generosity and liberal hospitality. Anyone who begged of him anything got what he wanted. On Fridays he gave vast amounts in charity. He made arrangements for the feeding of the travellers and the wayfarers. He awarded special stipends to the orphans and the widows. Because of his liberal policies, the means at the disposal of Sa'ad b Abi Waqas did not satisfy his needs. He was accordingly compelled to obtain a loan from the Baitul Mal. The Baitul Mal was under the charge of Ibn Masud. Ibn Masud was known for his scrupulous honesty and for his strictness in financial

1. Ibid.
2. Ibid.

matters. He allowed the loan to Sa'ad b Abi Waqas on the condition that it was to be repaid within a stipulated period. It was further laid down that the amount should be returned within the specified period and that no extension should be allowed under any circumstances.

Dispute Between Sa'ad b Abi Waqas and Ibn Masud[1]

Sa'ad b Abi Waqas was not able to repay the loan within the stipulated period and Ibn Masud insisted on immediate repayment. Sa'ad b Abi Waqas wanted an extension in the time for the repayment of the loan. Ibn Masud refused to allow any extension on the ground that in accordance with the terms of the grant of the loan no extension was admissible. The issue became the subject-matter of a dispute between Ibn Masud and Sa'ad b Abi Waqas. Hot words were exchanged between the two highest functionaries in the province. In the dispute some persons sided with Ibn Masud while some persons favoured Sa'ad b Abi Waqas. Such differences created a crisis and the provincial administration came to be paralysed.

Deposition of Sa'ad b Abi Waqas[2]

When the matter was reported to Hadrat Othman he expressed displeasure and wanted Sa'ad b Abi Waqas and Ibn Masud to settle the matter among themselves amicably. Some well-wishers tried to intervene but no way could be found to resolve the crisis. Sa'ad b Abi Waqas pleaded his inability to repay the loan immediately, while Ibn Masud pleaded his inability to allow any extension. The crisis deepened and ultimately Hadrat Othman had no option but to depose Sa'ad b Abi Waqas from the governorship of Kufa. Some of the malcontents made this order a matter of criticism against Hadrat Othman. It was contended that as there were two parties to the dispute, penal action should have been taken against both the parties and not against one of them only. It was argued that Hadrat Othman had unduly favoured Ibn Masud who was originally a slave of his step father Uqba b Abi Muheet. If the facts of the case are considered dispassionately, it would be seen that there was no dereliction on the part of Ibn Masud. He merely insisted on the repayment of the loan according to the terms governing the grant of

1. Ibid.
2. Ibid.

the loan. Ibn Masud merely performed his duty as the custodian of the Baitul Mal and there performing his duty'zealously.

WALID B UQBA

On the disposition of Sa'ad b Abi Waqas from the governorship of Kufa, Hadrat Othman appointed Walid b Uqba as the Governor of Kufa. Walid b Uqba was an uterine brother of Hadrat Othman. After the death of Affan, the father of Hadrat Othman, his mother Urwa had married Uqba b Abi Muheet. Uqba b Abi Muheet was one of the inveterate enemies of Islam. Among the Quraish he was in the forefront in the persecution of the Muslims. He was taken captive by the Muslims in the battle of Badr and was executed.

Walid became a Muslim at the time of conquest of Makkah. Thereafter he was commissioned by the Holy Prophet to collect taxes from the Banu Mustaliq tribe. When Walid reached the settlement of Banu Mustaliq they came out in large numbers to meet him. He got the impression that the Banu Mustaliq meant some mischief. He returned to Madinah and reported to the Holy Prophet that the Banu Mustaliq had apostatised and were not willing to pay the taxes.

Later it transpired that the impression of Walid was false. The Banu Mustaliq had not apostatised, on the other hand they had gathered in strength to greet him as an emissary of the Government of Madinah. The Holy Prophet felt annoyed at the conduct of Walid. On this occasion a verse of the Holy Qur'ãn was revealed enjoining the Muslims that when any news was reported, they should verify it in the first instance.

Walid was, however, intelligent and a man of considerable ability. Later he made amends for his lapse in the matter of the collection of taxes from Banu Mustaliq and his services were utilised for sundry purposes. Hadrat Umar employed him for the collection of taxes from the Banu Taghlib tribe in Jazira and he discharged his duties most conscientiously.

When Hadrat Othman became the Caliph, Walid came to Madinah and remained by the side of Hadrat Othman. In his book on Hadrat Othman, Raza Misri relates that once when Walid came to Hadrat Othman he took his particular seat but when Hakam b. Al 'Aas, the uncle of Hadrat Othman, came Hadrat Othman vacated his own seat for his uncle. Thereupon Walid b Uqba composed the verses:

"I have seen what respect one's uncle commands,
And before the uncle the stature of the brother is diminished,
Perhaps the brother's fault is that he is young in age,
I hope that in course of time 'Amr and Khalid (sons of Hadrat Othman) would respect me as uncle
As Hadrat Othman respects his uncle Hakam."

Walid as Governor of Kufa

When Walid went to Kufa to take over charge as Governor, Sa'ad b Abi Waqas said to him, "By Allah I do not know whether after us you have become wiser or before you we have become more foolish". Walid said, "It is neither this nor that, it is only the vicissitudes of time that shifts the centre of power from one person to another." Sa'ad said "Whatever the case I fear that you would convert the caliphate to monarchy."

As Governor Walid became very popular. His rule was mild and just. His house had no door, everybody had free access to him. He took pains to redress the grievances of the people. He sanctioned stipends for the poor, the widows and the orphans and the people admired him for his generosity.

In the case of revolts in Armenia and Azarbaijan, Walid led his forces in person; suppressed the revolts, restored law and order and amassed great booty.

Complaints Against Walid b Uqba

Walid b Uqba remained the Governor of Kufa for a period of five years and during this period he was very popular among the people and there were no complaints against him.

Thereafter the events took a sudden turn and the position of Walid as Governor became uneasy. One night some young men beat to death a citizen of Kufa, Ibn Hesiman Khuzaii by name. Three young men Zubair b Jandab Azdi, Mawan b Abi Lawah Asadi and Shabil b Abi Al Azdi were accused of the murder. Abu Sharih Khuzaii and his son who were the neighbours of Ibn Hesiman watched the murder from their house.

When the case was reported to Walid he held a public trial. The details of the case are not known. We do not know what was the cause of the dispute between the murdered person and his murderers. The only eye-witnesses of the tragedy were Abu Sharih Khuzaii and his son. They narrated that they heard Ibn Hesiman cry, for help. Thereupon the murderers had said to him, "Do not cry, for one stroke of the sword will suffice for you." As Abu Sharih and his son had watched the tragedy from some distance in the dark they were not in a position to fully recognise the murderers.

In view of this shortcoming in the evidence, the heirs of the deceased were asked to declare fifty oaths as required by the injunctions of the Shariah that the persons accuses of the murder were really the murderers of Ibn Hesiman. They took the prescribed fifty oaths and Walid gave the verdict that the accused were guilty of murder. The death sentence was referred to Hadrat Othman for confirmation and when the confirmation orders were received the three accused persons were hanged.

Thereupon 'Amr b 'Asim Tamimi composed the following verse:

"O mischief mongers do not murder your neighbours like this,
During the caliphate of Hadrat Othman,
Beware that the Caliph would penalise the miscreants,
According to the injunctions of Islam,
For verily Hadrat Othman always acts,
In accordance with the commands of the Holy Qur'ān
Which regulates the conduct of the Muslims in all matters."

While the general public felt satisfied at the execution of the murderers, the fathers of the three murderers namely Jandab Azdi, Abi Lawah Asadi and Abi Al Azdi felt dissatisfied. Their grouse was that the charge of murder had not been established against their sons and that Walid had executed them as he has some personal grudge against them. They carried on propaganda against the Governor and they were able to win some persons to their cause. The party worked underground and their secret agents spied on Walid with a view to ascertain his weaknesses and defame him.

As a result of the working of this party, Walid came to be accused of some imaginary grievances. When Walid was the Collector in Jazira he had come across Abu Zubayd Taii, a poet of great eminence. As Walid was also a poet, he freely associated with Abu Zubayd. Abu Zubayd was a Christian and he was given to drinking. While in Jazira there was no complaint that Walid had associated with Abu Zubayd in any drinking but Abu Zubayd had to pay some loan and he was not in a position to clear his debt. Walid came to the help of Abu Zubayd by repaying the loan out of his own pocket. That made Abu Zubayd indebted to Walid. When Walid became the Governor of Kufa, Abu Zubayd came to Kufa and stayed with Walid as his guest. At the instance of Walid, Abu Zubayd became a Muslim. He wrote some verses in praise of Islam. During the nights Walid and Abú Zubayd spent long hours together talking on literary matters. The conspirators whipped up a campaign that during the nights Abu Zubayd and Walid indulged in drinking some persons secretly raided the house of Walid to catch hold of some liquor but they found nothing objectionable.

A sorcerer appeared in Kufa who claimed that he could enter through the body of an ass from its tail and come out from its mouth. Walid asked the sorcerer to give a public demonstration of his feat. The conspirators whipped up a vilification campaign against Walid. They were critical that the Governor was patronising sorcery. On the occasion of the public demonstration the conspirators appeared in large number and raised the cry that the demonstration was un-Islamic. They rushed at the sorcerer and killed him. Thereupon Walid apprehended the murderers of the sorcerer and put them in jail. The case was reported to Hadrat Othman. He directed that the murderers be released and warned not to take the law in their hands. On release the conspirators intensified their campaign of vilification against Walid. They changed their tactics. They began to associate with Walid and pretended that they were sorry for the past misunderstandings and that in future they would be faithful and loyal to him. Walid took them at their word. These persons amused Walid with their anecdotes and stories. One night these persons kept awake till late hours telling him some interesting stories. When overpowered by sleep Walid dozed, they took off the official ring from his finger and departed for Madinah.

In Madinah they complained before Hadrat Othman that Walid was guilty of intoxication. In evidence of the charge that in a fit of intoxication Walid had thrown away his official ring. They also charged that Walid led the prayers in a state of intoxication and in the state of such unconsciousness he offered four rakaats in the morning prayers instead of the prescribed two rakaats.

Trial of Walid b Uqba

Walid b Uqba was summoned to Madinah and put to trial. The charge against him was that he had drunk and that he had led the morning prayers in a state of intoxication. The prosecutors were asked whether they had seen Walid drink. They said that they had not seen him drinking but he had vomited in their presence and they had seen drops of wine sticking to his beard. They added that on a particular day Walid in a state of unconsciousness led the morning prayers in four rakaats and then asked the congregation, "Are you satisfied or should we offer some rakaats." Walid denied the charge. No direct evidence had established the charge. In the absence of evidence the matter had to be decided by oath taking. The prosecutors took the solemn oath that Walid had drunk and that he had led the prayers in a state of intoxication. The accounts that have come down to us provide that thereafter Hadrat Othman sentenced Walid b Uqba to the penalty of flogging.

There is considerable discrepancy on the accounts that have come to down to us. According to one account it is related that Walid objected that the charge against him had not been established as the witnesses were interested and prejudiced. It is stated that Hadrat Othman counselled Walid to bear the hardship with patience. According to one account Hadrat Ali asked his son Hasan to flog Walid. Hasan refused to do so. According to one account it was Abdullah b Jafar b Abu Talib who flogged Walid. According to another version Saeed b 'Aas flogged Walid.

It is also related that the poet Hatiya composed some verses in the defence of Walid. He said:

"When Hatiya is presented in the court of Allah
He will give evidence that Walid is innocent.
Only jealous persons have complained against Walid and made false accusations.
In fact, Walid was not fond of office, nor did he depend on it."
A poet of the rival camp said:
"What to say of Walid,
He would lead the prayers in a state of intoxication,
And lengthen the prayers.
If he continues in office
He would lengthen the morning prayers to ten rakaats."

Objective Assessment

When the entire episode of the deposition and penalisation of Walid b Uqba is studied objectively one is apt to conclude that the accounts that have come down to us are distorted and remote from reality. The tale appears to have been embroidered both by those who were critical of Hadrat Othman and those who wanted to defend. Those who were hostile to Hadrat Othman took pains to establish that the person appointed by Hadrat Othman to high offices was guilty of heinous crimes and hence Hadrat Othman was guilty of appointing undeserving person to high offices.

On the other hand those who stood for the defence of Hadrat Othman and wanted to show that Hadrat Othman was just and impartial, held that even when a brother of Hadrat Othman was found guilty, Hadrat Othman did not hesitate to subject him to the penalty of law.

As a matter of fact, the accounts that have come down to us with regard to this episode do not stand the test of historical scrutiny. The case against Walid was not established and according to the norms of justice he could not be penalised on the ground of mere hearsay or the evidence of interested witnesses. During his five years rule Walid had been most popular. Only a few persons conspired against him and it is inconceivable that such high functionary of the State should have been publicly disgraced merely because of a conspiracy against him when the charge was not established.

Walid had the support of the Bani Umayya and they were in sufficient strength and power. They could not submit to the public disgrace of one of their leaders. It is well-known that Hadrat Othman had a great regard for his relatives. He could not have condemned his brother to such disgrace when the charge itself was not established.

The truth of the matter is that the charge against Walid was not established. As such no penalty was imposed and there was no flogging. Hadrat Othman merely deposed Walid b Uqba for administrative reasons.

SAEED B AL 'AAS[1]

On the deposition of Walid b Uqba, Saeed b Al 'Aas was appointed the Governor General of Kufa in 651 C.E. He belonged to the Umayyad section of the Quraish. His father was 'Aas b Umayya b Abd Shams. His mother was Umm Kulsum bint 'Amr b Abdullah b Abi Qais. His father was killed by Hadrat Ali at the battle of Badr. Saeed was then only two years old. Hadrat Othman took care of the child. Saeed was intelligent and well read. When he grew up he accepted Islam and went to Muawiyah in Syria. Hadrat Umar recalled him to Madinah and entrusted him some important duties. When Hadrat Othman constituted a board for the recension of the Holy Qur'ãn, Saeed was one of the members. Saeed was a young man of great qualities. He never turned down a beggar. When a beggar called on him and he had perchance nothing to pay, he would give the beggar a chit on the basis whereof he could recover the amount specified in the chit, from him later. He invited friends to a feast every Friday and gave them expensive presents and gifts. He was eloquent and was known for his scholarship.

Saeed's First Address at Kufa[2]

On taking charge as the Governor General of Kufa, Saeed addressed the congregation in the mosque. He said:

> "I swear by Allah that I have not come to you on my free will. I had no desire for the office and I did not ask for it. I was ordered to accept this office and I had no option but to comply. The office of the governorship is a great challenge and I have accepted it in the interests of the State. I see that disorder is continueing in Kufa. It will be my foremost duty to establish law and order and crush all attempts to foment disorder. In this task I will value your cooperation but I will discharge my obligations even if such cooperation is not forthcoming. O men of Kufa, beware that if you take to the path of righteousness you will find me your best supporter but if you choose to follow the path of mischief, I will have no option but to subject you to the penalty of law. I, therefore, warn you in your own interests that you should abandon your ways of the past and tread the path that behoves a good citizen. I appeal to you in the name of Islam not to disturb

1. *Othman b Affan*: Raza Misri.
2. Ibid.

the peace of the land. If you have any legitimate grievances, apprise me of such grievances and I assure you that I will leave no stone unturned in redressing such grievances."

Saeed's Survey of the Situations in Kufa[1]

Saeed surveyed the situation in Kufa. His finding was that agitation and mischief were aboard in Kufa. The peace-loving and law-abiding citizens were sitting shut up in their houses, while the society in Kufa had come to be dominated by agitators and mischief mongers. He apprised Hadrat Othman of the situation. Hadrat Othman advised him to patronise the law abiding citizens and neutralise the activities of the mischief-makers by a diplomatic handling of the situation. In accordance with the advice of Hadrat Othman, the first line of action of Saeed was to placate those from whom any mischief could be expected. Saeed invited such persons and admitted them to his society. Saeed would hold meetings with such people almost every night and consulted them on the affairs of the State. Saeed's strategy was to give such persons a sense of participation in the affairs of the State thereby neutralising their power of mischief-making. On the other hand the plan of such persons was to subvert the administration from within.

Disturbances in Kufa

In spite of Saeed's efforts to maintain peace and win over the mischief-makers to the cause of law and order, things soon came to head culminating in disturbances. One night when Saeed held his usual meeting with these persons, a reference was made to the liberality and generosity of Talha bin Ubaidullah. It was said that Talha was very liberal in charity and he distributed thousands of dirhams among the poor every week. Saeed said that Talha b Ubaidullah owned a very large estate "Nashstaj", which brought him very large income and as such he could indulge in manifestations of charity. Saeed added that if he were an estate holder, his generosity would surpass the generosity of Talha. Thereupon one of the persons in the gathering Khanis b Falan Asadi said, "I wish you owned the royal Persian estate in Iraq "Maltat", so that you could give us the manifestation of your generosity. There was some further talk on the subject and thereafter the tempers flared up. These people felt that Khanis was inciting Saeed to acquire the estate of Maltat.

---

1. Ibid.

Their view was that this estate should be distributed among the people. That led to an altercation and Khanis was given good beating.

On another occasion Saeed in an unwary moment said that Sawad (the area between the Tigris and the Euphrates) was the garden of the Quraish. These people protested in strong terms. They said that this area in Iraq belonged to Iraq and the Quraish had no right to dominate over the people of Iraq in that way. That led to a rift between Saeed and the people whom he usually invited to his night sittings. These people included Ashtar, Ibn Zi Alhabka, Jandab, Sasama, Ibn al Kawa, Kameel and Aamar b Zaabi.

Saeed discontinued his nightly meetings. Now these persons held their own meetings and at such meetings they carried on poisonous propaganda against Saeed and Hadrat Othman. Some poets wrote verses vilifying Saeed. One of the poets said:

> "Escaping from Walid I took shelter with Saeed. But it was like a person who took shelter in a cave and was killed. The Quraish put us every year to a trouble. Every now and then a new Amir is imposed on us. A burning fire is before us from which we apprehend danger. There is no fire before the Quraish. As such there is nothing to withhold the Quraish from their tyrannies. May Allah save us from them."

It appears that in order to carry out their subversive designs the conspirators raised the bogey of the tyranny of the Quraish. This poisonous propaganda slowly spread among the people of Kufa and the people began to harbour imaginary grievances against the Quraish. Saeed and Hadrat Othman became the target of criticism.

Saeed reported this unsatisfactory state of affairs to Hadrat Othman. Hadrat Othman directed that the ring leaders of the conspirators be sent to Syria.

Deposition of Saeed b Al 'Aas[1]

In Syria, Amir Muawiyah tried to deal with these conspirators diplomatically. He provided them with various facilities and conferred many favours on them. He held several sittings with them and tried to make them see reasons. The conspirators continued their campaign of vilification against the Quraish and even demanded the

---

1. Ibid.

deposition of Amir Muawiyah. Amir Muawiyah reported the matter to Hadrat Othman and he directed that these men be sent to Jazira where the ruler was Abdur Rahman.

Abdur Rahman was the son of the famous General Khalid b Walid. He treated with these conspirators harshly. The strong measures adopted by Abdur Rahman had a salutary effect and the conspirators offered repentance. Abdur Rahman sent one of these conspirators Ashtar to Madinah and sent a message to Hadrat Othrnan through him that as they had repented they might be allowed to return to Kufa.

In Madinah, Ashtar saw Hadrat Othman and offered repentance on his own behalf and on behalf of the other conspirators. At that time Saeed b Al 'Aas was also in Madinah. Hadrat Othman accepted the repentance of Ashtar and the other conspirators and allowed them to return to Kufa.

Ashtar and the other conspirators returned to Kufa, while Saeed was till in Madinah. Back in Kufa, the conspirators violated their pledge and once again resorted to a campaign of vilification. This time Saeed b Al 'Aas was the main target of criticism. Addressing the people at the gate of the main mosque in Kufa, Ashtar said that he had been to Madinah, where he had come to know that Saeed b Al 'Aas had recommended to Hadrat Othman that strong measures should be taken against the people of Kufa. They were to be enslaved and deported and their properties were to be confiscated.

The deputy that Saeed b Al 'Aas had left at Kufa tried to explain to the people that all this talk of enslavement and confiscation of properties was false and there was no such move in any quarter. The people paid no head to him and raised slogans demanding the deposition of Saeed b Al 'Aas. The persons who were pro-Government had to remain confined to their houses, while the streets of Kufa came to be flocked by agitators vociferous in their demand for the deposition of Saeed b Al 'Aas.

Over a thousand persons from Kufa decided to go to Madinah to place their demand before Hadrat Othman. Hadrat Othman listened to them at Madinah. He tried to explain to them that all their grievances were imaginary and Saeed b Al 'Aas had made recommendation to which they were objecting. They, however, stuck fast to their demand for the deposition of Saeed b Al 'Aas. Hadrat

Othman felt that argument with the rebels was of no avail. In order to pacify them he said, "If you do not want Saeed as your Governor, whom do you want?" They said, "Abu Musa Asha'ri may be appointed as our Governor." Hadrat Othman said, "All right, I accept your demand in the interests of peace although I know that no blame rests on Saeed b Al 'Aas. I depose him and appoint Abu Musa Ash'ari as your Governor. Now go back and be at peace. Now that I have given you the Governor of your own choice, obey him and let there be no more of unnecessary agitation."

This action of Hadrat Othman has been made the subject of criticism in some quarters. There is one school of thought which is critical of Hadrat Othman for making a wrong choice in the appointment of Governors. As a matter of fact there was nothing wrong with the appointment of Saeed b Al 'Aas. He was a talented young man whose talents had been acknowledged by Hadrat Umar. Saeed won brilliant victories in Tabaristan and that was a feather in his cap.

The other school of thought criticises Hadrat Othman for deposing Saeed when he was not at fault. Although Saeed was not at fault there was nevertheless strong agitation against him, right or wrong. In such circumstances if Saeed was to continue in office, it meant the imposition of a Governor on the people whom they did not want. In the circumstances, in the interests of public administration, the only course open to Hadrat Othman was to recall Saeed from Kufa and appoint in his stead the man they wanted. Hadrat Othman hoped that by such action he would take the wind out of the sails of the rebels.

ABU MUSA ASH'ARI

Abu Musa Ash'ari During the Caliphate of Hadrat Umar[1]

Abu Musa Ash'ari was the Governor of Basra during the caliphate of Hadrat Umar. During this period, some complaints were made against him to Hadrat Umar. The main complaints against him were:

(1) that out of the captives he had kept sixty persons for himself,

(2) that he had paid one thousand dinars to a poet,

(3) that he had a maid Aquila who was paid a stipend which

1. *Hadrat Umar Farooq*: Prof. Masudul Hasan.

was twice the stipend paid to other Muslims, and

(4) that he had entrusted most of his work to a young man Ziyad.

Hadrat Umar held a regular enquiry into these charges. Abu Musa Ash'ari offered his defence as follows:

(1) He had kept these slaves for himself, they were under his charge till they were ransomed. The amount of the rensom was duly credited to the Baitul Mal.

(2) He had paid the poet out of his own money and not out of the Baitul Mal.

(3) There was something exceptional and extraordinary with the physical make up of the maid for she consumed twice as much as a common person. Under the circumstances it was necessary to assign her two shares.

(4) The young man Ziyad was very intelligent and as Governor he was justified in making use of his intelligence in public interests.

Hadrat Umar after a detailed enquiry exonerated Abu Musa Ash'ari of all the charges levelled against him and allowed him to continue in his office.

Another Complaint[1]

On another occasion a person complained that Abu Musa Ash'ari had given him a lesser share than what he was entitled to. When the man saw Abu Musa he behaved rudely. Abu Musa felt annoyed and had him struck with twenty lashes. He also had his hair shaved. The man complained to Hadrat Umar and Hadrat Umar asked him to lay his complaint before a congregation in the mosque at Basra. When the man laid his complaint before the congregation in the main mosque at Basra, Abu Musa admitted his mistake and said to the man "You can have your revenge. You may strike me with twenty lashes and have my hair shaved." The man felt satisfied and withdrew his complaint.

Deposition of Abu Musa Ash'ari[2]

When Hadrat Othman became the Caliph, he let Abu Musa

---

1. *Othman b. Affan*: Prof. Raza Misri.
2. Ibid.

Ash'ari continue as the Governor of Basra. He continued to hold this office for three years during the caliphate of Hadrat Othman. During the year 647 C.E. there were some disturbances in Fars and some forces had to be sent there to restore law and order. There was shortage of animals at the time and addressing the people Abu Musa stressed the virtue of undertaking Jihad on foot. The people were impressed with the preaching of Abu Musa Ash'ari and they volunteered to undertake Jihad on foot in case there was a shortage of animals.

When on the scheduled date, Abu Musa Ash'ari came out of his palace to lead the people to battle, he rode on a richly caprisoned horse and his camp equipage was loaded on forty pack animals. The people flared up at this display of luxury on the part of Abu Musa Ash'ari and the dichotomy in what he preached and what he practised. Some of the persons held the reins of the horse of Abu Musa Ash'ari and said: "Alight and walk with us on foot or furnish us horses as well to ride." That annoyed Abu Musa Ash'ari. Harsh words were exchanged between Abu Musa Ash'ari and some of the persons and he had some persons lashed for their insolence. The reaction of the people to this act on the part of the Governor was violent. They refused to march to the battle-field under his leadership, who did not practise what he preached.

A deputation representing the people of Basra left for Madinah and there they lodged a complaint before Hadrat Othman against the conduct of Abu Musa Ash'ari. The news writer from Basra also sent a report which was not favourable to the Governor. Abu Musa had held the office of the Governor for over six years and because of the length of the term of office he had come to develop a sort of superiority complex which created a gulf between the people and the Governor. Abu Musa Ash'ari had grown in years and was prone to prefer a life of ease. Hadrat Othman gave a patient hearing to the deputationists. They pressed the need of deposing Abu Musa Ash'ari from his office. Hadrat Othman after hearing all the complaints against Abu Musa Ash'ari came to the conclusion that he was not guilty of any dishonesty or dereliction of duty. He, however, felt that Abu Musa had held the office for long and it was in public interests that there should be a change. He asked the desputationists: "In case Abu Musa is removed, whom would you like to be Governor?" They said that any young man in whom the Caliph had confidence would be better than the old Abu Musa Ash'ari.

Hadrat Othman thereupon passed orders deposing Abu Musa Ash'ari form the governorship of Basra and appointing Abdullah b 'Aamir in his place.

Abu Musa Ash'ari as the Governor of Kufa[1]

In 655 C.E. when Saeed b Al 'Aas was deposed from the governorship of Kufa, the people of Kufa demanded the appointment of Abu Musa Ash'ari as their Governor. Hadrat Othman accepted the demand and appointed Abu Musa Ash'ari as the Governor of Kufa. In his address on the occasion of the assumption of office Abu Musa secured an undertaking from the people of Kufa that they would not indulge in agitation and would be loyal to Hadrat Othman. The people of Kufa, however, did not fulfil their undertaking and they sent a contingent to Madinah to besiege the house of Hadrat Othman and press for his abdication. Although Abu Musa Ash'ari did nothing to oppose Hadrat Othman, he did nothing to help him either. He preferred to be neutral and watch developments.

ABDULLAH BIN 'AAMIR

Appointment as the Governor of Basra

When Abu Musa Ash'ari was deposed from the governorship of Basra, Hadrat Othman appointed Abdullah b 'Aamir as the Governor of Basra. The people of Basra wanted that a young man should be appointed as the Governor and in deference to this wish of the people, Abdullah b 'Aamir, a young man of twenty-five, was appointed to the office. 'Aamir, the father of Abdullah, was a maternal uncle of Hadrat Othman. Abdullah was thus a cousin of Hadrat Othman.

Conquests of Ibn 'Aamir

Abdullah b 'Aamir in spite of his young age was a man of exceptional merits. He was a man of sterling qualities. He was a good administrator and a skilful general. Soon after assuming charge as Governor, Abdullah b 'Aamir embarked on a campaign of extensive conquests. He first undertook campaigns in the province of Fars. After suppressing revolts in Fars, Abdullah b 'Aamir undertook campaigns in Kirman. The command of the forces in Kirman was entrusted to Mujasshaa b Musa Salmi. Kirman was soon reconquered.

---

1. The views expressed in this section are based on my own assessment and research.

Campaigns were next undertaken in Seestan. Rabeah b Ziyad Harithi was appointed to command the forces in Seestan. Seestan was reconquered. Thereafter Afghanistan was conquered and the borders of India were reached. Thereafter Abdullah b 'Aamir led the Muslim forces in person in Khurasan. The Muslim forces captured the forts which were the gates of Khurasan. Thereafter Abdullah b 'Aamir led the Muslim forces to Quhistan. Quhistan was conquered after some fighting. Ibn 'Aamir sent numerous columns in various directions. One column conquered the territory of Rustaqzam in Nishapur. Another column conquered the area of Bakharz. Another column conquered the area of Juban. Another column under Aswad b Kulthum Adwi was sent against Bahaq. Aswad was killed in action but the city was conquered by the Muslims. Thereafter other cities in Nishapur were brought under control. Thereafter the city of Abushahr was reduced after a long seige. Thereafter Nishapur was conquered. Ibn 'Aamir appointed Qais b Hatim Salmi as the ruler of Nishapur. Ibn 'Aamir sent another column under Abdullah b Khazam Salmi to Nasaa. The city was conquered and the peace was negotiated on the usual terms. The next campaign was against Sarakhs which fell to the Muslims after some fighting. From Sarakhs one column advanced to Kaif and another to Bina. Both the cities were conquered after some fighting. Tus was next to fall. Columns were thereafter sent to Herat, Badghes and Bushang which cities also fell to the Muslims. The cities of Taghun and Yaghun fell after some fighting. Thereafter the Muslim forces advanced to Merv. The ruler of Merv surrendered and agreed to pay tribute. Another column advanced to Taghiristan which country was conquered after some fighting. Next the territory of Mervroz was captured. A column under Aqraa b Habis Tamimi was sent to Juzjan. The territory of Juzjan was conquered by the Muslims after a good deal of fighting. The territories of Talqan and Faryab were next conquered. The Muslims thereafter advanced to Balkh which city was captured after a seige lasting for sometime.

Thereafter Abdullah b 'Aamir crossed the Oxus and subdued a greater part of Transoxiana. After these conquests Abdullah b 'Aamir returned to Nishapur. The achievements of Abdullah b 'Aamir were most astounding. Within a few years he had conquered Fars, Kirman, Seestan, Kabul, Khurasan and a greater part of Transoxiana. The conquests exceeded the conquest made by any other conqueror in history.

After the successful completion of his campaigns, Abdullah b 'Aamir donned the *Ihram* in Nishapur and proceeded to Ka'aba to perform Hajj and offer thanks to Allah. After performing the Hajj, Abdullah b 'Aamir proceeded to Madinah to see Hadrat Othman. Before Abdullah b 'Aamir reached Madinah, Hadrat Othman had been martyred. That was a great shock for Abdullah b 'Aamir. When Zubair, Talha and Hadrat Ayesha raised the call for the vengeance for the blood of Hadrat Othman, Abdullah b 'Aamir joined them. The confederates succeeded in capturing Basra because of the influence that Abdullah b 'Aamir commanded with the people of Basra. In the "Battle of the Camel" which was fought in December 656, the confederates were defeated and Basra was captured by Hadrat Ali.

Assessment of Abdullah b 'Aamir

In most of the accounts that have come down to us, Hadrat Othman is accused of nepotism and appointing his cousin Abdullah b 'Aamir, a young man of twenty-five years as the Governor of Basra. The critics forget that Abdullah b 'Aamir proved to be the most successful Governor in history. No other Governor in the history of the world ever made conquests on as large a scale as Abdullah b 'Aamir. It is unfortunate that full details of the exploits of Abdullah b 'Aamir have not been preserved in history. Only fragmentary accounts of his victories are given in history books and it appears that the achievements of Abdullah b 'Aamir and Hadrat Othman in the matter of these extensive victories have been suppressed under some intellectual conspiracy. What is regrettable is that while Hadrat Othman and his relatives who served under him are blamed for their favouritism and tribal predilections, their unique achievements have been belittled and passed over. As a matter of fact, Abdullah b 'Aamir deserves to be honoured as one of the top ranking Generals of Islam.

MARWAN BIN HAKAM

The Evil Genius[1]

In most of the accounts that have come down to us, Marwan b Hakam is painted as the "evil genius" who was responsible for the troubles of Hadrat Othman. The issue needs objective examination.

1. *Othman b Affan*: Raza Misri.

Marwan was the son of Hakam. Hakam was the paternal uncle of Hadrat Othman. When Hadrat Othman was converted to Islam, Hakam put considerable pressure on Hadrat Othman to retract from his faith in Islam. Hadrat Othman remained firm in his faith in Islam and thereafter Hakam left Hadrat Othman to himself. Hakam and his son Marwan were converted to Islam at the time of the conquest of Makkah. Hakam and Marwan then came to Madinah. In Madinah, the Holy Prophet felt annoyed at the conduct of Hakam and exiled him to Taif. Marwan consequently came to be called "Ibn Tarid", the son of the expelled one. It is reported that Hadrat Othman interceded with the Holy Prophet for the recall of Hakam from exile. The Holy Prophet agreed to rescind the orders of exile but before the orders were passed the Holy Prophet was dead. In the time of Hadrat Abu Bakr and Hadrat Umar, Hadrat Othman requested for the recall of Hakam. As no evidence other than the evidence of Hadrat Othman was available to the effect that the Holy Prophet had agreed to rescind the orders of exile, the Caliphs did not agree to recall Hakam from exile. When Hadrat Othman became the Caliph he recalled Hakam from exile. As Caliph, Hadrat Othman was competent to act on the basis of information available to him. In some quarters, Hadrat Othman was criticised for rescinding the order passed by the Holy Prophet, Hadrat Othman declared that the Holy Prophet had agreed to his recall. Hadrat Othman was not the man to speak a lie and whatever he said must be true. The orders of exile were recalled after more than twelve years and as every sentence must be for a specified period, Hadrat Othman was justified in passing the orders of recall after twelve years. Hakam did not stay in Madinah for long and went back to Makkah and Taif. Hadrat Othman requested Hakam to leave Marwan at Madinah in order to assist him. Marwan accordingly remained at Madinah and he acted as Hadrat Othman's Minister and Secretary. It cannot be denied that as Caliph Hadrat Othman needed assistance in running the affairs of the State. He could appoint only such persons to such office who enjoyed his absolute confidence.

It may be recalled that in the time of Hadrat Othman, there were no developed institutions for running the affairs of the State. Loyalties depended on blood relationship and tribal considerations alone. In the circumstances of the age in which he lived Hadrat Othman had no option but to invoke the assistance of his relatives. It is alleged that Hadrat Othman allotted one fifth of the revenues of Egypt to Marwan. The allegation is preposterous. If there had been any substance in the allegation Marwan should have been extraordinarily rich. As a matter of fact he was a man of ordinary means and this shows that no undue payments were made to him. It is probable that some allowances may have been paid to Marwan out of the public funds but such payment was justified because Marwan served as Minister or Secretary to the Caliph. Marwan is generally painted as the evil genius of Hadrat Othman. Sir William Muir has explained in his book regarding the history of the Caliphs that such allegations are based on partisan motives and are devoid of substance. It is made out that on several occasions Hadrat Ali gave his mind to Hadrat Othman and Hadrat Othman promised to follow the advice of Hadrat Ali but that on the advice of Marwan, Hadrat Othman would again revert to his objectionable ways. All such allegations were made with a view to projecting Hadrat Othman as a man of fickle and feeble character who had no will of his own and was led by the nose by unscrupulous advisers. As a matter of fact, Hadrat Othman was neither feeble nor fickle, nor were his advisers unscrupulous. They were as good Muslims as other persons and they served the State as best as they could.

Marwan's Role in the Martyrdom of Hadrat Othman[1]

In most of the accounts that have come down to us, an impression is created that Hadrat Othman was killed because he unduly shielded Marwan. It is related that the delegation which came from Egypt merely complained against Abdullah b Sa'ad, the Governor of Egypt. Hadrat Othman wrote a strong letter to Abdullah b Sa'ad to redress the grievances of the people. It is alleged that Abdullah b Sa'ad instead of redressing the grievances of the people scourged the persons who had complained against him and had one of them executed. Thereupon the Egyptians came to Madinah for the second time. They saw some of the Companions and explained their grievances to them. It is reported that Talha b Ubaidullah saw Hadrat Othman and spoke some harsh words to him about the laxity of his administration. Hadrat Ayesha is also reported to have criticised Hadrat Othman. Hadrat Ali is reported to have advised Hadrat Othman to depose Abdullah b Sa'ad from the governorship of Egypt. Hadrat Othman agreed to the demand and wanted the

1. Ibid.

Egyptians to name the person whom they wanted to be appointed as the Governor of Egypt. They suggested Muhammad b Abu Bakr and Hadrat Othman passed orders deposing Abdullah b Sa'ad and appointing Muhammad b Abu Bakr in his place. The Egyptians felt satisfied at this order and they returned to Egypt. After they had proceeded a few stages from Madinah they came across a slave of Hadrat Othman. On search he was found carrying a letter to Abdullah b Sa'ad not to give effect to the orders of deposition passed against him. He was instructed to put the rioters to death. That made the Egyptians return to Madinah. They saw Hadrat Ali and Hadrat Ali took them to Hadrat Othman. Hadrat Othman took a solemn oath denying all knowledge about the letter. It was suspected that the letter was in the hand of Marwan. The Egyptians wanted that Marwan should be handed over to them. Hadrat Othman refused and thereupon the rioters besieged Hadrat Othman in his house. The siege lasted for some days and ultimately Hadrat Othman was martyred. It is alleged that when Hadrat Ali heard of the murder of Hadrat Othman he said that he wanted the murder of Marwan and not that of Othman. This account tends to give the impression that Hadrat Othman lost his life because he showed undue favour to Marwan.

Research has established that the story about the alleged letter is a concocted story and is remote from reality. It appears from Tabari that when the rioters came to Madinah, Abdullah b Sa'ad was ousted from power by a revolt led by Muhammad b Abi Hudhaifa. Muhammad b Abi Hudhaifa was opposed to Hadrat Othman and as such there was no occasion to require that the rioters should be murdered.

Even if the story of the letter were true, Marwan who was the Minister could not be handed over to the rioters merely because they suspected that he has written the letter. Marwan could not be condemned unless a regular trial was held and he was found guilty. If the rioters had demanded the trial of Marwan, Hadrat Othman would have agreed to such a trial but he could not hand over a high functionary of the State to the fury of the rioters without trial.

4

CONQUESTS OF HADRAT OTHMAN

BYZANTINE INVASION OF EGYPT

Byzantine Occupation of Alexandria[1]

In Alexandria there was a considerable population of the Byzantines who owed nominal allegiance to the Muslims and whose loyalties lay with the Government of Byzantium.

With the death of Hadrat Umar and the deposition of 'Amr b Al 'Aas from the governorship of Egypt the Byzantines of Alexandria felt that it was the right moment to throw off the yoke of the Muslims. The Byzantines of Alexandria moved the Emperor of Byzantium, Constans to invade Egypt and reconquer it from the Muslims.

Early in 646 C.E., a large Byzantine force landed at Alexandria. There was only a small Muslim garrison in Alexandria generally remained faithful to the Muslims but they were not in a position to offer any resistance to the Byzantines. The Byzantine forces occupied Alexandria without much difficulty.

Recall of 'Amr b Al 'Aas[2]

From the base at Alexandria, the Byzantines planned to reconquer the whole of Egypt. The Muslims of Egypt sent a delegation to Madinah to wait on Hadrat Othman and prevail on him to restore 'Amr b Al 'Aas to the command of Egypt for he alone could save Egypt for the Muslims.

---

1. *Muslim Conquest of Egypt and North Africa:* Lt. General A.I. Akram.
2. Ibid.

Hadrat Othman summoned 'Amr b Al 'Aas and appealed to him to take over the command of Egypt. He stipulated some terms which were accepted by Hadrat Othman. 'Amr b Al 'Aas was made the Governor of Upper as well as Lower Egypt and he was also to be the supreme commander of the military forces in Egypt. Abdullah b Sa'ad was to hold a subordinate position under 'Amr b Al 'Aas.

Battle of Naqyus[1]

On taking over charge 'Amr b Al 'Aas reviewed the situation and decided that instead of attacking Alexandria forthwith the Byzantines should be drawn inside the country and then given a battle.

The Byzantine force advanced from Alexandria and marched to Fustat with a view to capturing it. The Muslim force under 'Amr b Al 'Aas marched from Fustat to meet the Byzantines half way. The two forces met at Naqyus.

The battle began with a duel between the Byzantine General and a Muslim warrior Haumal bin Abu Madhhij. As a result of the duel both the contestants died. Thereafter the two forces clashed. In spite of their superiority in strength, the Byzantines were defeated and they retreated to Alexandria.

Siege of Alexandria[2]

The Muslims pursued the retreating Byzantines and laid siege to Alexandria. The siege dragged on for sometime. The Byzantines within Alexandria became the victims of mutual dissensions. Ibn Bassama, a gate-keeper of one of the gates, contacted the Muslims and offered to open the gate for the Muslims, in case he was granted amnesty. 'Amr b Al 'Aas accepted the offer. One night the gate was opened and the Muslim force rushed inside the city. In a hand to hand fight that followed the Byzantines were defeated and the Muslims recaptured the city. On occupying the city, 'Amr b Al 'Aas had the walls of the city demolished to prevent the enemy from taking shelter within the city. The Copts who had remained loyal to the Muslims were duly compensated for the losses they had suffered because of the invasion of the Byzantines. After reorganising the administration of Alexandria, 'Amr b Al 'Aas returned in triumph to Fustat.

---

1. Ibid.
2. Ibid.

Deposition of 'Amr b Al 'Aas[1]

When Abdullah b Sa'ad was made the Governor of Lower as well as Upper Egypt, he managed to increase the revenues substantially. When 'Amr b Al 'Aas became the Governor, the revenues decreased again. At the fall of revenues, Hadrat Othman decided that while 'Amr b Al 'Aas should remain the Governor, Abdullah b Sa'ad should hold independent charge of the revenue department. To this arrangement, 'Amr b Al 'Aas did not agree. He said that such an arrangement would amount to his holding the cow by the horns while someone else milked it. The controversy assumed a bitter turn. Hadrat Othman placed two alternatives before 'Amr b Al 'Aas, either he should guarantee a stipulated amount of revenue each year or he should agree to Abdullah b Sa'ad holding independent charge of the Revenue Department. 'Amr b Al 'Aas did not agree to any of these alternatives. Thereupon Hadrat Othman deposed 'Amr b Al 'Aas from the governorship of Egypt. Abdullah b Sa'ad became the Governor and he stipulated that a certain sum would be guaranteed as the revenue for each year. This difference between Hadrat Othman and 'Amr b Al 'Aas is regrettable. It appears that as the conqueror of Egypt, 'Amr b Al 'Aas had developed a certain sense of pride and haughtiness which prevented him to see things in their proper perspective. As the Caliph, Hadrat Othman had every right to insist that Egypt should raise revenues commensurate to its importance and as the Governor 'Amr b Al 'Aas should have collaborated in the implementation of such measures. As 'Amr b Al 'Aas protested against these measures, Hadrat Othman had every right to depose him.

MUSLIM CONQUEST OF NORTH AFRICA

Campaign against North Africa[1]

After the withdrawal of 'Amr b Al 'Aas, when Abdullah b Sa'ad settled down as the Governor of Egypt, he sent raiding parties to the west. As a result of these raids the Muslims got considerable booty. The success of these raids made Abdullah b Sa'ad feel that a regular campaign should be undertaken for the conquest of North Africa. North Africa was originally under Byzantine control but after

---

1. *Othman*: Taha Hussain.
2. *Hadrat Umar Farooq*: Prof Masudul Hasan.

the withdrawal of the Byzantines from Egypt, North Africa had declared its independence under its king Gregory. The dominions of Gregory extended from the borders of Egypt to Morocco.

Jihad against North Africa[1]

Abdullah b Sa'ad sought the permission of Hadrat Othman to undertake Jihad against North Africa. In Madinah, Hadrat Othman summoned a meeting of the Majlis-i-Shura to consider the question. After discussion it was decided that a campaign against North Africa should be undertaken. It was also decided that a force from Madinah should be sent to assist the Egyptian forces under Abdullah b Sa'ad. A force of 10,000 warriors was raised in Madinah and sent to Egypt under the command of Harith b Al Hakam in the fall of 647 C.E. The Madinah force included Ma'bad b Abbas, Abdul Rahman b Abu Bakr, Abdullah b Umar, Ubaidullah b Umar, Abdullah b Zubair, Abdullah b 'Amr Al 'Aas and Marwan b Al Hakam.

March to Tripoli[2]

The Muslim forces assembled in Barqa in Cyrenica, the last outpost of the Muslims and from there marched to Tripoli. Muslims invaded Tripoli. The siege lasted for sometime and ultimately the town fell to the Muslims.

The Battle of Subetula[3]

From Tripoli the Muslim forces marched to Subetula, the capital of Gregory. The Muslim forces numbered 30,000. The forces of Gregory were twice the strength of the Muslim forces. The two forces clashed outside Subetula. The war dragged on for several days without leading to any tangible result.

Gregory had a daughter Sabiyya, renowned for her beauty and bravery. Gregory announced that whosoever killed Abdullah b Sa'ad, the Commander of the Muslim forces, would be married to Sabiyya as his reward and would be declared as the heir to the Crown. This declaration caused some anxiety among the Muslims and Abdullah b Sa'ad fearing for his life remained confined to his camp. That led to a state of stalemate in the fortunes of the war.

---

1. *Othman b Affan*: Raza Misri.
2. Ibid.
3. Ibid.

One day Abdullah b Zubair saw Abdullah b Sa'ad in his camp and advised him to make a counter declaration to the effect that whosoever killed Gregory would be married to Sabiyya, the daughter of Gregory. This counter declaration became a cause of great concern in the camp of Gregory.

A few days passed and still the stalemate continued. Then Abdullah b Zubair with the help of a Berber came to know of a secret way to the camp of Gregory. He decided to take the bold step of penetrating to the camp of Gregory and killing him. He ordered a regiment of the cavalry to follow him and remain at striking distance. According to plan, Abdullah b Zubair managed to reach the camp of Gregory and before anyone could realise what had happened, he severed the head of Gregory when the forces of Gregory rushed to get hold of Abdullah. The Muslim cavalry rushed at the forces of Gregory and made minced meat out of them. The battle of Sabetula was won by the Muslims.

Sequel to the Battle of Subetula[1]

After the battle of Subetula the people of North Africa sued for peace. They agreed to pay an annual tribute. Instead of annexing North Africa, the Muslims preferred to make North Africa a vassal state. When the stipulated amount of the tribute was paid, the Muslim forces withdrew to Barqa.

True to the declaration, Sabiyya, the beautiful daughter of Gregory, was awarded to Abdullah b Zubair. In this battle immense booty fell into the hands of the Muslims. When the booty was distributed, according to the prescribed formula, the share of each warrior came to as much as 3,000 dinars.

Hadrat Othman had declared at the outset of the campaign that if Abdullah b Sa'ad succeeded in his mission he would be given one fifth of the booty out of the State share. Abdullah b Sa'ad kept one fifth of the State share of the booty for himself and sent the rest to Madinah through Marwan b Al Hakam.

When the news of the victory of Subetula reached Madinah, the Muslims rejoiced and Hadrat Othman led a prayer of thanksgiving. When Marwan b Al Hakam reached Madinah with the booty, he prevailed upon Hadrat Othman to sell the entire booty to him for five lakh dinars. Hadrat Othman was in a generous mood and he

1. Ibid.

conceded to the request of Marwan. According to some accounts even the amount of five lakh dinars was paid by Hadrat Othman out of his own pocket.

The people felt bitter at the disposal of the booty in this way. The people were also critical of the award of one fifth of the State share of the booty to Abdullah b Sa'ad. A delegation from Egypt came to Madinah to see the Caliph. They complained against the misappropriation of the booty by Abdullah b Sa'ad. Hadrat Othman said that there was no misappropriation as he had himself announced that in case Abdullah b Sa'ad was victorious he would get one fifth out of the State share as his reward. The delegation said that even if it was so, there was no justification for such a high reward to Abdullah b Sa'ad. The battle was won through the feat of Abdullah b Zubair and there was nothing conspicuous about the services of Abdullah b Sa'ad.

Hadrat Othman said that if the people of Egypt felt dissatisfied at the grant of the reward, he could ask Abdullah b Sa'ad to return it. The delegation said that the people of Egypt were very bitter at the grant of the reward. Thereupon Hadrat Othman wrote to Abdullah b Sa'ad that the share of the booty kept by him should be distributed by him among the poor of Egypt.

The delegation demanded that as they had complained against Abdullah b Sa'ad, he was prone to be vindictive and as such he should be deposed. Hadrat Othman said that as Abdullah b Sa'ad was not to be blamed for anything there was no justification for his deposition. He, however, wrote to Abdullah b Sa'ad that he should not take any action against the members of the delegation for having made a complaint against him.

Unfortunately the account that has reached us is distorted and confused. Extensive conquests had been made under Abdullah b Sa'ad and immense booty had fallen to the share of each person. Abdullah b Sa'ad who had the Muslims to victory must have been very popular with the soldiers and it is difficult to believe that immediately in the wake of the victory, the soldiers should be dissatisfied against their commander who had led them to victory and send a delegation to Madinah to complain against him. Again it is unbelievable that the Head of the State should promise a reward for a certain achievement and rescind the order when the achievement is made, merely because certain person chooses to represent against such reward. Obviously these stories have been concocted because of partisan considerations merely to condemn the administration of Hadrat Othman on one pretext or the other.

CAMPAIGNS AGAINST NUBIA

The First Invasion of Nubia[1]

In 641 C.E. during the caliphate of Hadrat Umar when 'Amr b Al 'Aas was the Governor of Egypt, an expedition under Uqba b Nafe' was undertaken against Nubia. The Nubians were very mobile and as such no regular battle was fought. The operations consisted of skirmishes, haphazard engagements and hit-and-run raids. The Nubians were expert archers and they caused considerable havoc among the ranks of the Muslims. Most of the Muslim soldiers lost their eyes. The war proved inconclusive and the Muslim forces were pulled out of Nubia without achieving any result.

Second Invasion of Nubia[2]

Ten years later, when Abdullah b Sa'ad was the Governor, the Muslim forces invaded Nubia for the second time. The Muslim forces advanced into Nubia and besieged Dongola, the capital of Nubia. Here history repeated itself. The Nubian archers known as the "Archers of the Eye" let loose a shower of arrows aimed at the eyes of the Muslim warriors. The Nubians were expert marksmen and their arrows caused a good deal of consternation among the Muslim ranks.

As the Muslims were not able to overpower the Nubians, they accepted the Nubian offer of peace. According to the treaty that was signed, each side agreed not to make any aggression against the other. Each side agreed to afford free passage to the other party through its territories. Nubia agreed to provide 360 slaves to Egypt every year, while Egypt agreed to supply grain to Nubia according to demand.

---

1. Ibid.
1. Ibid.

NAVAL BATTLES

Hadrat Umar and Naval Warfare[1]

During the caliphate of Hadrat Umar, Muawiyah had sought the permission of Hadrat Umar to undertake naval warfare. Hadrat Umar consulted 'Amr b Al 'Aas who was then the Governor of Egypt. 'Amr b Al 'Aas reported unfavourably in the following terms:

> "O Commander of the Faithful, I have seen a numerous people going upon it overpowered by a few. When it is calm it tends the heart and when it is in motion, it twists the brain. It weakens confidence and strengthens doubt. There is nothing there but sky and water. People at sea are like a worm in a log of wood. If their boat inclines they sink and if they survive they are dazed."

Hadrat Umar rejected the proposal of Muawiyah to undertake war on the sea in the following terms:

> "I have heard that the Syrian Sea rises higher than the highest thing on earth and it seeks Allah's permission day and night to spread over the earth and drown it. So how can I send forces over this terrible Kafir. By Him Who sent Muhammad with the truth, I shall never send any Muslim upon it."

Naval Activities under Hadrat Othman[2]

Hadrat Othman withdrew the restriction of naval warfare. He permitted Muawiyah to invade the island of Cypress. The island was captured by the Muslims. The success of the Cypress campaign set the stage for the undertaking of naval activities by the Government of Egypt as well. Abdullah b Sa'ad built a strong navy. He proved to be a good naval commander and under him the Muslims won a number of naval victories.

The first naval clash between the Byzantine navy and the Egyptian navy took place on the Egyptian coast in 651 C.E. In this naval action, the Byzantines who were the aggressors were repulsed with a heavy loss.

1. Ibid.
2. Ibid.

The Battle of the Masts[1]

The Byzantines came again three years later in 654 C.E. The Byzantine fleet comprised as many as 500 vessels. Against this strength the Egyptian fleet had 200 vessels only. The Byzantine fleet was commanded by the Byzantine Emperor Constans in person. To start with, the archers from each side shot arrows at the other side. This led to some damage on the sides. Then the fleet of the two sides moved closer until their masts came to touch one another. Because of the proximity of the masts, the battle came to be known as *Zat us Sawari*—the battle of the Masts. As the two fleets came to touch one another a fierce hand to hand fight with swords and daggers took place on board the ships. In this type of warfare the Muslims commanded superiority. There were heavy casualties in the Byzantine camp and the Byzantines suffered defeat. Intense booty fell into the hand of the Muslims. So great was the slaughter that the sea was virtually dyed with the blood of the wounded and the dead. So great was the remorse of the Byzantine Emperor Constans at his defeat that he did not have the courage to return to Constantinople. He sought refuge in the island of Syracuse but here too the infuriated people rose against him and he was assassinated.

The battle of *Zat us Sawari* was a landmark in the history of Islam. It established the superiority of the Muslims on land as well as the sea. The Mediterranean Sea now became virtually a lake of the Muslims.

When Hadrat Othman came to know of this naval victory, he led a prayer of thanksgiving in the Prophet's mosque at Madinah. Hadrat Othman felt happy that he had the honour of being the Caliph when the Muslims first won their naval victory and became a naval power.

CONQUEST OF SPAIN

According to the general books of Islamic history the conquest of Spain is attributed to Tariq b Ziyad and Musa b Naseer in 711-712 C.E. in the time of the Umayyad Caliph Walid b Abdul Malik. According to Tabari, Spain was conquered some sixty years earlier during the caliphate of Hadrat Othman.

---

1. Ibid

Tabari's Account[1]

According to the account of Tabari, when North Africa had been duly conquered by Abdullah b Sa'ad b Abi Sarah, two of his Generals Abdullah b Nafiah b Husain and Abdullah b Nafi' b Abdul Qais were commissioned to invade Spain by sea. On this occasion Hadrat Othman is reported to have addressed a letter to the invading force. In the course of the letter, Hadrat Othman said:

> "Constantinople will be conquered from the side of Spain. Thus if you conquer Spain you will have the honour of taking the first step towards the conquest of Constantinople. You will have your reward in this behalf both in this world and the next."

Kaab al Ahbar, an eminent companion and a counseller of Hadrat Othman is reported to have said:

> "The people who conquer Spain after crossing the sea will be identified on the Doomsday on account of the special light that would radiate from them."

Campaigns in Spain[2]

No details of the campaigns in Spain during the caliphate of Hadrat Othman are given by Tabari or any other historian. The account of Tabari is merely to the effect that an Arab force aided by a Berber force landed in Spain and succeeded in conquering it. We do not know where the Muslim force landed, what resistance they met and what parts of Spain did they actually conquer. Anyhow it is clear that the Muslims did conquer some parts of Spain during the caliphate of Hadrat Othman. Presumably the Muslims established some colonies on the coastland of Spain. There are reasons to presume that these Muslims entered into trade relations with the rest of Spain and other parts of Europe.

Interesting Revelation

The aforesaid passage of Tabari makes an interesting revelation. It means that when in 711-712 C.E. regular campaigns were undertaken for the conquest of Spain by Tariq b Ziyad and Musa b Naseer the Muslims were already familiar with Spain and such familiarity helped in the process of conquest.

---

1. Tabari: *History of Islam.*
2. Ibid.

Another point which emerges from this account is that Hadrat Othman contemplated the conquest of Constantinople *via* Spain. At that time there were only two great powers in the ancient world namely the empire of Persia and the empire of the Byzantines. The empire of Persia was completely subjugated during the time of Hadrat Othman. Syria, Palestine, Egypt and North Africa were wrested from the Byzantines but the Byzantines still held Constantinople, Asia Minor and some parts of Europe. It appears that Hadrat Othman contemplated the complete subjugation of the Byzantine empire as well and his strategy was to launch a two-pronged attack against Constantinople—one from the east *via* Syria and Asia Minor and the other from the west *via* Spain. The attack from the west envisaged the subjugation of the continent of Europe. If there had been no internal dissensions within the ranks of the Muslims, Hadrat Othman was likely to have embarked on his ambitious plan of the conquest of Europe and Constantinople.

When the Muslims completely subjugated Persia during the caliphate of Hadrat Othman and when the Muslims after conquering North Africa succeeded in getting a foothold in Spain, the Byzantines must have felt alarmed at the rising tide of the Muslims. It may also be borne in mind that Hadrat Umar had forbidden the Muslims to venture across the seas but Hadrat Othman had withdrawn that restriction. During the time of Hadrat Othman the Muslims beat the Byzantines on the sea several times. During the time of Hadrat Othman the situation had thus become very critical for the Byzantines. In open warfare the Byzantines were no match for the Muslims. The Byzantines therefore encouraged schemes for the subversion of Islam from within. It appears to me that those who conspired against Hadrat Othman were really playing in the hands of the Byzantines and other foreign powers. Hadrat Othman beat the enemy on the battle-ground but he could not beat them in the matter of intrigues and underhand subversive activities.

CONQUEST OF ISLAND OF CYPRESS

Muawiyah's Proposal

When Muawiyah became the Governor of Syria, he suggested to Hadrat Umar the desirability of undertaking a naval expedition and conquering the island of Cypress in the Mediterranean. He argued that in any campaign against Constantinople, Cypress could serve as base.

Hadrat Umar's Decision[1]

On receiving the proposal of Muawiyah, Hadrat Umar asked the opinion of 'Amr b Al 'Aas, the Governor of Egypt, on the point. He was particularly asked to express his view about naval warfare on the sea.

In figurative language, 'Amr b Al 'Aas described naval action on the sea in the following terms:

> "Verily, I saw a huge creature floating on the sea, on which men seemed to be diminutive things. Huge billows as high as mountains rise. If the sea is still it rends the heart. If it swells it terrifies the senses. With it the faculties become numb and the calamities augment. Those inside it are like worms in a log. If it inclines to one side, they are drowned, if it escapes they are confounded."

On receiving this reply from 'Amr b Al 'Aas, Hadrat Umar turned down the proposal of Muawiyah. He wrote to Amir Muawiyah:

> "Let the sea remain a barrier between us and the enemy. By Allah I will not set a true believer upon it."

Amir Muawiyah did not agree with the logic of fear from the sea. He had, however, no option but to remain quiet.

Conquests of Cypress[2]

When Hadrat Othman became the Caliph, Amir Muawiyah reported his proposal to undertake a naval expedition and conquer Cypress. Muawiyah advanced detailed arguments in favour of his proposal. Hadrat Othman agreed to the proposal but laid down the condition that only such persons should participate in the naval expedition who volunteered themselves and no person should be forced to join the expedition against his will.

Muawiyah fitted a strong naval fleet under the command of Abdullah b Qais. Another fleet was sent by Abdullah b Abi Sarah from Egypt. Muawiyah raised a force of volunteers. Among other persons, the volunteers included eminent companions like Abu

---

1. *Hadrat Umar Farooq*: Prof. Masudul Hasan.
2. *Othman b Affan*: Raza Misri.

Dhar Ghifari, Ubadah b Samit, his wife Umm Haraam, Abu Darda and Shaddad b Aus.

The Muslim force landed on Cypress in 649 C.E. There was only a small Byzantine garrison on the island which was overpowered without any difficulty. The islanders submitted to the Muslims and agreed to pay a tribute of 7,000 dinars per year.

The conquest of Cypress was the first naval conquest of the Muslims. When the conquest of the island was reported to Hadrat Othman he felt satisfied with the result of the first naval expedition. That made Hadrat Othman feel that the fears of Hadrat Umar about naval warfare were unfounded and that in future the Muslims would have to conduct campaigns on the sea as well as the land. He accordingly permitted Muawiyah as well as Abdullah b Abi Sarah to build up strong navies in Syria and Egypt.

Umm Haraam[1]

Among the persons who landed on the soil of Cypress was Umm Haraam. She was a venerable Ansar lady, the wife of an Ansar chief Ubadah b Samit. In the Hadith it is related that the Holy Prophet frequently visited the house of Ubadah b Samit. It is related that one day the Holy Prophet visited the house of Ubadah and had his noon sleep there. As he woke up, there was a smile on his face. Umm Haraam enquired of the Holy Prophet the reason for his smile. The Holy Prophet said that in a dream he had seen some of his followers floating on the Mediterranean and they looked like kings. Umm Haraam enquired, "Holy Prophet, will I be one of them". The Holy Prophet said, "Yes you will be one of them but you will be martyred and would die in the distant land". True to the prophesy of the Holy Prophet Umm Haraam was one of the persons who landed on the island of Cypress. After landing on the island, she proceeded inland on a pony. She fell from the pony on the way and died. She was buried on the island. Her tomb on the island became a seat of pilgrimage for the Muslims.

Abu Darda[2]

In this campaign the Muslims captured a large number of war prisoners. As Abu Darda saw these prisoners, he wept bitterly.

---

1. *Muslim Conquest of Egypt and North Africa*: Lt. General A.I. Akram.
2. Ibid.

Someone asked Abu Darda as to why he was weeping when it was an occasion for the Muslims to rejoice Abu Darda said, "I am weeping at the fate of people who disobey Allah. When they disobey Allah they come to grief like these people. I fear for the Muslims, lest by disobeying Allah they may also invite such a grim fate for themselves."

Abdullah b Qais[1]

After the conquest of Cypress Abdullah b Qais, the commander of the Muslim naval forces, continued his cruise in the Mediterranean Sea. He is accredited with having fought fifty naval battles in all of which he was victorious. In all these battles not a single Muslim was killed or drowned. The details of these battles have not been preserved in history. Presumably most of these naval actions took place along the coast of Asia Minor. Because of these victories the exploits of Abdullah b Qais came to acquire the character of a legend. As a result of his victories he won great booties. He was known for making large bounties. Even the enemy profited from his charities.

He was a terror for the naval forces of the enemy but on account of his beneficent activities he enjoined popularity among the common men even in the enemy territory.

Once he landed with a few companions at Forma in the enemy territory. A few persons gathered around him and he gave them large bounties. Among these persons was a beggar woman. Returning home she told the authorities that Abdullah b Qais had landed on their territory and they could take him captive. A force was sent to apprehend Abdullah b Qais. They failed to take him captive. They could only take hold of his dead body.

The beggar woman was asked, "How did you know that he was Abdullah b Qais?"

She said, "He looked like a merchant but he gave bounties like a king and from what I had heard about Abdullah b Qais, I felt convinced that such a liberal person could not be any one but Abdullah b Qais, the Commander of the Seas".

1. Ibid.

CAMPAIGNS IN SYRIA, ARMENIA AND ASIA MINOR

Byzantine Attack on Syria[1]

When after the death of Hadrat Umar, Hadrat Othman came to power, the Byzantines made a bid to reconquer what they had lost to the Muslims during the caliphate of Hadrat Umar. The Byzantines made a multi-pronged attack on the Muslim dominions. One attack was made on Alexandria in Egypt, another attack was planned on Syria. The Byzantines mustered a strong force of 80,000 men and planned a wholesale invasion of Syria. Amir Muawiyah, the Governor of Syria, had an army of 10,000 soldiers with him. He accordingly requested for aid from Hadrat Othman. Hadrat Othman asked Walid b Uqba, the Governor of Kufa, to send a contingent to the aid of Syria. A contingent from Kufa was sent to Syria under the command of Salman b Rabia.

The Syrian contingent under Habib b Maslama and the contingent from Kufa under Salman b Rabia met the Byzantines in battle and defeated them. Details about the action are not available but a story has come down to us highlighting the valour of Muslim women. It is related that the Byzantine army was four times larger than the army of the Muslims. Under the circumstances Habib b Maslama, the Commander of the Muslim army, devised the plan to steal across to the camp of the Byzantine Commander and kill him before the Byzantines could know what had happened. When, in accordance with plan, Habib managed to reach the camp of the Byzantine Commander he was surprised to see that his wife dressed in male attire had forestalled him and reached the camp of the enemy. The husband and wife together killed the Byzantine Commander. That turned the tide of the battle and the Muslims won an astounding victory.

Campaigns in Armenia[2]

After defeating the Byzantines, the Muslim army penetrated into Armenia. During the time of Hadrat Umar a multi pronged attack had been made on Armenia. A column under Bukair b Abd had attacked Bab. Shahrbaz, the ruler of Bab, had surrendered and

---

1. *The Muslim Conquest of Egypt and North Africa*: Lt. General A.I. Akram.
2. Ibid.

peace was negotiated on the usual terms of paying 'Jizya'. Another column under Habib b Maslama conquered Tiflis. Another column under. Hudhaifa overpowered the Al Lan mountainous area. Another column under Abdur Rahman b Rabeah reduced Baida.

In the time of Hadrat Othman, Armenia rose in revolt like other regions. Habib b Maslama was the victor of Armenia under Hadrat Umar. After the defeat of the Byzantines, Habib b Maslama was commissioned by Hadrat Othman to suppress the revolt in Armenia. Habib penetrated into Armenia and occupied Tiflis. Thereafter he marched upto the Black Sea and the whole of Armenia was reconquered. The Muslim column under Salman subjugated the districts of Sharwan and Jabal. Details about the campaigns in Armenia are not available. It appears that there was not much of fighting and that on the approach of the Muslim armies, the Armenians laid down arms and accepted the usual terms of the payment of Jizya.

Campaigns in Asia Minor[1]

After the re-conquest of Armenia, the Muslim army undertook campaigns in Asia Minor. The Byzantines evacuated all forts between Antioch and Tarsus and these forts were occupied by the Muslims. Under Hadrat Othman, the frontier with the Byzantines came to be extended upto the Tarsus.

In the meantime the Muslims had conquered the islands of Cypress and Rhodes. With the naval bases at Rhodes and Cypress and the military bases at Tarsus, the Muslims made raids into the Byzantine territory every year. Full details about such raids are not available but it is clear that these raids had much of nuisance value and precluded the Byzantines from taking the offensive.

RE-CONQUEST OF FARS

Conquest of Fars under Hadrat Umar[2]

The province of Fars in Persia was conquered by the Muslims during the caliphate of Hadrat Umar.

A column of the Muslim army led by Mujashe b Masud advanced in the district of Ardsheer Khurra. A confrontation between the Muslim and the Persian forces took place at Tawwaj. The Persians

1. Ibid.
2. *The Muslim Conquest of Egypt and North Africa*: Lt. General A.I. Akram.

resisted the Muslim advance but they suffered defeat and they agreed to pay tribute. From Tawwaj the Muslim forces proceeded to the town of Sabur. The Persians shut themselves within the city and closed the gates. The Muslims besieged the town. The siege did not last long for the Persians laid down their arms and sued for peace. Peace was made on the payment of tribute.

Another Muslim column took the field under the command of Othman b Abul Aas. It started the campaign from where the column under Mujashe b Masud had left. The Muslim forces advanced to Jor, a city to the south of Shiraz. The Persian forces at Jor offered resistance but it was overcome by the Muslims and the city was captured. From Jor the Muslim forces struck north and occupied Shiraz without firing a shot. From Shiraz the Muslim forces struck north east and occupied Persepolis, the ancient capital of Persia.

With Persepolis as the base another Muslim column under Sariyah bin Zuneim penetrated further into the hilly tracts of the province. The Muslims captured the town of Fasa and then they advanced to Darab which also fell to them.

Another column led by Suhail b Adi marched to Kirman. A feeble resistance was offered by the Persians which was soon overcome by the Muslims. From Kirman the Muslims advanced to Jeeraft which city was taken by assault. Thereafter the Muslim forces advanced to Sirjan which city also fell to them after some show of resistance.

As a result of these campaigns the Muslims became the masters of Fars.

Re-conquests of Fars under Hadrat Othman[1]

During the caliphate of Hadrat Othman, the people of Fars revolted against the Muslim rule. No details about the revolt are available. Obviously the Persians wanted to throw off the yoke of the Muslims. Under Hadrat Othman, the process of the re-conquests of Fars had to be taken up afresh.

The accounts of the campaigns that were undertaken to reclaim Fars available in the source books are too sketchy and brief. It appears that the revolt began at Persepolis. The Muslim garrison at Persepolis under the command of Abdullah b Ma'amar was outnum-

---

1. *Othman b Affan*: Raza Misri.

bered and could not cope with the situation. In the confrontation that took place between the Muslims and the Persians the Muslims suffered defeat and were driven away from Persepolis. Hadrat Othman directed Abdullah b 'Aamir, the Governor General of Basra, to take immediate steps to retrieve the situation. Abdullah b 'Aamir marched at the head of a large force to Persepolis. The Persians closed the gates of the city. The Muslim forces besieged the city and took it by assault. The citizens surrendered and agreed to pay tribute.

From Persepolis, the Muslim forces advanced to Aljabard. Some feeble resistance was offered which was overcome and the city was captured by the Muslims. Peace was made on the usual terms of the Persians agreeing to pay tribute.

Thereafter the Muslim forces advanced to Jor. The Persians gave battle but they were defeated and the city was captured by the Muslims. Peace was made on the usual term of the payment of Jizya.

While the main Muslim forces was still at Jor, the people of Persepolis broke into revolt once again. They expelled the Muslim ruler from the city and re-established the Persian rule. Abdullah b 'Aamir rushed from Jor to Persepolis. Persepolis had strong walls and the Persians shut themselves within the city. The Muslims besieged the city and succeeded in demolishing the walls. The Persians were thus forced to come out of the city. A violent battle took place outside the city. In the hand to hand fight the Persians were no match for the Arabs. The Persian forces suffered great slaughter and they ultimately laid down arms. As the people of Persepolis had revolted repeatedly and no reliance could be placed on their promises very stringent terms were imposed this time. Immense booty fell into the hands of the Muslims. All leaders among the Persians who were guilty of instigating the revolt were hunted out and executed.

With the fall of Persepolis, other cities in Fars also submitted unconditionally. Thus the Muslims once again became the masters of Fars. Hadrat Othman appointed Shareek b Aaor Harithi as the Governor of Fars. Shareek restored law and order. He sent missionaries of Islam to various cities. Shareek's analysis of the situation was that the Persians had revolted for they still followed their old religion and that the only way to peace was that the people should be converted to Islam so that they were cut off from their old associations. As a result of the efforts of the Muslim missionaries conversions to Islam took place on a large scale. Under the orders of Hadrat Othman, mosques were built in the various cities of Fars and these became the centres for the promotion of Islam.

CAMPAIGNS IN SEESTAN

Conquest of Seestan[1]

Seestan, the eastern province of Persia and the home of the legendary hero Rustam of *Shahnama* fame was conquered by the Muslim forces sent to Seestan. The Muslim advance had been obstructed by the Persian forces at the frontier. After a violent fight the Persian forces had been repulsed. The Muslims had thereafter advanced to Zaranj, the capital of the province which fell after a prolonged siege. Thereafter the Muslims suppressed all opposition and became the masters of the entire province.

Re-conquest of Seestan[2]

Sometime around 649 C.E. a wave of unrest swept across Persia and Seestan, like other provinces, revolted against the authority of the Muslims. Hadrat Othman had, therefore, to embark on a plan of the re-conquest of Persia and Seestan. Abdullah b 'Aamir, the Governor of Basra, was charged by Hadrat Othman with the responsibility of reconquering Persia. Abdullah b 'Aamir launched a multi pronged attack and sent columns of Muslim warriors under seasoned commanders to various parts of Persia.

A column was sent to Seestan under the command of Rabe'ah b Ziyad. The first confrontation took place at Zaliq, a border town. The Muslims attacked the Persians on the day of the Persian festival Mehrgan. Taken by surprise the Persians suffered a heavy defeat. The chief of the city was taken captive and he sued for peace. Rabeah stuck a pole in the ground and wanted the Persians to lay a heap of gold and silver upto the top of the pole. The condition was fulfilled and peace was concluded.

Thereafter the Muslim forces advanced to the town of Qarquqya, five miles from Zaliq. The town was captured after some resistance.

1. *Muslim Conquest of Egypt and North Africa*: Lt. General A.I. Akram.
2. Ibid.

Thereafter the Muslim forces advanced to Zaranj. The Persians shut themselves within the walled city. The Muslims besieged the city and blockaded all passages thereto. After sometime when the citizens began to starve, their chief Abruwaiz sought an interview with the Muslim commander Rabe'ah. When the Persian chief was admitted to the Muslim camp he found Rabe'ah sitting on a Persian corpse and reclining against another. This weird scene struck terror in the heart of the Persian chief. He felt that the Muslims were aided by some supernatural power and it was futile to resist them. He offered his submission and besides agreeing to pay an annual tribute, he presented to the Muslim commander one thousand slave girls and one thousand gold cups.

After staying at Zaranj for sometime, the Muslim forces proceeded to subjugate the rest of the province. Crossing the valley of Sanurwaz the Muslim forces advanced to the city of Qarbatin. It was the region to which the legendary hero Rustam had belonged. The people were warlike and they fought against the Muslims. They were, however, defeated and had to accept the sovereignty of the Muslims. After settling the affairs of the outlying regions, Rabe'ah returned to Zaranj with 40,000 captives. Immense booty fell to the Muslims in these campaigns.

Rabe'ah stayed as Governor at Zaranj for sometime and reorganised the administration. After two years Rabe'ah left Zaranj for Basra. As soon as Rabe'ah left Seestan, the Persians rose in revolt against the Muslim rule and expelled the representative of Rabe'ah from Seestan.

Abdur Rahman b Sumra[1]

As a consequence of the Persian revolt, the process of the conquest of Seestan had to be repeated. This time after obtaining the approval of Hadrat Othman, Abdullah b 'Aamir appointed Abdur Rahman b Sumra to command the Muslim forces in the invasion of Seestan. Abdur Rahman b Sumra led the Muslim forces to Seestan and after crossing the frontier and overcoming resistance in the border towns advanced to Zaranj. The old story of siege, blockade and surrender was repeated. Abdur Rahman b Sumra made peace on the Persians undertaking to pay an annual tribute of 2 crore dirhams. The Persians also presented one lakh slaves.

1. Ibid.

From Zaranj the Muslim force advanced into the interior of the province and all towns were subjugated. Most of the towns surrendered without offering resistance. In their onward march the Muslim force advanced to the place known as the "Zor's hill", which fell after some resistance. Here was the temple of Zor which was an important place of pilgrimage. In the temple was the idol of "Zor", which had the body of gold and the eyes of precious rubies. As Abdur Rahman entered the temple and stood before the idol, the chief priest of the temple sighed and said, "Alas! we have witnessed this evil day because by our sins we had annoyed the deity." Abdur Rahman told him that whom they regarded as their deity was a helpless thing which was incapable of doing them any good or bad. Thereafter Abdur Rahman broke the idol. He let the chief priest have the gold and rubies that made the idol. Turning to the chief priest he said, "I do not crave this gold and silver. I have broken your idol merely to show you that the idol whom you worship is helpless to defend itself." The chief priest thereupon abandoned the religion of his forefathers and became a Muslim. All other persons followed suit and Abdur Rahman had a mosque constructed at the site of the temple.

Thereafter Abdur Rahman crossed the border and conquered Ghazni and Kabul. After making these conquests Abdur Rahman returned to Zaranj and stayed there as Governor till the end of the caliphate of Hadrat Othman.

RE-CONQUEST OF TABARISTAN

Conquest of Tabaristan under Hadrat Umar[1]

The province of Tabaristan in Persia lay to the south of the Caspian Sea. The province was so named because almost every citizen carried with him an axe—*Tabar*.

Tabaristan was conquered by the Muslims during the caliphate of Hadrat Umar. After the conquest of Rayy, the Muslim commander Nuaim b Muqarrin sent an expedition to Tabaristan under the command of his brother Suwaid b Muqarrin. Suwaid proceeded to the city of Qumas in the first instance. The people of Qumas did not choose to fight. On the approach of the Muslims, they opened the

1. Hadrat Umar Farooq: Prof : Masudul Hasan.

gates of their city and submitted to the Muslim rule on the usual terms. From Qumas the Muslim forces proceeded to Jurjan. It was an important town on the main highway to Merv. The Persian garrison under the command of Rozban offered feeble resistance which was soon overcome by the Muslims. The citizens surrendered and accepted submission to the Muslim rule on the usual terms.

From Jurjan the Muslim forces marched to Dehistan. When the people of Dehistan learnt that Jurjan had surrendered to the Muslims, they also found safety in submitting to the Muslim rule. Peace was made on the citizens agreeing to pay tribute.

From Dehistan the victorious Muslim forces marched to Amul. The Persian garrison at Amul was commanded by Sipehdar, a seasoned warrior. The city was strongly fortified. Sipehdar accordingly decided to defend the city. The Persians shut themselves in the city and closed the gates. The Muslims invested the city. The siege dragged on for sometime and the Persians began to suffer from lack of water and provisions. Sipehdar opened negotiations with the Muslim commander. Peace was made on the Persians agreeing to the usual terms. With the fall of Amul, the Muslims became the masters of the whole of Tabaristan.

Re-conquest of Tabaristan under Hadrat Othman[1]

During the caliphate of Hadrat Othman the people of Tabaristan like the people of the other provinces of Persia revolted against the authority of the Muslim rule. Hadrat Othman directed Sa'ad b Al 'Aas, the Governor General of Kufa, to suppress the revolt. Sa'ad b Al 'Aas led a strong force of 80,000 warriors to Tabaristan under his personal command. The forces included such eminent persons as Abdullah b Abbas, Abdullah b Umar, Abdullah b Zubair and Abdullah b Umar b Al 'Aas.

The Muslim forces advanced in the first instance to Qumas. The Persians at Qumas were not in a position to fight against such a large Muslim force. They surrendered and peace was made subject to their payment of an annual tribute. From Qumas the Muslims advanced to Jurjan. The Persian garrison offered some resistance but finding such resistance useless they surrendered. A tribute of 20 lakh dirhams was imposed on the people and peace was made.

1. *Othman b Affan*: Raza Misri.

Thereafter the Muslim forces advanced to Tamlisa. It was situated on the sea coast. It was a fortified town and contained a large Persian force. The Persian forces offered stiff resistance. So stiff and violent was the resistance of the Persians that Saeed b Al 'Aas had to offer *Salat-i-Khauf*, prayers offered on the occasion of great danger. A violent battle took place outside the city which was not conclusive. The Muslims increased their pressure and at last the Persian garrison surrendered. The peace terms agreed upon were ambiguous and one of the terms agreed upon was liable to the interpretation that immunity was to be allowed to one man only. Availing of the ambiguity of the term when the Persians surrendered and laid down arms, all male persons except one were executed. Women and children were made slaves. Immense booty fell into the hands of the Muslims. The harsh treatment meted out to the people of Tamlisa struck terror into the hearts of the people of other towns and they lost the will to resist the Muslims.

The Muslim forces thereafter overran Gilan and other parts of Tabaristan. Even the hilly tract which had not been conquered during the caliphate of Hadrat Umar was brought under Muslim rule. Having reconquered the whole of Tabaristan Saeed b Al 'Aas planned to march to Khurasan but when he came to know that Ibn 'Aamir, the Governor General of Basra, was already in Khurasan, Saeed returned to Kufa

Ka'ab b Jamil wrote some verses in the honour of Saeed b Al 'Aas. He said:

"The bravery of young Saeed was notable,

He overpowered the whole of Tabaristan,
And that was a great feat,
He even penetrated the hills,
Heretofore inaccessible to the Muslims.
He led a force of 80,000 warriors,
And his efforts were crowned with success.
As a General and Administrator,
He has surpassed his predecessors,
Verily, he is a great man."

RE-CONQUEST OF AZARBAIJAN

First Conquest of Azarbaijan[1]

Azarbaijan lay to the west of the Caspian Sea. The region was so called because of the large number of its fire temples.

During the caliphate of Hadrat Umar when the Muslims overpowered Persia, a column of the Muslim forces under Hudhaifa b Alyaman invaded Azarbaijan. The Muslim forces marched to Jurjan, where the local garrison surrendered after some resistance.

From Jurjan the Muslim forces advanced to Ardbeel, the capital of the province. The citizens did not choose to fight. They surrendered and agreed to pay the usual "Jizya".

Thereafter the Muslim forces marched northward along the western coast of the Caspian Sea. In a confrontation at Bab, a port on the Caspian Sea, the Persians were defeated and the town was captured by the Muslims.

After sometime on the transfer of Hudhaifa the people Azarbaijan revolted and they met some initial success. As a consequence, the Muslims had to abandon the advanced posts in Azarbaijan.

Thereafter Hadrat Umar sent two columns to Azarbaijan to recapture the lost territories. One column was led by Bukair b Abdullah while the other column was led by Utba b Farqad. The column under Bukair b Abdullah advanced to Jurmizan. Here a battle was fought against the Persians led by their chief Isfandiyar. The town was captured by assault and Isfandiyar was taken captive. Thereupon the Persians took to the hills and shut themselves in the hill forts. The Muslim column under Utba b Farqad clashed with the Persian forces led by Bahram, a brother of Isfandiyar. The Persians were defeated. The Muslims once again became the masters of Azarbaijan.

Utba b Farqad was appointed as the Governor of Azarbaijan. He suppressed all revolts and restored law and order.

Azarbaijan During the Caliphate of Hadrat Othman[2]

When Hadrat Othman became the Caliph, Utba b Farqad was the Governor of Azarbaijan. Hadrat Othman made no change and

---

1. *Hadrat Umar Farooq*: Prof. Masudul Hasan.
2. *Othman b Affan*: Raza Misri.

Utba b Farqad continued as the Governor of Azarbaijan. For military purposes Azarbaijan was included in the command of Kufa. When Walid b Uqba became the Governor General of Kufa he recalled Uqba b Farqad from Azarbaijan. With the withdrawal of Uqba b Farqad the people of Azarbaijan once again broke into revolt. Thus in the caliphate of Hadrat Othman the process of the conquest of Azarbaijan had to be taken up all over again.

The main military station commanding the region was Kufa where about 40,000 warriors were stationed. There were substation at Rayy and Ardbeel where 6,000 and 10,000 soldiers were stationed. Hadrat Othman directed Walid b Uqba, the Governor General of Kufa, to undertake military operations in Azarbaijan. Details of the operations are not available. In the source books the accounts are very brief and sketchy. It appears that Walid b Uqba made a two-pronged attack on Azarbaijan. One column advanced to Azarbaijan from the side of Armenia under the command of Abdullah b Shabil b Auf Ahmsi. This column conquered Mauqan, Talisan, Al Basira and a few other towns. The main Muslim army advanced to Azarbaijan under the personal command of Walid b Uqba, The rebels could not withstand the might of the Muslim forces. One by one all the towns surrendered and the Muslims once again became the masters of the whole of Azarbaijan. The Muslims amassed a good deal of booty. Peace was restored on the people of Azarbaijan undertaking to be faithful and loyal and agreeing to pay an annual tribute of eighty lakh dirhams.

RE-CONQUEST OF KHURASAN

Conquest of Khurasan During the Caliphate of Hadrat Umar[1]

Khurasan was conquered by the Muslims during the caliphate of Hadrat Umar. For undertaking campaigns against Khurasan, Hadrat Umar appointed Ahnaf b Qais to the chief command. Ahnaf b Qais led the Muslim army from Isfahan. From Isfahan two routes led to Khurasan. The main route was *via* Rayy and Nishapur. The other route which was less frequented led to Herat by passing Nishapur and then to Merv. Ahnaf b Qais followed the less fre-

1. *Hadrat Umar Farooq*: Prof. Masudul Hasan.

quented route. On the march to Khurasan the first encounter took place at Tabas. The Persian garrison offered feeble resistance which was overcome and the city was captured by the Muslims. The next encounter took place at Tun. Here too the Persian garrison surrendered after offering some show of resistance. Thereafter the Muslim army invested Herat. Here the Persian garrison offered stiff resistance. The siege lasted for a month and finding further resistance useless the Persians surrendered. From Herat the Muslim army marched to Nishapur. The people of Nishapur did not choose to fight and surrendered on the condition of paying a tribute. From Nishapur the Muslim army advanced to Tus which was captured after some show of resistance. Thereafter the Muslim army advanced to Merv. Yazdjurd, the Persian emperor, fled from Merv to Balkh. The Persian resistance at Merv was overcome and the Muslims became the masters of Merv.

Yazdjurd obtained reinforcements from Farghana and made a stand at Balkh. The Muslim army advanced to Balkh but before beginning the battle they took steps to separate the Turks and the Persians. The Turkish army took the field after there heralds had sounded the bugle. Ahnaf b Qais adopted the strategy to prevent the heralds from sounding the bugles. Ahnaf b Qais along with a reserve hid themselves at a convenient place and when the first herald came to sound the bugle, they caught hold of him and killed him, before he could sound the bugle. The second and third heralds met the same fate. The war bugles thus did not sound that day. When the Turkish commander enquired into the cause as to why the bugles had not been sounded he found that all the heralds had been killed. He considered this to be a bad omen. He asked the Turkish forces to break the camp and return to their country. The Muslim forces thereafter attacked the Persians who were defeated and Balkh was captured. Yazdjurd crossed the Oxus and sought refuge with the Turks. Ahnaf b Qais returned from Balkh to Merv. Hadrat Umar ordered that the Muslims should consolidate their conquests in Khurasan but should not cross the Oxus and undertake any campaigns in Transoxiana.

Revolt in Khurasan[1]

On the death of Hadrat Umar, like the rest of Persia, Khurasan also revolted and broke away from the authority of the Muslims.

1. Ibid.

Yazdjurd, the Persian emperor, made Merv his headquarter and once again made preparations to measure swords with the Muslims and drive them out of Persia. Before Yazdjurd could lead the Persian forces against the Muslims, Yazdjurd fell a victim to the treachery and disloyalty of his own people and he was killed in 651 C.E.

Re-conquest of Khurasan[1]

On the death of Yazdjurd, Hadrat Othman directed Abdullah bin 'Aamir, the Governor General of Basra, to undertake campaigns for the re-conquest of Khurasan. Abdullah b 'Aamir took the field in person and marched at the head of a large force to Khurasan.

The vanguard of the Muslim forces was led by Ahnaf b Qais. Crossing the Khurasan border he laid siege to two forts that served as the gates to Khurasan. The Persian garrisons there offered some resistance which was soon overcome and the forts were captured by the Muslims. After garrisoning these forts, Ibn 'Aamir spread Muslim columns in various directions and thus a multi-pronged attack was launched on Khurasan. The strategy of the Muslims was that the Persians should not be allowed to combine their forces.

A Muslim column advanced to the town of Rustaq Zam and captured it by assault. Another column captured the town of Bakharz. A third column invested the town of Juban and captured it after a short siege. Another column under Aswad b Kulsum advanced to Bayak. The Persians shut themselves in the city and closed the gates. The siege dragged on for some days with no tangible results. One night Aswad b Kulsum managed to enter the city through a drain. The Muslim army followed him. A severe hand to hand fight took place in the city. Aswad b Kulsum fell fighting. His brother Udham b Kulsum then took the standard and charged the enemy with violence. The Persians surrendered and the Muslims became the masters of Bayak. Thereafter the Muslims advanced to Tabisan which was captured after some show of resistance by the Persians.

Having conquered the region around Nishapur the Muslim force advanced to the main city of Nishapur. The city was divided into four sectors and each sector was under a Persian chief. These chiefs decided to defend the city. They shut themselves in the city and closed the gates. The Muslims invested the city. The siege dragged on for some days and the Muslims intensified the blockade. In the

---

1. *Othman b Affan*: Raza Misri.

meantime the Persian chiefs quarrelled among themselves. One of the chiefs entered into negotiations with the Muslims. He offered to open one of the gates for the Muslim army to enter provided he was granted immunity. The Muslims accepted the offer. One night one of the gates of the city was opened whereby the Muslim army entered the city. The Persians were taken by surprise and the Muslims became the masters of Nishapur. After consolidating their position at Nishapur the Muslims conquered other pockets around Nishapur. These included Pusht, Ashband, Rukh, Zar, Khawaf, Osparain and Arghian.

Thereafter the Muslim forces advanced to Abrshahr. The Persians chose to defend the city. The Persians shut themselves in the city and closed the gates. The Muslims besieged the town and the siege dragged on for more than a month. The Muslims succeeded in winning over one of the watchmen. One night he opened the gate and the Muslim army entered the city. The Persians taken by surprise surrendered and agreed to pay an annual tribute. Thereafter a Muslim column was sent to Nish which fell to the Muslims after feeble resistance. Thereafter the Muslim column advanced to Nasaa which fell to the Muslims after some fighting. Thereafter the town of Abiur was captured. The Muslim force next advanced to Sarakhs. The city was besieged. After some days the chief entered into negotiations with the Muslims for the peace. He wanted safety for one hundred persons. The offer was accepted. In the list of one Hundred persons that he submitted he forgot to include his own name. The city of Sarakhs surrendered and after granting immunity to one hundred persons the other male adult population of the city including the chief was put to death. The victor of Sarakhs was Abdullah b Khazam Salmi. The Muslims won immense booty here. Among the women taken captive was a daughter of the chief who was a great beauty. Ibn Khazam married her after she was converted to Islam and was renamed Misa.

From Sarakhs a column was sent to Kaif and Bayna. Both the towns were captured.

By this time the Muslims had reconquered a greater part of Khurasan. That weakened the will to resist in the case of the chiefs of the other parts of Khurasan. Before the Muslim forces could advance to Tus, the chief of Tus, Kanaztuk waited on Ibn 'Aamir and offered his submission on the payment of tribute. The offer was accepted. Ibn 'Aamir sent a column to overpower Herat. Before this force could reach Herat, the chief of Herat waited on Abdullah b 'Aamir and offered submission on the usual terms with regard to Herat, Badghis and Bushang. This offer was also accepted. When the Muslim column reached Herat there was no fight. The two towns of Taghun and Yaghun in Herat, however, chose to fight. They were captured after some fighting.

Thereafter the Muslim force advanced to Merv. The chief of Merv, Shah Jahan by name, waited on Ibn 'Aamir and offered his submission. Peace was made on the people of Merv agreeing to pay an annual tribute. In the peace treaty it was also stipulated that some lands would be allotted to the Muslims for their settlement in Khurasan. A town in the neighbourhood of Merv, Sang by name which was the residence of some military men refused to surrender. The Muslims advanced against the town and conquested it by force.

After the treaty of Merv the whole of Khurasan had become subject to the suzerainty of the Muslims. The remoter part of Khurasan known as Taghiristan alone remained independent. Ibn 'Aamir commissioned Ahnaf b Qais to undertake campaigns in Taghiristan. In its advance in Taghiristan the Muslim force had its first encounter with the Persian force at Najirid. The Persians were defeated and peace was made on their undertaking to pay an annual tribute. Ahnaf stayed at Najirid for sometime and then advanced to Marvul Roz. Here resistance was offered to the Muslim force but it proved to be of no avail. The chief sued for peace, which was made on his agreeing to undertake the payment of an annual tribute. Thereafter the Muslim column advanced to Bugh which was captured after some fight. At some distance from Bugh the Persians rallied again and put up stiff resistance. They were, however, defeated. Many were taken captive who were killed. The rest of them fled to Jurjan. The Muslims pursued them to Jurjan which town was occupied after some fight. Thereafter the Muslim force advanced to Balkh. There was not much of fighting at Balkh and the city surrendered and agreed to pay an annual tribute. With the fall of Balkh, the Muslims became the masters of the whole of Khurasan. The campaigns in Khurasan lasted for some three years from 651 to 654 C.E.

Campaigns in Transoxiana[1]

After consolidating the Muslim authority in Khurasan, Abdullah bin 'Aamir crossed the Oxus and invaded Transoxiana. Details of these campaigns are not known but the source books tell us that a greater part of Transoxiana submitted to the suzerainty of the Muslim rule. Abdullah b 'Aamir returned triumphant to Nishapur. Through his military campaigns lasting for some three years, he had not only reconquered Khurasan, but also conquered a greater part of Transoxiana as well, which had been heretofore beyond the access of the Muslims. Abdullah b 'Aamir had successfully fulfilled the mission entrusted to him by Hadrat Othman and on the occasion of the Hajj he started from Nishapur to Makkah clad in the *Ihram*—the pilgrim's garb.

After Abdullah b 'Aamir had left Khurasan, Qaran, the chief of the Turks, invaded Khurasan. His army was swelled by rebels from Herat, Balkh and other places in Khurasan. The Turks had a large army over forty thousand in strength. Against this the Muslims could muster a force of 4,000 warriors only. It was difficult for the Muslims to meet the enemy in the open. To save the situation the Muslims resorted to a stratagem. The Muslim forces of 4,000 decided to take the initiative and attack the enemy at night. The Muslims marched with torches tied on their lances. The soldiers advanced in such a way that it gave the impression as if a sea of fire was moving ahead. The enemy was taken by surprise and panic struck they left the field. In the confusion that followed a large number of the Turks were killed and a large number taken captive. The Muslims won a decisive victory and they amassed extensive booty.

YAZDJURD

Yazdjurd in History[2]

Yazdjurd, the last of the Sassanid emperors of Persia is one of the most tragic figures of human history. He was born under an unlucky star; misfortune dogged his steps throughout his life. He died young at the age of forty-one. For the first half of his life, he had to live in hiding as an exile. For the second half of his life, though a

1. *History*: Tabari.
2. Muslim Conquest of Persia: Lt. General A.I. Akram.

king in name, he had to run for life from pillar to post and post to pillar. His death took place under tragic circumstances. He fell a victim to the treachery and disloyalty of his own people. His people even did not allow him a burial.

Chosroes Parwez[1]

Yazdjurd's grandfather was Chosroes Parwez. He was a mighty monarch and during his reign the Sassanids were at the helm of their power. Parwez built a fabulous palace for his favourite Christian wife Shirin and around it he created an earthly paradise. The name of Shirin is associated with the well-known romance of Shirin and Farhad. Historical research has now established that the story of the love affair of Shirin and Farhad is mere fiction which has no founding in fact. Parwez had three thousand women in his harem. He had eighteen children. The eldest boy of these was Shahryar, born of his favourite wife Shirin.

Prediction of the Astrologers[2]

The court astrologers predicted that one of his sons would have a son at whose hands the Sassanian empire would come to grief and Persia would become subject to foreign rule. Parwez felt much perturbed at this prediction. He placed a sexual embargo on his sons and decreed that none of them was to marry. His sons chafed at this decree. Shahryar his eldest son was secretly married by Shirin to a beautiful girl of a noble family. Of this union a son was born who was named Yazdjurd. The birth of the prince was kept a guarded secret.

Restoration and Exile of Yazdjurd[3]

Five years passed away and by that time Parwez had forgotten all about the prediction. Availing of the opportunity, Shirin told him about the birth of a grandson. He expressed the desire to see the child. The child was brought and Parwez became fond of him. After sometime Parwez recalled the prediction and decided to kill the child. Shirin pleaded for the life of the child. Parwez ultimately agreed to spare the life of the child, provided he was exiled away from the court. Yazdjurd was accordingly exiled to Seestan.

---

1. Ibid.
2. Ibid.
3. Ibid.

Enthronement of Yazdjurd[1]

Eleven years later, Parwez was overthrown by his second son Sheeruya. Parwez was first put in the dungeon and later blinded and killed. Sheeruya had all royal princes killed except his son Ardsheer. As Yazdjurd remained in hiding, he escaped from the massacre. To avoid discovery, Yazdjurd moved from Seestan to Persepolis. Sheeruya the regicide could hold the throne for a short period of six months only. He was succeeded by his son Ardsheer who also ruled for a short time. Thereafter there was a succession of some princesses. Their rule was also shortlived. In the absence of any other prince, Yazdjurd was discovered and crowned in 632 C.E. He was a young man of twenty-one at that time.

Misfortunes of Yazdjurd[2]

At the outset of his reign misfortune stalked the footsteps of Yazdjurd. He came to power at the time when the Muslims were poised to burst across the horizon and embark on their career of conquests. In 633 C.E. the Muslims under Khalid b Walid conquered a greater part of Iraq then under Persian rule.

When Khalid b Walid was transferred to the Syrian front, the Persians were able to recapture most of their territories in Iraq. Under Hadrat Umar, the Muslims once again launched the attack against the Persians. At the battle of Qadissiyia in 636 C.E. the Persians suffered a decisive defeat. This battle marked the beginning of the end of the Sassanian empire. Yazdjurd vacated Madain, the capital of the Persians in Iraq. The Persians suffered another defeat at the battle of Jalula. Thereafter Yazdjurd fell back on Isfahan. The Persians met another reverse at the battle of Nihawand. This battle decided the fate of Persia and Yazdjurd. By 642 C.E. it was clear that the days of the Sassanian empire were numbered and it could not survive.

After the battle of Nihawand the Muslims advanced to Isfahan and Yazdjurd left for Rayy. At Rayy he realised that the Governor was disloyal to him. With a few followers, Yazdjurd left for Persepolis.

In 643 C.E. the Muslims invaded Fars. Yazdjurd left Persepolis for Kirman. When the Muslims captured Kirman, Yazdjurd fled to

1. Ibid.
2. Ibid.

Seestan. When the Muslims continued their pursuit and overpowered Seestan, Yazdjurd fled to Merv.

His overwhelming misfortunes made his people lose confidence in his leadership. The people of Merv wanted him to make peace with the Muslims and thereby save whatever little was left of the empire. To this course he did not agree. The people of Merv seized his treasure and drove him away from the city.

The Battle of Merv[1]

Yazdjurd crossed the Oxus and sought refuge with the Khaqan of Farghana. After the death of Hadrat Umar, the Persians revolted against the Muslims and a greater part of Persia was lost to the Muslims. Availing of this opportunity, Yazdjurd with the help of a Turkish force reoccupied Merv.

Conspiracy against Yazdjurd[2]

In spite of the reoccupation of Merv, Yazdjurd was not able to have a firm hold on administration. Neizak Tarkhan was the strongest and the most powerful chief in Khurasan and when Yazdjurd wanted to win him over to his side, Neizak demanded that Yazdjurd should marry one of his daughters to him. Yazdjurd considered such demand to be an affront and he gave a rude reply to Neizak. Thereupon Neizak led a force against Yazdjurd. Mahrweih, the Governor of Merv, was won over by Neizak. When the battle was at its thickest and the forces of the Shah appeared to have the upper hand, Mahrweih with a large detachment crossed over to the side of Neizak. That turned the tide of the battle. The forces loyal to Yazdjurd fought heroically but they were outnumbered and were soon overpowered.

Death of Yazdjurd[3]

When after his defeat, Yazdjurd wanted to retreat to Merv, he found the gates of the city closed against him. Abandoned by all, Yazdjurd fled to the countryside and sought shelter in a miller's hut. Yazdjurd sent the miller to the market to get some food for him. There he told some of the persons about his guest. The intelligence was carried to Mahrweih, the Governor of Merv. He sent a small force to

---

1. Ibid.
2. Ibid.
3. Ibid.

the miller's hut to cut off the head of the guest of the miller who was none other than Yazdjurd. When the force reached the miller's hut, Yazdjurd was identified and the commander of the force ordered his head to be cut off. Yazdjurd pleaded in vain for mercy. His head was cut off and taken to the Governor. The headless body was thrown in the river Murghab. The dead body was found in the river by some Christian monks. They carried it to the Christian graveyard at Merv and buried it there. That was the end of Yazdjurd and the Sassanian empire. Thus the prediction of the astrologers of the court of Chosroes Parwez was duly fulfilled.

5

AGITATION AGAINST HADRAT OTHMAN

ABDULLAH BIN SABA

The Holy Prophet and the Jews[1]

When the Holy Prophet migrated to Madinah, there was a considerable number of Jews there. They were wealthy and commanded great influence as they controlled all trade. The Holy Prophet laid down the policy of "Live and let live" with reference to the Jews. He accordingly entered into a treaty of mutual cooperation and collaboration with them. According to the terms of the treaty, the Jews were to religious freedom and there was to be no interference in religious affairs. The Muslims and the Jews were to be on friendly terms and were to help each other in the promotion of objects of common interests. It was stipulated that the Muslims and the Jews would jointly defend Madinah against any enemy. The Jews were not to give protection to the Quraish of Makkah and in the event of any attack by the Quraish, both the Muslims and the Jews were to join hands in the defence of the city.

Betrayal of Jews

The Jews knew that in their holy books, there were references to the advent of a prophet in Arabia. They were, however, under the impression that the expected prophet would rise from their midst. When the Holy Prophet rose from the ranks of the Quraish in Makkah, the Jews recognised in him all the signs of prophethood foretold in their sacred books. When the Holy Prophet came to

1. *History of Islam*: Prof. Masudul Hasan.

Madinah the Jews thought that he would be subservient to them and would have to depend upon them. When the Holy Prophet followed an independent policy based on the supremacy of Islam, the Jews followed the policy of betrayal and embarked on a campaign of ridicule and vilification. Only a few Jews accepted Islam. Even some out of them were hypocrites, whose object in accepting Islam was to disrupt Islam from within. Those Jews who did not accept Islam remained hostile to Islam at heart.

Banu Qainuqa[1]

After the battle of Badr in 624 C.E. a dispute arose between the Muslims and the Jews of Banu Qainuqa. All attempts to settle the dispute peacefully failed and the Muslims were forced to accept the challenge of the Jews. The Banu Qainuqa shut themselves in their strongholds and the Muslims laid siege to their strongholds. The siege lasted for a fortnight and then brought to bay, the Jews surrendered. The Muslims wanted to kill the Jews for their treachery but on the intercession of Abdullah bin Ubayy, the Holy Prophet agreed to spare their lives but exiled them from Madinah,

Banu Nadeer[2]

On the occasion of the battle of Uhud, the Jews of Banu Nadeer restored to treachery. They entered into secret negotiations with the Quraish and even planned to assassinate the Holy Prophet. After the battle of Uhud, these Jews were asked to explain their conduct and when they could offer no satisfactory explanation they were served with an ultimatum of war. They accepted the ultimatum and shut themselves in their strongholds. After a few days they surrendered. They were required to leave Madinah. They were allowed to take away whatever movable property they could except arms.

Banu Quraiza[3]

In the battle of the Trench, the Jews of Banu Quraiza acted treacherously. Their treachery was established and they were given the ultimatum. Instead of appeasing the Muslims they chose to adopt an attitude of defiance. They were besieged and they ultimately surrendered. An arbitrator was appointed to determine their fate. The arbitrator gave the award that in accordance with the Jewish law all

1. *Digest of the Holy Qur'ān*: Prof. Masudul Hasan.
2. Ibid.
3. *Hadrat Abu Bakr Siddiq*: Prof. Masudul Hassan.

male Jews should be killed and all children and women should be taken captive as slaves. This award was duly executed. All Jewish slaves were purchased by Hadrat Othman. Most of these slaves accepted Islam and Hadrat Othman liberated them. It is reported that Hadrat Othman used to liberate a slave every Friday.

The Khyber[1]

Even after expulsion, the Jews did not stop intriguing against the Muslims. After the Hudaibiya pact with the Quraish, the Jews of Khyber entered into conspiracy with some of the tribes to attack Madinah. The Holy Prophet anticipated the move of the Jews and marched with a force to Khyber. The Jews were overpowered.

The Apostasy Campaigns[2]

In the apostasy campaigns the Jews secretly aided the apostates and incited the tribes who had accepted Islam to apostatise. The designs of the Jews were frustrated and the apostasy campaigns ended in victory for the Muslims. Then under Hadrat Abu Bakr and Hadrat Umar the Muslims embarked on a campaign of conquests. Within a short time the Muslims were masters of Iraq, Persia, Syria and Egypt. That alarmed the Jews. The Jews were now no longer in the position to come in direct confrontation with the Muslims. They, therefore, changed their strategy and instead of a direct attack on Islam they restored to a campaign for the subversion of Islam from within.

ABDULLAH B SABA[3]

The movement of the Jews for the subversion of Islam from within was spearheaded by Abdullah b Saba. He was a Jew of Yemen. At one time the Jews had ruled over Yemen. The movement launched by Abdullah b Saba aimed at the restoration of the glory of the Jews by subverting Islam from within. Abdullah b Saba came to Madinah and was converted to Islam. He posed as a champion of Islam and pretended to live a life of piety according to the injunctions of Islam. He had considerable funds raised by the Jews at his disposal and this money he distributed among the poor. Within a short time Abdullah b Saba became popular with the Muslims.

---

1. Ibid.
2. Ibid.
3. *Othman b Affan*: Raza Misri.

Subversive Activities of Abdullah b Saba[1]

From Madinah, Abdullah b Saba went to Basra. There he stayed with Hakim b Jabala, a brigand. There he indulged in the propaganda that those who robbed the rich were not outlaws; they merely aimed at narrowing down the differences between the rich and the poor. He insinuated that as a matter of fact, the Government which depended upon the support of the rich was a tyranny. The common men came to feel that Abdullah b Saba was their well-wisher. Abdullah b Saba thus poisoned the political atmosphere at Basra. The Governor of Basra kept a watch on the activities of Abdullah b Saba. From the reports that he received it transpired that Abdullah was preaching doctrines which were very dangerous. The Government of Basra accordingly expelled Abdullah b Saba from the province of Basra.

Abdullah b Saba in Kufa[2]

From Basra, Abdullah b Saba came to Kufa. Here he pretended to lead a virtuous life and the people were attracted to him. In Kufa, most of the people favoured Hadrat Ali. Abdullah b Saba exploited this position in a subtle way. Addressing the persons who were pro-Ali, Abdullah b Saba said, "Every prophet has *Wasi.* Moses had his brother Aaron as his *Wasi.* Similarly the Prophet of Islam had Ali as his *Wasi.* In the presence of the *Wasi* no one else had the right to the caliphate". By his subtle talks he exhorted the people of Kufa to rise to a man to overthrow Othman and instal Ali as the Caliph. In his talks he dwelt on the sins of omission and commission of Hadrat Othman. He observed that Othman had imposed his near of kin as Governors in various provinces. He distorted facts and even the good things done by Hadrat Othman were presented in bad light. Posing as a great Muslim he would say, "Look here, Othman calls himself as a Caliph of the Prophet and yet he has burnt copies of the Holy Qur'ān. There could be no sacrilege greater than that." He would further say: "O people, do you know what innovations in your religion your present Caliph has introduced. On the occasion of the Hajj, the Holy Prophet, Abu Bakr and Umar offered only two rakaats of prayers but he raised the number of rakaats to four. He has deviated from the precedent set up by the Holy Prophet and has forfeited the right to be the Caliph. "He would multiply the list of such imaginary innovations and sigh at subversion of Islam by the Caliph. Arguing in a

1. Ibid.
2. Ibid.

crooked way he would say, "O Muslims, under the circumstances it is not for you to undertake Jihad across the borders of the Muslim dominions; the real Jihad lies against the Caliph who has played fast and loose with Islam". Those who listened to him fell under the impression that Abdullah was a true Muslim who was prepared to take up cudgels on behalf of Islam. When the activities of Abdullah b Saba were reported to the Governor of Kufa he asked Abdullah to leave the province.

Abdullah b Saba in Syria[1]

On expulsion from Kufa, Abdullah b Saba came to Syria. Here he came across Hadrat Abu Dhar Ghifari. Hadrat Abu Dhar Ghifari was an eminent companion of the Holy Prophet who was held in high esteem by the people. He, however, propounded ultra socialist doctrines and vehemently denounced the luxurious way of living of the rulers. That made him very popular with the poor. Abdullah b Saba exploited this position in Syria and posed himself as a devoted follower of Abu Dhar Ghifari. Meeting Abu Dhar Ghifari, Abdullah b Saba said, "Look Sir, the Governor calls the 'Baitul Mal' the property of Allah. That is a device to avoid its distribution among the people." The argument appealed to Abu Dhar Ghifari and when he saw Muawiyah he was critical of the amassing of funds in the treasury; he wanted the immediate distribution of available funds among the people. When Muawiyah pointed out the unpractical aspect of the proposal, hot words were exchanged between Muawiyah and Hadrat Abu Dhar Ghifari. When it came to the notice of Muawiyah that Abdullah b Saba was at the back of these ultra socialist thoughts, he ordered Abdullah to leave Syria.

Abdullah b Saba in Egypt[2]

From Syria Abdullah b Saba came to Egypt. Here he found the atmosphere more congenial. Muhammad b Abu Bakr and Muhammad b Hudhaifa were already carrying on hostile propaganda against Hadrat Othman. Abdullah b Saba took advantage of this position and posing as a pious Muslim he projected doctrines aimed at the subversion of Islam. Posing as a staunch Muslim he said, "I wonder at the wisdom of the Muslims. They believe that Jesus is alive, while they hold that Muhammad is dead. If Muhammad is the last of the prophets, how can he die? He must be alive till the Doomsday. And

1. Ibid.
2. Ibid.

again if Muhammad is the last of the prophets, why should Jesus come back again to usher in an era of peace and justice?" The common men who listened to him came to regard him as a staunch Muslim and felt that there was considerable weight in what he said. By such activities the Jews were able to wage a war against Islam on the intellectual plane. Abdullah b Saba sent secret emissaries to major towns in the Muslim empire and through cunning device and subtle talks these emissaries misled the people and made them feel that they had been wronged.

HADRAT ABU DHAR GHIFARI[1]

Hadrat Abu Dhar Ghifari was an eminent companion of the Holy Prophet and was among the early converts to Islam. His original name was Jandab b Janadah and he belonged to the Ghifari tribe who had their settlements between Makkah and Syria. The Ghifari tribe was converted to Islam through the efforts of Hadrat Abu Dhar Ghifari. When the Holy Prophet migrated to Madinah, Hadrat Abu Dhar also came to Madinah and there devoted himself exclusively to prayers and religious meditation. He adopted a more or less ascetic way of life, shunned luxury and stood for austerity. He is described as the first socialist in Islam. After the death of the Holy Prophet he went to Syria and undertook Jihad. He was outspoken and he freely criticised the administration where he felt that there was anything wrong. The Holy Prophet said of him that nothing could deter him from speaking whatever he considered to be the truth.

Hadrat Abu Dhar and Amir Muawiyah[2]

During the times of Hadrat Abu Bakr and Hadrat Umar, Hadrat Abu Dhar Ghifari did not have much to criticise. When Hadrat Othman came to office, the people progressively took to a luxurious way of life and this became a matter of great criticism with Hadrat Abu Dhar Ghifari. He vehemently denounced the palaces, the expensive costumes, the rich dishes and the luxurious indulgences of Amir Muawiyah and his court. He thundered, "The gold and silver that you hoard would be heated red one day in the fire of hell and struck against your forehead." He cursed those who hoarded wealth. He wanted the rich people to distribute all their surplus

1. *Khulafa-i-Rashdin and Sahaba Karam*: Muhammad b Saad.
2. Ibid.

wealth among the poor. He held that one should have only as much money which was just enough for one day's bread. On the same analogy he advocated that nothing should be kept in the Baitul Mal and all that was there should be distributed among the people. The doctrine preached by him that no one should possess more money than what was sufficient for a day's expense appealed to the common man. Large groups assembled round him and listened to his preachings.

Amir Muawiyah saw Hadrat Abu Dhar Ghifari and brought home to him the point that the doctrine preached by him was unpractical and dangerous. He argued that the Baitul Mal belonged to Allah and money had to be kept for use in the way of Allah from time to time. Abu Dhar stuck to his own way of thinking and vehemently urged that the Baitul Mal was not the property of Allah, it was the property of the Muslims and should be distributed among them.

One day Amir Muawiyah sent a purse containing one thousand dinars. Hadrat Abu Dhar distributed the amount among the poor immediately. When Amir Muawiyah came to know that Hadrat Abu Dhar Ghifari had kept nothing for himself and had distributed the entire amount among the poor, he felt much concerned, for Hadrat Abu Dhar Ghifari actually practised what he preached and as such his preachings would be a source of danger to the State. Amir Muawiyah brought the matter to the notice of Hadrat Othman and Hadrat Othman directed Amir Muawiyah to send Hadrat Abu Dhar Ghifari to Madinah. Amir Muawiyah accordingly sent Hadrat Abu Dhar Ghifari to Madinah.

Hadrat Abu Dhar Ghifari in Madinah

Hadrat Abu Dhar Ghifari had come to Madinah after some ten years. During this period a great change had taken place in the environments. Palatial buildings had sprung up and the city had expanded upto the hill of "Sala'a". Hadrat Abu Dhar Ghifari stayed in the Prophet's mosque and addressing the people he said, "O the people of Madinah, you have departed from the ways of the Holy Prophet. You are after amassing wealth; you have raised palatial buildings and have become the victims of luxury. I give you the tidings of troubled times that lie ahead, for the Holy Prophet said that when the city expanded to the Sala'a hill there would be trouble for the people."

Hadrat Othman saw Abu Dhar Ghifari and pointed to him the fallacy in his view point. He pointed out that Islam condemned asceticism and monasticism. Islam stood for both this world and the world hereafter, Islam stood for a proper synthesis between this world and the next world. As such it was not advisable that what was in the Baitul Mal should be distributed immediately among the people. Money had to be necessarily kept for meeting the needs of the administration and the requirements of the State. The State was under an obligation that the real needs of the people were met. Hadrat Othman pointed out that he had raised the stipends of the people and these were enough to meet their needs. Some persons were critical that he had been lavish in raising the amount of the stipends. Hadrat Othman made out the point that in the circumstances to preach the doctrine that nothing should be kept in the State treasury and should be distributed immediately was not only unpractical, it was dangerous as well.

Ka'ab Ahbar, an eminent companion who was also present on the occasion, joined in the discussion. He observed that it was inadvisable to condemn the rich for hoarding. The obligation on them was to pay Zakat and after they had paid Zakat they could use their money in any way they liked and they could not be condemned for hoarding money or violating any injunctions of Islam. Hadrat Abu Dhar Ghifari did not agree with this view. Hot words were exchanged between Hadrat Abu Dhar Ghifari and Hadrat Ka'ab Ahbar. In a fit of fury Hadrat Abu Dhar Ghifari struck Hadrat Ka'ab Ahbar with his staff. Hadrat Othman took strong notice of this conduct on the part of Hadrat Abu Dhar Ghifari and said, "O Abu Dhar may Allah have mercy on you, hold your tongue and your hand".

Hadrat Abu Dhar Ghifari thereupon wanted permission to live outside Madinah. Hadrat Othman permitted him to live wherever he liked. Hadrat Abu Dhar Ghifari chose Rabza as the place of his residence. Hadrat Othman sanctioned a stipend for Hadrat Abu Dhar Ghifari. He granted him some camels and placed the services of a slave at his disposal. Hadrat Abu Dhar settled at Rabza with his wife and daughter. He built a mosque at Rabza and spent the remaining years of his life in prayers and religious meditation. Abu Dhar died in 652 C.E. A curious story is narrated about his death. On the day he was to die he asked his daughter to see whether any men were visible on the horizon coming that way. She saw some persons in the distance and informed her father accordingly. Thereupon he lay on the bed with his face to the Ka'aba. He told his daughter that he was now going to die and that when the men she had seen reached there, they should be given his salutation and asked to arrange for his burial. She was further asked to prepare meals for the guests and they should be fed after they had buried him.

Thereafter Hadrat Abu Dhar Ghifari died. It was a peaceful passing on from one life to another. When the people she had seen arrived at the hut, the daughter of Hadrat Abu Dhar Ghifari gave them the salutation of his father. That was a caravan of fourteen persons led by Abdullah bin Masud. On enquiring where was Hadrat Abu Dhar Ghifari, she said that he was in the hut and had died. Abdullah b Masud and his men arranged for the burial of Hadrat Abu Dhar Ghifari. Abdullah b Masud recalled that the Holy Prophet had said about Hadrat Abu Dhar: "He would live alone and die in solitude." When Hadrat Othman came to know of the death of Hadrat Abu Dhar Ghifari, he shifted the wife and daughter of Hadrat Abu Dhar Ghifari to Madinah, provided them with accommodation and sanctioned a special stipend for them. Later he also arranged for the marriage of the daughter of Hadrat Abu Dhar Ghifari. Hadrat Othman always spoke high about Hadrat Abu Dhar Ghifari. He used to say: "May Allah have mercy on Abu Dhar Ghifari. He was a great soul, who was more a citizen of the next world than that of this world."

Exile of Hadrat Abu Dhar Ghifari [1]

In the accounts that have come down to us, there is a good deal of confusion in the matter of the relationship between Hadrat Othman and Hadrat Abu Dhar Ghifari. In the books which have a critical stance with reference to Hadrat Othman it is made out that Hadrat Othman was too harsh with Hadrat Abu Dhar Ghiffari and that he had exiled him. In the books generally favourable to Hadrat Othman it is stated that Hadrat Othman did not exile Hadrat Abu Dhar Ghifari and that Hadrat Abu Dhar Ghifari had on his own accord chosen to reside at Rabza. If all the evidence is examined dispassionately the conclusion that emerges is that there is no truth in the story about the exile of Hadrat Abu Dhar Ghifari by Hadrat Othman. Rabza was only three miles from Madinah and if Hadrat Othman had exiled him he would have exiled him to some remoter place in the

1. *Othman*: Taha Hussain.

interior of the country. Again there is evidence to the effect that Hadrat Abu Dhar Ghifari came to Madinah from Rabza on some occasions. If he had been exiled he could not have gone to Madinah. There is also evidence to the effect that Hadrat Othman had gifted some camels to Hadrat Abu Dhar and also placed a slave at his disposal. He had also sanctioned a stipend in favour of Hadrat Abu Dhar Ghifari. If Hadrat Abu Dhar Ghifari had been the victim of the hostility of Hadrat Othman, he would not have been allowed such privileges. The truth of the matter is that Hadrat Abu Dhar Ghifari being of an ascetic bent of mind preferred the solitude of the desert to the busy life of Madinah which had developed into a metropolis. Both Hadrat Othman and Hadrat Abu Dhar Ghifari were great Muslims and although they had different outlooks on life, there was no ill-will between the two.

ABDULLAH BIN MASUD

Early Life[1]

Abdullah b Masud was an eminent companion of the Holy Prophet. He was among the early converts to Islam. He migrated to Abyssinia and was supported there by Hadrat Othman. On return from Abyssinia he migrated to Madinah. He entered into brotherhood with Muadh b Jabal of the Ansars. He participated in all the campaigns undertaken by the Holy Prophet. On the occasion of the battle of Badr, he had the distinction of cutting off the head of Abu Jahl, the arch enemy of Islam. In Madinah he became an attendant of the Holy Prophet. Whenever the Holy Prophet came to the mosque Abdullah b Masud held his shoes. On Fridays Abdullah b Masud while leading the Holy Prophet to the pulpit carried his sceptre in front of him.

After the Death of the Holy Prophet[2]

After the death of the Holy Prophet, Abdullah b Masud migrated to Syria and there participated in the various border campaigns against the Byzantines. During his caliphate, Hadrat Umar appointed him as the Qadi and the treasurer of the Baitul Mal at Kufa. Abdullah b Masud was an authority on the Holy Qur'ān and at Kufa

1. *Ashab-e-Rasul Ke Karname*: Nabi Ahmad Suha.
2. Ibid.

he established a school where he lectured on the Qur'ãn. He was scrupulously honest and enjoyed great fame as an eminent Muslim and a religious scholar.

Abdullah b Masud and Hadrat Othman[1]

After the death of Hadrat Umar when Hadrat Othman became the Caliph, Abdullah b Masud addressed the citizens of Kufa in the mosque and exhorted them to take the oath of allegiance to Hadrat Othman as he was the best choice for the caliphate. In the second year of his caliphate, Hadrat Othman appointed Sa'ad b Abi Waqas as the Governor of Kufa. Soon a quarrel arose between Sa'ad and Abdullah. Sa'ad took some loan from the Baitul Mal and failed to return it within the stipulated period. Abdullah b Masud insisted on the repayment of the loan. The dispute grew and culminated in the deposition of Sa'ad b Abi Waqas. After Sa'ad, Walid b Uqba was appointed as the Governor of Kufa. At one time Abdullah b Masud used to shepherd the goats of Uqba b Abi Muheet, the father of Walid. To start with the relationship between Walid and Abdullah b Masud was very cordial but later differences grew between the two.

When Abdullah b Masud came to know of Hadrat Othman's reform about the recension of the Holy Qur'ãn, Abdullah b Masud was critical of the exercise. He regarded himself as an authority on the Holy Qur'ãn and he felt aggrieved that in the standard text his viewpoint had not been accommodated. He began to criticise Hadrat Othman. According to the accounts that have come down to us Abdullah b Masud levelled the accusation that some of the verses against the Bani Umayyads had been suppressed.

Walid b Uqba also took some loan from the Baitul Mal. He failed to return the loan within the stipulated period and that became the subject-matter of dispute between Walid and Abdullah. Walid complained to Hadrat Othman and Hadrat Othman is reported to have taken objection to his conduct against the Governor. Thereupon Abdullah b Masud resigned his office and confined himself to his house where he freely criticised Hadrat Othman and his administration. Walid reported the matter to Hadrat Othman and Hadrat Othman directed Walid to send Abdullah b Masud to Madinah.

---

1. *Othman b Affan*: Raza Misri.

Abdullah b Masud in Madinah[1]

It is alleged that when Abdullah b Masud came to Madinah, he saw Hadrat Othman in the mosque. Some hot words were exchanged between the two and Hadrat Othman had Abdullah b Masud expelled from the mosque. Hadrat Othman is further said to have stopped the stipend of Abdullah b Masud. It is further stated that Abdullah b Masud wanted to go to Syria for undertaking Jihad but Hadrat Othrnan did not grant him the permission. Abdullah b Masud died in Madinah in 654 C.E. two years before the assassination of Hadrat Othman. According to one account when Abdullah b Masud fell sick, Hadrat Othman visited him and the two were reconciled. According to another account Abdullah b Masud died without being reconciled to Hadrat Othman.

Analysis of the Accounts[2]

If all the accounts that have come down to us about the relationship between Hadrat Othman and Abdullah b Masud are analysed, it will be seen that all these accounts are highly coloured and remote from reality. There can be no two opinions on the point that Hadrat Othman's exercise about the recension of the Holy Qur'ãn was in the best interests of Islam. Hadrat Othman had set up a board of eminent companions and the standard text was compiled after due deliberations and considerations of all the view points. There are reasons to hold that Abdullah b Masud submitted his view point before the board and this was duly considered. If for any reason any of the points urged by Abdullah b Masud had not been accepted, Abdullah b Masud could not be justified in making this a ground for agitation. Again Hadrat Othman took no decision in the matter at personal level. He merely accepted the recommendations of the board. As such there was no justification for making this a cause of personal grievance against Hadrat Othman. The allegation that Hadrat Othman had some verses which were unfavourable to the Umayyads suppressed is preposterous. A man of the calibre of Hadrat Othman could never dream of tampering with the word of Allah.

It appears that, in the matter of the administration of Baitul Mal, Abdullah b Masud was too fastidious. In the matter of administration a more rational view had to be taken and if Hadrat Othman did not

---

1. Ibid.
2. This view is based on my own analysis.

approve of his over-sensitiveness in some cases, Hadrat Othman as Caliph had every right to do so and no blame can rest on him.

It appears that the later writers because of partisan considerations indulged in the exercise of condemning Hadrat Othman for picking up quarrels with all eminent companions. It is inconceivable that Hadrat Othman could have expelled Abdullah b Masud from the mosque. The allegation is false firstly because such conduct could not be expected of a man like Hadrat Othman and secondly because no Muslim could be expelled from the house of Allah.

The truth of the matter is that Abdullah b Masud himself resigned from the office of the treasurer of the Baitul Mal. Hadrat Othman called him to Madinah and looked after his needs. Soon after his arrival in Madinah Abdullah b Masud fell sick and died. Hadrat Othman attended him during his sickness and there was no ill-will between the two. Hadrat Othman led the funeral prayer of Abdullah b Masud and the story that there was any dispute between the two on account of the recension of the Holy Qur'ān is fictitious and false.

ABDUR RAHMAN BIN AUF

Early Life[1]

Abdur Rahman bin Auf was born around 580 C.E. and was younger than the Holy Prophet by ten years. He was one of the early converts to Islam. He was related to Hadrat Othman and was married to a step sister of Hadrat Othman. In the battle of Uhud he received twenty-one wounds while defending the Holy Prophet. On this occasion he also lost some of his teeth. He was a trader and a shrewd businessman. It is related that when he came to Madinah his Ansar brother Sa'ad proposed to give half of his property to him. Sa'ad had two wives and he proposed to divorce one of them so that Abdur Rahman could marry her. Abdur Rahman thanked his brother and said that he did not need his property or any of his wives. He merely wanted him to show him the way to the market and he would make his own fortune. Soon Abdur Rahman was able to build a great fortune. He amassed considerable wealth and came to be regarded as one of the richest men in Madinah.

---

1. *Ashab-e-Rasul Ke Karname*: Nabi Ahmad Suha.

Abdur Rahman and Hadrat Othman[1]

Abdur Rahman b Auf was one of the six persons who had been nominated by Hadrat Umar to choose the Caliph from among themselves. Abdur Rahman withdrew his candidature and played the part of a truthful arbitrator in resolving the dispute. Abdur Rahman gave his verdict in favour of Hadrat Othman and Hadrat Othman was accordingly elected as the Caliph.

Some of the accounts that have come down to us tend to give the impression that in the later part of the caliphate of Hadrat Othman some differences developed between Hadrat Othman and Abdur Rahman b Auf and Abdur Rahman even regretted his choice of Hadrat Othman as the Caliph. It is related that some camels were assigned to the Baitul Mal as Zakat and Hadrat Othman distributed these camels among his relatives. It is alleged that when Abdur Rahman came to know of such distribution, he made the persons to whom these camels had been given to return them to the Baitul Mal.

Assessment[2]

When the account about the camels which has come down to us is examined objectively it appears to be fictitious. It appears that the story was invented by interested quarters to create the impression that even the person who played the dominant role in securing the caliphate for Hadrat Othman came to regret his choice because of the wayward conduct of Hadrat Othman. Even if the allegation about the distribution of camels was correct it is inconceivable that Abdur Rahman should have taken the law in his hand and asked for the return of the camel over and above the head of Hadrat Othman. If there were any truth in the story, Abdur Rahman should have lodged the complaint with Hadrat Othman and Hadrat Othman should have directed the return of the camels. It is again inconceivable that the recipients of the gifts would have returned the gift merely at the behest of Abdur Rahman.

Abdur Rahman died in 652 C.E., four years before the assassination of Hadrat Othman. The agitation against Hadrat Othman grew in 654 C.E. only and as such there was nothing to complain during the lifetime of Abdur Rahman b Auf. We can thus safely hold that there is no truth in the allegation that differences developed

---

1. *Othman b Affan*: Raza Misri.
2. This is based on my own assessment.

between Hadrat Othman and Abdur Rahman b Auf and the latter regretted his choice of Hadrat Othman at any stage.

TALHA B UBAIDULLAH

Early Life[1]

Talha b Ubaidullah belonged to the Taym section of the Quraish. He was closely related to Hadrat Abu Bakr. He became a Muslim at the young age of fifteen and was among the early Muslim converts. He migrated to Madinah in 622 C.E., along with the family of Hadrat Abu Bakr.

He played an important part in the battle of Uhud. He received numerous wounds in his effort to save the Holy Prophet. He pulled the Holy Prophet from the ditch in which he had fallen. He was also very active in the battle of the Trench. He was one of the persons to whom Holy Prophet had given the tidings of paradise. He was one of the six members of the board which had been constituted by Hadrat Umar to choose his successor.

Hadrat Othman and Talha[2]

At the time of the death of Hadrat Umar, Talha was out of Madinah. When he returned to Madinah, the oath of allegiance had been taken to Hadrat Othman. Talha felt annoyed that the new Caliph had been elected in his absence. He showed some hesitation in offering allegiance to Hadrat Othman but Hadrat Othman placated him and he offered allegiance to Hadrat Othman. It is reported that Talha owed some money to Hadrat Othman and Hadrat Othman gifted the money to him. According to some of the accounts that have come down to us, it appears that on another occasion Hadrat Othman made a liberal gift to Talha out of the Baitul Mal. Full details of such gift are not available. Talha was a rich trader and there could be no occasion for making a gift to him from the Baitul Mal. Most probably the story of a gift to Talha out of Baitul Mal is a fiction which has no foundation in fact. Talha may have obtained some loan from the Baitul Mal for business purposes and would have returned it.

---

1. *Ashab-e-Rasul Ke Karname*: Nabi Ahmad Suha.
2. *Othman b Affan*: Raza Misri.

Siege of Hadrat Othman and Talha[1]

It appears that later some differences rose between Hadrat Othman and Talha and Talha supported the rioters. It is reported that one day during the course of the siege, Hadrat Othman called out to the rioters and said, "Is Talha among you." Talha was present among the rioters but he did not respond to the call. When Hadrat Othman repeated the call for the third time, Talha responded to the call. Thereupon Hadrat Othman said, "I did not expect that you would be among the rioters and would not respond to my call." Hadrat Othman then asked Talha to recall that once when they were alone with the Holy Prophet, the Holy Prophet had said, "Othman will be my companion in the paradise." Talha corroborated that what Hadrat Othman had said was correct. Thereupon he left the company of the rioters and went home.

Battle of Camel[2]

When after the assassination of Hadrat Othman, Hadrat Ali became the Caliph. Talha and Zubair took the allegiance to Hadrat Ali but soon they repudiated such allegiance and supported the demand for vengeance for the blood of Othman. Talha, Zubair and Hadrat Ayesha occupied Basra and the battle of the Camel was fought between the supporters of Hadrat Ali and the supporters of Talha, Zubair and Hadrat Ayesha outside Basra. In this battle, Hadrat Ali won and the cause of Talha and Zubair was lost. Talha escaped from the battle-field but fell a victim to an arrow shot by Marwan b Hakam. It is reported on the authority of Alqama b Waqas that in Basra, Talha said that he was guilty of a lapse in the matter of his conduct towards Hadrat Othman and he wanted to atone for such lapse by supporting the demand for the vengeance for the blood of Hadrat Othman.

Taha Hussain's View[3]

From the accounts that have come down to us, the conduct of Taha appears to be inexplicable. Hadrat Othman made some gifts to Talha and Talha supported Hadrat Othman. Later Talha joined the rioters and opposed Hadrat Othman. Taha Hussain has expressed the view that as long as Hadrat Othman met the demands of Talha,

---

1. Ibid.
2. *History of the Saracens*: Ameer Ali.
3. *Othman*: Taha Hussain.

Talha supported him but when Hadrat Othman did not or could not meet the demands of Talha, Talha joined the opposition. Talha was an eminent companion of the Holy Prophet, whom the Holy Prophet had given the tidings of paradise. He was one of the six persons whom Hadrat Umar regarded as his probable successors. We cannot therefore conceive that such an eminent person could be unscrupulous enough to change sides on account of personal motives. It is also inconceivable that such eminent persons like Talha and Zubair should first offer allegiance to Hadrat Ali and then repudiate it and resort to war. It appears that all the details relevant to the matter at issue are not available with us and in the absence of such details it is difficult for us to pass any judgement about the conduct of Talha.

UMMAIR AND KAMMIL

Dhabi b Harith

When Walid b Uqba was the Governor of Kufa one Dhabi b Harith borrowed a hunting dog named "Qarhan" from an Ansar family. There was something extraordinary about the dog; it was an expert in the hunting of the deer. Dhabi wanted to purchase the dog but the owner of the dog refused to part with the dog for any consideration. On one pretext or the other Dhabi b Harith did not return the dog to the owner. That led to a dispute. Thereupon the Ansars took away the dog by force. Dhabi wrote some pungent verses satirising the Ansars. The Ansars complained to Hadrat Othman. Hadrat Othman gave the verdict that satirising the Ansars, whose services to Islam Allah Himself had appreciated, was a great sacrilege. Under the orders of Hadrat Othman, Dhabi b Harith was arrested and lodged in the jail at Kufa. Dhabi died in the jail. Thereupon his son Ummair b Dhabi vowed vengeance. He gathered a group of persons around him who had to complain of some wrong on the part of Government. One of such persons was Kammil b Ziyad who also smarted under some grievance against the Government. When Ibn Saba launched his subversive movement, Ummair and Kammil joined the movement and carried on propaganda against Hadrat Othman and his Government. They preached the cult that as long as Hadrat Othman was the Caliph, the people could not expect any justice

Conspiracy to Murder Hadrat Othman

When the country came to be rocked by agitation against Hadrat Othman, Ummair and Kammil entered into a conspiracy to murder Hadrat Othman. They accordingly decided to go to Madinah with a view to assassinating Hadrat Othman. Ummair fell sick on the way and he returned to Kufa. Kammil, however, decided to proceed to Madinah. In Madinah, Kammil lay in ambush at a strategic point between the house of Hadrat Othman and the Prophet's mosque. One day as Hadrat Othman was proceeding to the mosque, he caught sight of Kammil lying in ambush under suspicious circumstances and before Kammil could dare attack Hadrat Othman, Hadrat Othman attacked him with a lance in self defence and wounded him. Kammil cried "Amirul Mominin! you have wounded me for no cause." Hadrat Othman asked him to declare on oath whether he was not lying there in ambush to murder him. Kammil took the oath that he had no intention of murdering the Caliph. Men around Hadrat Othman wanted that a further probe should be made into the antecedents of Kammil so that his guilt could be determined. Hadrat Othman said that as Kammil had taken the oath in the name of Allah that he had no evil design, the matter rested with Allah and Kammil and he would not make any further probe into the matter. He told Kammil that he could have his *Qasaas* from him for wounding him. Kammil said that in the circumstances, he freely forgave the Caliph and withdrew his claim for *Qasaas*. Thereafter Kammil returned to Kufa.

Siege of the House of Hadrat Othman[1]

In spite of the magnanimity of Hadrat Othman, Kammil on return to Kufa continued his activities against Hadrat Othman. When in 656 C.E., a contingent from Kufa left for Madinah, both Ummair and Kammil were included therein. When Hadrat Othman was assassinated Ummair and Kammil insisted that the dead body of Hadrat Othman should be mutilated. Years later when Hajjaj became the Governor of Kufa, he tried Ummair and Kammil for the murder of Hadrat Othman and had them executed.

---

1. Othman b Affan: Raza Misri.

'AMMAR BIN YASIR

'Ammar b Yasir and Hadrat Othman[1]

'Ammar b Yasir is one of the companions of the Holy Prophet who is regarded as a critic of Hadrat Othman. Whatever accounts have come down to us are too biased and prejudiced to be reliable. 'Ammar's father Yasir belonged to Yemen. He migrated to Makkah and became attached to the Bani Makhzum section of the Quraish. 'Ammar's mother Samia served as a maid. 'Ammar accepted Islam at an early age. At his instance his father and mother also accepted Islam. As the family was poor and had few social contacts in Makkah they were persecuted by the Quraish for their acceptance of Islam. 'Ammar was made to lie on burning sand and was required to recant from Islam on pain of death. 'Ammar, however, remained firm in his faith. It is reported that the Holy Prophet accompanied by Hadrat Othman often visited 'Ammar when he was being persecuted by the Quraish and advised him to be patient. 'Ammar migrated to Abyssinia and there are grounds to believe that in Abyssinia, Hadrat Othman materially helped 'Ammar. Later like other Muslims, 'Ammar migrated to Madinah. In the building of the Prophet's mosque at Madinah, 'Ammar carried double the number of bricks as compared with other Muslims. This was much appreciated by the Holy Prophet. 'Ammar took part in all the battles fought during the time of the Holy Prophet.

After the Holy Prophet[2]

After the death of the Holy Prophet, 'Ammar took part in the apostasy campaigns during the time of Hadrat Abu Bakr. In the battle of Yamama against the false prophet Musailma when the Muslims began to waver under the pressure of the enemy, 'Ammar mounted a hillock and summoned the Muslims to him. That proved to be a turning point in battle and the battle ended in victory for the Muslims. When Hadrat Umar became the Caliph, he appointed 'Ammar b Yasir as the Governor of Kufa. He could not hold the office for long and Hadrat Umar soon deposed him. It is related that when Hadrat Umar met 'Ammar after his deposition he asked him about his reaction to such deposition he said that he was neither happy when he was appointed as the Governor nor was he happy when he was deposed.

---

1. *Othman*: Taha Hussain.
2. Ibid.

'Ammar b Yasir During the Caliphate of Hadrat Othman[1]

'Ammar b Yasir belonged to the camp of Hadrat Ali and when Hadrat Othman was chosen as the Caliph, 'Ammar offered him his allegiance like other Muslims but he was not happy with the caliphate of Hadrat Othman. In course of time 'Ammar's opposition to Hadrat Othman increased. According to an account which is recorded in Taha Hussain's book on Hadrat Othman, Hadrat Othman appropriated some of the jewellery in the Baitul Mal. 'Ammar criticised Hadrat Othman for such conduct. It is reported that addressing the congregation Hadrat Othman said, "As the Caliph, I have the right to appropriate anything from the Baitul Mal. I will continue to do so, let anybody who object may." It is alleged that thereupon 'Ammar stood up and criticised Othman for such conduct. Hadrat Othman is reported to have lost temper and said, "You son of a maid servant, how dare you criticise me like that." It is alleged that at the instance of Hadrat Othman, 'Ammar was given a good beating and carried home from the mosque in an unconscious state. It is further alleged that in view of the growing discontent against Hadrat Othman some companions in Makkah addressed a letter to Hadrat Othman criticising his conduct and requiring him to make amends. It is stated that this letter was brought to Hadrat Othman by 'Ammar and that on reading this letter Hadrat Othman lost temper and kicked 'Ammar.

There is also the story that Hadrat Othman sent some persons as his representatives to the various provinces to enquire into the various allegations levelled against the administration. It is said that 'Ammar was sent to Egypt. While the representatives sent to other provinces submitted their reports to Hadrat Othman, 'Ammar did not submit any report and chose to join the rebels in Egypt. It is further alleged that 'Ammar returned to Madinah later and played an active part in poisoning the atmosphere against Hadrat Othman.

All the above accounts which have come down to us and are recorded in Taha Hussain's book *Othman* appear to be self-contradictory and therefore devoid of truth. It is unbelievable that a responsible person like Hadrat Othman could publicly say that right or wrong he would appropriate the Baitual Mal to his private use. It is also inconceivable that a man of such mild disposition as Hadrat

1. Ibid.

Othman should have publicly kicked an eminent companion, who had been Governor of a province.

Again if all this account of quarrels between Hadrat Othman and 'Ammar is correct, it is inconceivable that Hadrat Othman should have deputed 'Ammar b Yasir to Egypt to report about the affairs of the province when 'Ammar was against him. It appears that all stories of Hadrat Othman's differences with 'Ammar b Yasir have no foundation in fact. Differences between Hadrat Othman and 'Ammar b Yasir cropped up only when Hadrat Othman deputed 'Ammar b Yasir to Egypt and there he came under the influence of Muhammad b Hudhaifa and Muhammad bin Abu Bakr. All the facts that have come down to us about the differences between Hadrat Othman and 'Ammar b Yasir are so confusing and self-contradictory that much reliance cannot be placed on them.

CAMPAIGN OF VILIFICATION AGAINST HADRAT OTHMAN

International Situation[1]

During the caliphate of Hadrat Umar, the Muslim dominions had expanded considerably both in the east and the west. Hadrat Umar was a strong man but Hadrat Othman who succeeded him was known for his kindheartedness. The foreign powers felt that with Hadrat Othman as the Caliph, it would be possible for them to wrest the territories from the Muslims which they had conquered during the caliphate of Hadrat Umar. In pursuance of this programme to overthrow the Muslim rule, Persia rose in revolt in the east and the Byzantines attacked Egypt in the west to drive away the Muslims.

Developments, however, took place contrary to the expectations of the foreign powers. The Sassanian emperor Yazdjurd made another bid to recover Persia. Revolts broke out in all the provinces of Persia, national feelings against the Muslims rose high among the Persians, and Yazdjurd made strenuous efforts to rally the Persians in another bid to drive away the Muslims from the Persian soil. In spite of being a kind hearted and soft spoken man, Hadrat Othman proved to be a great General. He organised military campaigns with great skill. Within a few years the whole of Persia was reconquered,

1. *History of Islam*: Prof. Masudul Hasan.

Yazdjurd was killed and the Sassanian dynasty was extinguished. The Muslims under Hadrat Othman crossed the Oxus for the first time. The frontiers of the Muslim empire came to touch the frontiers of China in the north and India in the east.

In the west, in the momentum of the first attack, the Byzantines were able to conquer Alexandria. In the counter attack, the Muslims drove the Byzantines from Alexandria and the Byzantine plan to reconquer Egypt came to nought. Then the Muslims took the offensive. They conquered the whole of North Africa. Then they crossed the sea and obtained a foot-hold in Spain. Heretofore the Byzantines were the masters of the Mediterranean Sea. Under Hadrat Othman the Muslims grew into a naval power. The Muslims conquered the island of Cypress. They beat the Byzantines at the naval battle known as the "Battle of the Masts." The Muslims made several raids on the Byzantine coasts. The Byzantine capital itself was now threatened by a two-pronged attack, one from the east *via* Syria and Asia Minor and the other from the west *via* Spain and Europe.

The foreign powers became nervous at the success of the Muslim arms under the leadership of Hadrat Othman and now their only hope lay in aiding and patronising subversive movements within the territories of Islam.

Ibn Saba's Subversive Movement[1]

Ibn Saba's movement began as a religious movement. It aimed at the subversion of Islam by creating doubts among the Muslims with regard to certain matters of their belief. Ibn Saba's movement was patronised by the Jews and had its links with foreign countries. With the triumph of the Muslim arms, under the incitement of the Byzantines, Ibn Saba's movement became a political movement as well. The agents of Ibn Saba in various towns launched a campaign of vilification against Hadrat Othman and his government. The movement tried to sow discord among the Muslims on one pretext or the other. The non-Arabs were incited to object to the supremacy of the Arabs. Among the Arabs the differences between the northerners and the southerners were exploited. Differences were also exploited between the Quraish and the other Arabs. Differences between the Bedouins and the city dwellers were exploited. Among

1. *Othman b Affan*: Raza Misri.

the Quraish the differences between the Hashimites and the Umayyads were exploited. The people were fed on fictitious stories about the tyrannies of the Government of Hadrat Othman. Even whatever good had been done by Hadrat Othman was presented in false colour. As a result of such subtle propaganda the peace of the country came to be disturbed. No specific charges against Hadrat Othman or his government were forthcoming. Only vague and hearsay allegations floated from ear to ear. Because of the virulence of the propaganda the Muslim society became a victim of discontentment. In Madinah, the companions and other leaders of public opinion were flooded with anonymous letters containing vague allegations against Hadrat Othman and his government.

Allies for the Ibn Saba's Movement[1]

Ibn Saba won some allies from among the Muslims who had some grievances against Hadrat Othman right or wrong. 'Amr b Al 'Aas had been deposed by Hadrat Othman from the governorship of Egypt. He had a personal grievance against Hadrat Othman and in some way or the other he played into the hands of the Ibn Sabaites.

Muhammad b Abi Hudhaifa was a young man whose father had been martyred in one of the campaigns under Hadrat Abu Bakr. After the death of his father Muhammad came to live with Hadrat Othman who treated him as a son. Muhammad grew into a wayward young man. When Hadrat Othman became the Caliph, Muhamrmad aspired to be made the Governor of some province. When Muhammad requested Hadrat Othman to be made the Governor of some province, Hadrat Othman said that if he had considered him fit to be made the Governor he would have done that and that as he was still very young he should wait for some time till he acquired some maturity. That annoyed Muhammad and he wanted that he should be allowed to go elsewhere. Hadrat Othman permitted him to go wherever he liked. Muhammad proceeded to Egypt.

Muhammad b Abu Bakr was the son of Hadrat Abu Bakr. His mother was Asma, whom Hadrat Abu Bakr married after the death of her husband Jaffar b Abu Talib. After the death of Hadrat Abu Bakr, Asma married Hadrat Ali. Muhammad b Abu Bakr thus grew up under the guardianship of Hadrat Ali. When Hadrat Othman became the Caliph, Hadrat Ali felt unhappy at being passed over.

---

1. Ibid.

Muhammad b Abu Bakr therefore came to adopt at an early age an attitude which was critical of Hadrat Othman. Later Muhammad b Abu Bakr was a party to a case. Hadrat Othman gave his verdict against Muhammad b Abu Bakr. That annoyed Muhammad b Abu Bakr. He left Madinah for Egypt.

In Egypt Muhammad b Abi Hudhaifa and Muhammad b Abu Bakr came under the influence of Ibn Saba and came to indulge in propaganda against Abdullah b Sa'ad, the Governor of Egypt, as well as Hadrat Othman. They ingratiated themselves with the army and tried to seduce the soldiers from the cause of Hadrat Othman. When the Muslims won the naval battle known as the "Battle of the Masts" and felt proud of the victory, the two Muhammads tried to belittle this achievement by declaring that such victories were of no avail when the caliphate itself was indulging in anti-Islamic practices.

When Abdullah b Sa'ad came to know of this propaganda he reported the matter to Hadrat Othman and wanted his permission to take action against Muhammad b Abi Hudhaifa and Muhammad b Abu Bakr. Hadrat Othman withheld the permission saying that Muhammad b Abi Hudhaifa was his son and that because of his regard for Hadrat Abu Bakr he could not contemplate any action against his son.

In Egypt 'Amr b Al 'Aas had a party and as 'Amr b Al 'Aas was unhappy at his deposition, his party joined those who were critical of Abdullah b Sa'ad and Hadrat Othman. Thus Egypt became a hotbed of sedition against the administration of Hadrat Othman.

The movement of Ibn Saba won allies in Madinah and elsewhere. Ibn Sabaites declared that they were working for the caliphate of Hadrat Ali. That won for them the sympathies of the followers of Hadrat Ali. Hadrat Ali himself did not espouse their cause but the Ibn Sabaites had every reason to believe that as they were working for the cause of Hadrat Ali, his sympathies could not be denied to them. Most of the companions in Madinah chose to be neutral. Such companions as Abu Dhar Ghifari were critical of the luxurious style of living of those in power. The Ibn Sabaites exploited this position and tried to give out that they were with Abu Dhar Ghifari. They gave currency to some false reports about the harassment of Hadrat Abu Dhar Ghifari at the hands of Hadrat Othman and his government.

In Kufa, the people had demanded the deposition of Saeed b

'Aas and the appointment of Abu Musa Ash'ari. In the interests of peace Hadrat Othman yielded to the demand. In a letter addressed to the people of Kufa, Hadrat Othman hoped that as he had acceded to their demand there would be no more trouble from their side. On assuming office as Governor Abu Musa Ash'ari warned the people to desist from their subversive activities. He said that he would not lead them in prayer until they had assured him of their loyalty to Hadrat Othman. The people assured him of their loyalty to Hadrat Othman and gave a solemn undertaking that they would maintain peace and would not indulge in any agitation.

'AAMIR BIN ABDULLAH TAMIMI

'Aamir b Abdullah in Basra[1]

'Aamir b Abdullah Tamimi was an eminent Muslim. He settled at Basra. He was intensely religious and would pray the whole night. Being too much absorbed in religious devotions, he was cut off from the world around him. He became critical of the irreligious ways of life of the people around him and the people felt unhappy at his biting criticism. The Governor of Basra complained against him to Hadrat Othman and Hadrat Othman directed that 'Aamir b Abdullah be sent to Syria.

'Aamir b Abdullah in Syria[2]

In Syria, Abdullah Tamimi was lodged in the main mosque at Damascus and Muawiyah, the Governor of Syria, kept a watch over him. One of the complaints against 'Aamir was that he did not eat meat. One day Muawiyah invited 'Aamir to dinner at which meat was served. 'Aamir duly partook of the dish of meat. That convinced Muawiyah that this allegation against 'Aamir was false.

Another allegation against 'Aamir was that he did not offer Friday prayers. Muawiyah posted some persons to spy on the activities of 'Aamir with regard to Friday prayers. It was reported by these agents that 'Aamir did attend Friday prayers but he came last of all, took his seat in the last row and would then leave the mosque before others. Thus it was established that the allegation against him, that he did not offer the Friday prayers, was not established.

---

1. *Othman b Affan*: Raza Misri.
2. Ibid.

Muawiyah enquired of 'Aamir as to why he did not marry. 'Aamir said that he had no objection to marriage but he felt that as he spent most of his time in prayers, no woman would be happy with him. He said that if he came across any woman who would agree to pray with him, he would be glad to marry her. Muawiyah felt convinced that in the circumstances, 'Aamir could not be held guilty of his opposition to marriage.

Muawiyah reported to Hadrat Othman that the complaints against 'Aamir were not established. Hadrat Othman ordered that in the circumstances 'Aamir was free to return to Basra or go anywhere else at his discretion. 'Aamir refused to go back to Basra, the people whereof had complained against him. He remained in Syria and participated in the Jihad against Byzantine.

'Aamir in Kufa[1]

The people of Kufa invited 'Aamir to visit them. 'Aamir visited Kufa in response to the invitation. The people of Kufa welcomed him and humoured him in his eccentricities. They found that being intensely religious, 'Aamir was critical of the luxurious style of the government of Hadrat Othman. They also found that 'Aamir was bitter against Hadrat Othman for having exiled him from Basra for no cause. The people of Kufa exploited this position and fed 'Aamir on imaginary tales about the lapses of Hadrat Othman and his government. That aroused the indignation of 'Aamir and he declared that such a man had no right to be the Caliph. Someone suggested that the best Jihad for a man of the calibre of 'Aamir was to tell Hadrat Othman in the face that he was not fit to be the Caliph and should accordingly abdicate. 'Aamir said that he was not afraid of any one except Allah and that he had the courage to tell Hadrat Othman in the face that he was not fit to be the Caliph. The people of Kufa declared their faith in 'Aamir and chose him their emissary to go to Madinah and speak to Hadrat Othman. 'Aamir agreed to undertake the mission.

'Aamir in Madinah[2]

In Madinah, 'Aamir saw Hadrat Othman and told him bluntly that he was not fit to be the Caliph and should abdicate. Hadrat Othman said that as the Caliph his responsibility was to Allah and not to any

1. Ibid.
2. Ibid.

person. As Allah had clothed him with the office of the caliphate, he could not withdraw from the office at the behest of any person. He added that he had held the office for over ten years and during this period he had served the Muslims to the best of his ability. Extensive conquests had been made during his time. The State had become financially prosperous under him. He had increased the stipends of the people, the Baitul Mal was full and he had discharged the duties of his office honestly and conscientiously. Under the circumstances unless any specific charges were established against him, he could not resign. Any such move would amount to his running away from his post. 'Aamir insisted that charges or no charges, he had forfeited the right to rule and should abdicate on his own freewill or he would be deposed by force. That was pure sedition on the part of 'Aamir. Some hot words were exchanged between Hadrat Othman and 'Aamir, which created some bitterness. Hadrat Othman banned the return of 'Aamir to Kufa, he was sent to Syria and Muawiyah was asked to keep a watch on him.

FACING THE CHALLENGE OF THE SEDITIONISTS

The Political Atmosphere in Madinah

'Aamir b Abdullah Tamimi in pressing the demand for the abdication of Hadrat Othman had advanced no arguments. Hadrat Othman had turned down the demand for cogent reasons. Nevertheless these altercations poisoned the political atmosphere in Madinah. Barring a few persons who espoused the cause of Hadrat Othman strongly, the other companions were either critical or preferred to remain indifferent.

Hadrat Othman discussed the matter with Hadrat Ali. Hadrat Ali talked in cautious and diplomatic terms. He neither came forward to support Hadrat Othman through thick and thin, nor did he support the rebels. He was, however, critical of the leniency of Hadrat Othman. He said that because of such leniency on the part of Hadrat Othman, the Governors in the provinces had become headstrong and they were following policies which were not approved by the people. Hadrat Ali was also critical that under Hadrat Othman high office under the State had been monopolised by the Umayyads to the great dissatisfaction of the other sections of the people. Hadrat Othman gave his defence but this did not make Hadrat Ali change his views. On the other hand Hadrat Othman stuck to the view that he had done no wrong and he had become a victim of false propaganda.

The differences between Hadrat Othman and Hadrat Ali pointed to the fact that something had gone wrong with the Muslim polity and that the Muslims were no longer a united community. Such disruption in the ranks of the Muslims forbade some catastrophe. That set Hadrat Othman thinking and in order to overcome the crisis Hadrat Othman decided to summon a council of his Governors.

Council of Governors[1]

The Council of Governors met at Madinah. Hadrat Othman apprised them of his concern at the virulent propaganda that was being carried against the administration and wanted their suggestions for overcoming the crisis. Abdullah b 'Aamir, the Governor of Basra, suggested that the persons responsible for making the propaganda should be sent to the borders for undertaking Jihad. Muawiyah suggested that the Governors should be authorised to suppress the sedition movements within their provinces. Abdullah b Saad proposed that the miscreants should be won over by the grant of favours. 'Amr b Al 'Aas struck a different note. He had a personal grievance against Hadrat Othman because he had been deposed from the governorship of Egypt. He observed that there could be no improvement in the situation unless Hadrat Othman changed his policies and instead of favouring his relatives appointed the right men to the right job. Hadrat Othman directed the Governors that they should adopt all the expedients they had suggested according to local circumstances. He exhorted the Governors to be just and fair and redress the legitimate grievances of the people. They should, however, take stern measures against the seditionists. Hadrat Othman appealed to the people in general to remain united and maintain the integrity and unity of the Ummah. He said that the enemies of Islam were out to subvert Islam by creating dissensions in their ranks and they should be beware of the enemy. Those who wanted to create differences between the people and the administration could be no friends of the Muslims. Hadrat Othman took note of the criticism of 'Amr b Al 'Aas. He said that it was for the Caliph as Head of the State to appoint such persons to State offices in whom he had confidence

---

1. *Othman b Affan*: Raza Misri.

and if any person was deposed in public interest, he should not make such deposition a cause of personal grievance. He pointed out that in an Islamic state, high offices were mere burdens and one should neither covet them, nor feel aggrieved when deprived of any of such office. He added that he had never coveted the caliphate but once he had been made the Caliph there was no option with him but to discharge the onerous duties of the office according to the best of his ability. He assured all concerned that it would be his endeavour to redress the legitimate grievances of the people. He pointed out that at the same time it was the duty of the people not to indulge in false propaganda or lend ear to what was mere hearsay.

Investigation into the State of Affairs in the Provinces[1]

In spite of the good intentions on the part of Hadrat Othman and his Governors there was no diminution in the vilification campaign. The seditionists worked underground. They did not bring forward any specific grievance which the administration could redress, they merely tried to poison the atmosphere by spreading false rumours. The Holy Prophet had an official ring which was used for the authentification of official documents. After the Holy Prophet this seal was held by Hadrat Abu Bakr and then by Hadrat Umar. When Hadrat Othman became the Caliph he inherited the ring. In order to augment water supply for the citizens of Madinah, Hadrat Othman has a well dug, Arees by name. One day as Hadrat Othman was supervising the digging operations the official ring fell from his finger and was dropped in the well. Every effort was made to salvage the ring from the well but all such efforts proved abortive. This loss of the ring was made the subject-matter of propaganda against Hadrat Othman. It was made out that the Holy Prophet had withdrawn his favour from Hadrat Othman and a person who no longer enjoyed the favour of the Holy Prophet had no right to be the Caliph. Currency was given to many other fictitious stories of the so-called waywardness of Hadrat Othman and his government. Nobody could tell from where such stories emanated but nevertheless they became the common talk of the people and in the absence of any refutation, the people generally came to believe in the veracity of such rumours. The position became embarrassing and some of the companions suggested to Hadrat Othman that reliable agents should be deputed

1. Ibid.

to various provinces to investigate the matter and report about the truth of such rumours.

Investigation into Rumours[1]

Hadrat Othman sent his agents to some of the main provinces to look into the various reports about the rumours. Muhammad b Masalma was sent to Kufa, Usama b Zaid was sent to Basra, 'Ammar b Yasir was sent to Egypt, while Abdullah b Umar was sent to Syria. These emissaries made thorough investigations on the spot; they addressed the congregations in the mosque and they interviewed the leaders of public opinion. On return to Madinah the emissaries reported that all was well in Kufa, Basra and Syria. The people were satisfied with the administration and they had no legitimate grievance against the administration. Some individuals here and there had some personal grievances of minor character with whicn the people at large were not concerned. 'Ammar b Yasir, the emissary to Egypt, however, did not return to Madinah. In Egypt Ibn Saba, Muhammad b Abi Hudhaifa and Muhammad b Abu Bakr were very active in their campaign of vilification against Hadrat Othman. 'Ammar b Yasir was influenced by their subtle propaganda. Instead of returning to Madinah he chose to stay in Egypt and join the seditionists. The emissaries who had been deputed to Kufa, Basra and Syria submitted their reports to Hadrat Othman. The people were apprised of these reports and they felt satisfied that there was no substance in the rumours that were being spread. The people of Madinah felt concerned about the situation in Egypt. Abdullah b Sa'ad, the Governor of Egypt, reported about the activities of the seditionists in Egypt. He wanted to take action against Muhammad b Abu Bakr, Muhammad b Abi Hudhaifa and 'Ammar b Yasir. Hadrat Othman did not want Abdullah b Sa'ad to be harsh against these persons for whom he had great regard.

Hadrat Othman's Open Letter to His People[2]

In view of the reassuring reports, from Kufa, Basra and Syria, Hadrat Othman addressed an open letter to his subjects. He observed that he had deputed special emissaries to investigate into the rumours against the administration. These emissaries had made investigations on the spot and their report was that on the whole the

1. Ibid.
2. Ibid.

people were satisfied with the administration and they had no particular grievance. Hadrat Othman added that his mission in Egypt had not been successful and his emissary had chosen to stay in Egypt and not to return to Madinah. He was watching further development in Egypt. He observed that he had never coveted the office of the Caliph but when he had been made the Caliph he had to discharge the onerous duties of the office. He observed that as the Caliph he had taken pains to administer the State affairs in the best interests of the people according to the injunctions of Islam. He observed that while it was his duty to be just and fair, it devolved on the people to cooperate with him and not to be led astray by false propaganda. He wanted the people who had any grievance against the administration to assemble at Makkah on the occasion of Hajj. He assured them that all their legitimate grievances would be redressed. He directed the Governors and the "Amils" of various cities to come to Makkah on the occasion of Hajj.

Hadrat Othman's Address on the Occasion of the Hajj[1]

In response to the call of Hadrat Othman, the followers of Ibn Saba sent large delegations from various cities. They were thoroughly briefed and were armed with a catalogue of imaginary wrongs which they were required to present before the gathering.

Hadrat Othman presided at the Hajj functions and thereafter he addressed the people. After praising Allah and the Holy Prophet, Hadrat Othman said that he had summoned that meeting at the house of Allah to redress the grievances of the people, to foster accord between the people and the government and to remove misunderstandings if any. He said that of late some false rumours had been circulating against him and his government in a surreptitious manner. He said that Islam did not favour such underhand means. Islam stood for calling a spade a spade. He said that the object of the meeting was to promote a dialogue between the people and the rulers and take steps to redress the grievances of the people if any. He assured the people that he would espouse their just cause and as such they should come forward with their grievances so that these could be redressed. He said that in view of this assurance on his part the underhand propaganda against the government should cease for that was likely to undermine the integrity of the State.

1. Ibid.

He wanted the people to be his witness that before assuming the caliphate he was one of the richest man. As such the caliphate could not be an office of profit with him. He wanted the people to say whether what he had said was correct or not. Thereupon the congregation said, "Yes O Caliph of the Holy Prophet, you are correct".

Hadrat Othman continued: "You know after the Holy Prophet Hadrat Abu Bakr became the Caliph and after him Hadrat Umar became the Caliph. During this period the Muslim dominions expanded and the Muslim State was burdened with onerous responsibilities. Hadrat Abu Bakr and Hadrat Umar administered the affairs of the State with admirable skill. Thereafter the burden fell on me. I swear by Allah that I did not covet the office but once I have been made the Caliph, I have to discharge my functions. You know Hadrat Umar was a hard task master. After him you wanted some relaxation. In contrast I followed mild polices. At the outset of my rule I increased the stipends of the people. I treated the people as my children and my treatment was liberal and generous". Then Hadrat Othman paused and enquired of the people whether what he said was correct. They answered, "Yes, we testify to your kindness."

Hadrat Othman added, "You know after the demise of Hadrat Umar there were revolts in Persia and the Persians made a bid to overthrow the Muslim yoke. At one time we practically lost the whole of Persia. In this crisis your government was not found wanting. We directed campaigns in Persia. The whole of Persia was reconquered. Not only that but we extended the Muslim conquests. In the east we reached the borders of India. In the north we penetrated into Transoxiana and reached the borders of China. You know the Byzantines tried to reconquer Egypt and captured Alexandria. We drove them from the soil of Egypt. Thereafter we undertook campaigns in North Africa and captured the whole of North Africa. Thereafter we crossed over to Spain and established a foothold there. You know the Muslims had heretofore avoided wars on the sea. During my time the Muslims became a naval power for the first time. We conquered the island of Cypress. We defeated the Byzantines at the battle of the Masts. We conducted campaigns in Asia Minor and captured many Byzantine forts." Hadrat Othman paused and addressing the people said, "O ye people, swear by Allah whether what I have said is correct or not?" The people cired with one voice, "We testify that what you have said is correct".

Hadrat Othman further said, "Now O people look around you and say honestly whether you are not more prosperous than what were you yesterday. Look to Madinah itself. Has it not expanded and is such expansion not an indication of the prosperity of the people. Are the people of Makkah not more prosperous than what they were in the past. Is there any man in the State who is starved. Previously the companions were not allowed to leave Madinah. Have I not removed this restriction. Have I not allowed free purchase and sale of land. Have I not promoted your freedom of speech and movement? Look to your Baitul Mal. Does it not have more reserve than what it had previously? Look to the Prophet's mosque at Madinah. Have I not extended it. Again look to the Ka'aba. Have I not extended or embellished it? Please let me know whether this is correct or not". And the people said that verily this was correct.

Hadrat Othman continued: "If all that I have said is correct is it not uncharitable on the part of some of the people to indulge in unfounded propaganda. If you make the head of your State the victim of false propaganda you weaken the solidarity of the Ummah. Our strength lies in our unity and if any attempt is made to sow dissensions among the Muslims we will be playing in the hands of the enemy. I therefore appeal to you to be just and fair. If you seek justice you must be just yourself. I assure you that if you have any legitimate grievance it will be redressed. On the other hand if you have no real grievance but merely resort to frivolous allegations that will be neither in your interest nor in the interests of the State."

Hadrat Othman said, "Now I will dwell on the various allegations that are afloat against me or my government. I am criticised that on the occasion of the Hajj I offered four rakaats of prayers instead of availing of the concession of two rakaats in accordance with the precedent set by the Holy Prophet and my two predecessors. In this connection it may be borne in mind that the stipulated number of rakaats in such prayers is four but in the case of exceptional circumstances the prayer can be shortened to two rakaats. Now such exceptional circumstances cannot last for all times. I have married in Makkah and I reside here for some time in a year. I, therefore, felt that I was no longer entitled to the concession of shortening the prayer. If four rakaats were enjoined and I had shortened them I could have been held guilty but when I offer the full prayers and do not avail of a concession meant for exceptional circumstances, what is the wrong that I have done. Again it is said that I have been guilty of sacrilege in burning some copies of the Holy Qur'ãn. Do you know what happened to the Holy Books revealed to other prophets. Their followers produced variety of versions and in such diversity the original text was lost. I was anxious that the Holy Qur'ãn should not become a victim of such diversity. I, therefore, in consultation with the eminent companions had a standard text compiled and destroyed all other texts, so that the integrity of the text should be maintained for all times. O Muslims I ask you in the name of Allah whether this was a service or a disservice to the cause of Islam?" Hadrat Othman paused for a reply from the people and they said, "Yes, O-Caliph you have done a great service to the cause of Islam".

Hadrat Othman continued: "It is objected that I have appointed young persons to high offices and that most of the governors are my relatives. In appointing young persons I followed the precedent set by the Holy Prophet. He appointed Usama, a young man of seventeen, to lead the expedition against the Byzantines. It is true that some of the Governors are related to me. As Caliph I am responsible for the administration of the entire country. I have, therefore, to appoint persons in whom I have full confidence. Whether a person is related to me or not is not the material thing. The material thing is: how far have such persons discharged their functions. Is it not a fact that as Governor Muawiyah is most popular in Syria? Is it not a fact that Abdullah b Sa'ad conquered the whole of North Africa? Is it not a fact that he was the victor of the battle of the Masts? Is it not a fact that Uqba's son Walid was most popular in Kufa during the first five years of his rule and I removed him when voices were raised against his rule? Is it not a fact as the Governor of Basra Abdullah b 'Aamir reconquered the whole of Persia and even carried the Muslim arms to Transoxiana? O Muslims be just and fair. How can you deny the achievements of these Governors in the cause of Islam and merely condemn them because they are related to me? I assure you that I appointed them because I thought them to be the fittest persons. All of them came to my expectations and I maintain that I did not commit any wrong in appointing them as Governors. On the other hand Muhammad b Hudhaifa who was like a son to me wanted to be appointed to a post but I refused to do so, because I did not consider him fit to bear such responsibilities." Then Hadrat Othman paused and said, "Have I not narrated the true facts" and the people said, Yes, you have stated the facts as they are".

Hadrat Othman continued, "It is said that I have reserved the pastures for my camels. This is incorrect. I have reserved the State pastures for State camels and that was necessary. It is objected that I recalled my uncle Hakam from exile. The fact is that the Holy Prophet exiled him and then permitted his recall. It is objected that on the eve of the conquest of Makkah, Abdullah b Sa'ad was on the murder list but I intervened on his behalf. It is true that Abdullah b Sa'ad was guilty but he repented. Forgiveness is an attribute of Allah. On the occasion of the conquest of Makkah the Holy Prophet granted the Quraish general amnesty and in this context he forgave Abdullah b Sa'ad. Thereafter Abdullah b Sa'ad proved to be a staunch Muslim and he performed valuable services in the cause of Islam. Uqba's son Walid was certainly guilty of a lapse but the Holy Prophet forgave him. It is a tradition of the Holy Prophet that once a man is forgiven we have to judge him solely on the basis of his conduct after such forgiveness. These persons have nothing to their discredit after they had been forgiven. It is uncharitable on the part of Muslims to condemn these persons for their conduct for which they have been forgiven. If previous misconduct is to remain alive what is the purpose of forgiveness?"

Hadrat Othman said, "I have had my say. Now I am prepared to listen to you. If any one of you have any legitimate grievance against me or my government you are free to give expression to such grievance and I assure you that I will do my best to redress such grievance."

The seditionists had come fully prepared to give vent to their imaginary grievances but they realised that the people in view of the defence offered by Hadrat Othman were not in the mood to listen to any imaginary grievances. All the seditionists remained quiet and they did not have the courage to declare any grievance.

That was a great pyschological victory for Hadrat Othman.

Muawiyah's Advice[1]

On return to Madinah, Muawiyah saw Hadrat Othman. He said that although on the occasion of the Hajj the seditionists had not been able to declare any grievance, that did not mean the end of their

1. *Othman b Affan*: Raza Misri.

opposition. He feared that they would resort to other means to harm Hadrat Othman.

Muawiyah suggested that Hadrat Othman should accompany him to Syria. He said that the people of Syria were devoted to the Caliphate and the Caliph would have an atmosphere of peace there. Hadrat Othman said that as the Caliph of the Holy Prophet, he could not leave the city of the Holy Prophet.

Muawiyah observed that in the alternative he should be allowed to send some Syrian force to keep a guard on the Caliph. Hadrat Othman said that the presence of the Syrian force in Madinah would be an incitement to a civil war and he could not be a party to such a move.

Exasperated Muawiyah said, "My next suggestion is that in case you are murdered I should be authorised to demand *Qasaas* for your murder." Hadrat Othman said that he agreed to the suggestion and in case he was murdered, Muawiyah was free to demand vengeance for assassination.

6

MARTYRDOM OF HADRAT OTHMAN

UNREST IN MADINAH

The Situation in Madinah[1]

After the pilgrimage of 655 C.E. things remained quiet for sometime. With the dawn of the year 656 C.E. Madinah itself became a hotbed of intrigue and unrest. Muhammad b Abu Bakr and 'Ammar b Yasir returned from Egypt to Madinah. They were joined by 'Amr b Al 'Aas. They let loose a flood of propaganda and vilified the administration of Egypt. It was given out that the administration of Egypt was guilty of tyranny and oppression. 'Amr b Al 'Aas took pains to project the view that under Abdullah b Sa'ad, the Governor of Egypt, the taxes were most oppressive and while the she-camel had been forced to give more milk its young ones had been starved. Muhammad b Abu Bakr had personal grievances against Hadrat Othman and he condemned Hadrat Othman's government for its inefficiency. 'Ammar b Yasir had at the outset supported the candidature of Hadrat Ali for the caliphate and he was a bitter critic of the administration of Hadrat Othman. It cannot be said why Hadrat Othman chose to send him to Egypt to enquire into the affairs of the province when it was known that he was prejudiced against the caliphate of Hadrat Othman. Perhaps Hadrat Othman considered that a report by a person who did not belong to his camp was likely to be more assuring. 'Ammar b Yasir, however, did not submit any report. Instead in Egypt he joined with the malcontents and carried on propaganda against Hadrat Othman. When 'Ammar returned to

1. *Othman b Affan*: Raza Misri.

Madinah he did no see Hadrat Othman. Instead he became active in creating unrest in Madinah.

Marwan, a cousin of Hadrat Othman, acted as his Secretary. Another cousin of Hadrat Othman acted as the Superintendent of the markets in Madinah. Hadrat Othman paid them for their services from the Baitul Mal. This was made the subject of criticism. Hadrat Othman gave some gifts from the Baitul Mal to Zubair b Awwam and Talha b 'Ubaidah. It is not known what exactly was the occasion for the grant of such gifts but presumably such gifts were made because of their services. Criticism against Hadrat Othman took over a virulent form. People began to talk freely as to who would be the next Caliph. Many doggerels were composed supporting the candidature of Hadrat Ali, Zubair and Talha as the next Caliph.

Hadrat Ali's Dialogue with Hadrat Othman[1]

When the crisis deepened, Hadrat Ali saw Hadrat Othman and talked to him in diplomatic terms. He said:

> "I have been sent by the people to you. Many things are being said against you but I do not know how I should tell you what they say. I cannot think of any matter about which I can advise you, nor do I know of anything more than what you know. You are aware of all this. How should I give you any information, for I am not better informed than you, nor anything has been said in secret, about which I know but you do not. We are all nothing in front of you. You have seen the Holy Prophet, heard him and lived in close companionship with him. Neither Abu Bakr, nor Umar were superior to you in any way. In relationship to the Holy Prophet you were closer to him than all of us. The position attained by you was gained by none else. Under your caliphate the community has come to be faced with some problems. O Caliph, invoke Allah's help in solving these problems. I need offer you no advice. Take heed and remember that the nearest to Allah is a Caliph who is just and upholds the covenant of Allah as revealed to the Holy Prophet and discards all that was discarded by him. The worst man on earth is the Imam who is cruel and one who has gone astray himself and makes others go astray, who revives the discarded vices and discards virtues. All these things are clear to you. Right and wrong are far apart.

1. Ibid.

I have myself heard the Holy Prophet say that on the Day of Judgement, a tyrant Imam will be friendless and sent down to hell. He would revolve around it like a grinder and then be plunged into the bottomless pit. I want to remind you of Allah's powers and His revenge. His punishment is severe and powerful. Be careful that you do not become the murdered Imam for the flock for it is said that one of the Imams would be killed who would open door to dissensions within the community. Things would come to such a pass that the Muslims would be divided into various sections. Falsehood would gain such ascendancy that people would forget what is right."

Hadrat Othman's Reaction to the Address of Hadrat Ali [1]

Hadrat Othman listened patiently to the talk of Hadrat Ali and then said:

"Ali, I am grateful to you for having come and talked to me. I have always looked to you as my best support. You are a keen judge of men and matters and you are known for your perception of the truth. I had expected that in this crisis you would discern the truth and take measures to stop the false propaganda that is poisoning the atmosphere. Instead you have talked in the same vein as the malcontents. You have insinuated that as an Imam I had been cruel and tyrannical and that the punishment therefor is hell. This is uncharitable on your part. You have been apparently led away by the false propaganda that is being carried by some persons who have their own axe to grind. In my speech on the occasion of the Hajj 655 C.E. I dealt with all the allegations that had been levelled against me. All the persons assembled corroborated what I had said. No one had the courage to stand up and say anything to the contrary. It is unfortunate that in Madinah some further propaganda has been made. I have pondered over all what the people say and I will talk about this further in the Prophet's mosque."

Hadrat Othman's Address at the Prophet's Mosque [2]

On the following Friday, Hadrat Othman addressed the congregation in the Prophet's mosque. After praising Allah and the

1. Ibid.
2. Ibid.

Holy Prophet, Hadrat Othman said:

"It has come to my notice that many false things are being said against me and my administration. You know after the Holy Prophet, Hadrat Abu Bakr became the Caliph and after him Hadrat Umar became the Caliph. I served both of them and they were happy with me. After Hadrat Umar I was chosen as the Caliph. I swear by Allah that I did not covet the office. You know I was already very rich and the office of the Caliph could not be a matter of any material advantage for me. You know Hadrat Umar was harsh and stern. He was not hard with the people alone; he was hard with his own person. May Allah bless him. His services to the cause of Islam cannot be forgotten. When I became the Caliph, I felt that the people wanted some change in policies. I consequently followed liberal policies and relaxed some of the harsh measures that had been in force in the time of Hadrat Umar. I increased the stipends of the people. I withdrew the restraints that had been imposed in the time of Hadrat Umar. The rule of any Imam is to be judged on the basis of the prosperity of the people. Look around you and say honestly whether you are not more prosperous today than what you were at the time of my succession. The Muslim dominions today are much more extensive than what they were twelve years ago. The people now are wealthier and richer than what they were before. As a result of military operations there has been much of booty. All such booty has been distributed among the people according to the formula laid down by the Holy Prophet. After such distributions there are ample funds in the Baitul Mal to meet our future needs. I have served the people to the best of my ability. It is, however, a matter of regret to note that instead of appreciating the good that I have done, a malicious propaganda is being carried out in some quarters to malign me. I chose to be kind and liberal. I tried to be a benevolent ruler. It is very unfortunate that undue advantage has been taken of my liberality and my kindness has been mistaken for my weakness. It is given out that I am weak and fickle, that I am led by others around me. It is true that I have some persons around me who help me in State affairs but it is not correct that I play into their hands. I take all decisions myself. It is said that such and such persons are my evil genius who are leading me on the wrong path. Every person has the right to choose his own advisers and if I have to my own satisfaction chosen certain persons as my advisers, it is not for any one to say that I should not have appointed such and such a person as my adviser. You merely cavil at persons; you do not bring out in specific terms what wrong has been done. You take pleasure in distorting facts. You give currency to rumours and do not care to verify facts. You say that I gave one lakh dirhams to Harith b Hakam out of the Baitul Mal. I have married my son to his daughter and I gave him this money out of my pocket for financing the marriage. The money was not paid out of the Baitul Mal. You say that I gave one lakh dirhams to Marwan b Hakam out of the Baitul Mal. This is sheer falsehood. I have married my daughter to a son of Marwan and I gave one lakh dirhams in dowry. This money was paid out of my pocket and not from the Baitul Mal. It is said that I paid Abdullah b Khalid 3 lakh dirhams from the Baitul Mal. He has taken this money as a loan from the Baitul Mal and he will repay it according to the terms of the loan. It is said that I deposed Abdullah b Arqam from the office of the custodianship of the Baitul Mal because he had protested against my grants from the Baitul Mal. There is no truth in this allegation. Abdullah b Arqam had held this office for the last twenty-five years and being old he has retired of his own free-will. Again it is said that I have diverted funds from the Baitul Mal for the construction of private property. This is a tissue of falsehood. I have constructed my private property with my own money and all know that I have ample resources of my own. It is alleged that I have gifted the entire surplus money in the Baitul Mal to Zaid b Thabit, the new Treasurer. This is again a sheer lie. After distributing the money in the Baitul Mal, there was a surplus amount of 1,000 dirhams in the Baitul Mal. I asked Zaid b Thabit to utilise this amount for some public purpose and he utilised this amount for the repair of the Prophet's mosque.

O people I exhort you to fear Allah and not to indulge in false propaganda. All the Muslims are one community. Do not create dissensions among the Muslims. If you are tired of me, you may rest assured that being an old man, I do not have long to live. If you want me to abdicate, let you know that this is duly assigned to me by Allah and I would never run away from duty whatever the pressure used against me. If you think of employing any force against me, you should be beware that I have my supporters who will support me through thick and thin. I appeal to you not to be misled by false rumours. I assure you of full justice. I expect justice from you. Do not be unnecessarily critical. If you have any legitimate grievance I will certainly redress it; if you are swayed by imaginary grievances, that would lead to mere confusion."

ARMED REVOLT AGAINST HADRAT OTHMAN

Disorder in Egypt[1]

Hadrat Othman had hoped that after his speech in which he had explained his position and offered full defence for his actions, the false propaganda against him would cease. As the conspiracy against him was deep rooted there was no diminution in the virulence of the campaign against him. That was because the agitation against Hadrat Othman was not being led on the basis of any principle; it was prompted by ulterior motives to overthrow his government. In Madinah, Muhammad b Abu Bakr, 'Aamir b Yasir and 'Amr b Al 'Aas whipped up the vilification campaign against Hadrat Othman and fed the people on false tales about the atrocities committed on the people of Egypt. In a fit of revengeful fury, 'Amr b Al 'Aas declared that he would inflame even the shepherds of the desert to rise against Hadrat Othman.

As the politics of Egypt figured most in the propaganda against the caliphate, Hadrat Othman summoned Abdullah b Sa'ad, the Governor of Egypt, to Madinah to consult him as to the course of action to be adopted. Abdullah b Sa'ad came to Madinah leaving the charge of the affairs in Egypt to his deputy. In the absence of Abdullah b Sa'ad, Muhammad b Abu Hudhaifa staged a *coup d'etat* and captured power in Egypt. On hearing of the revolt in Egypt, Abdullah hastened back to Egypt. Hadrat Othman was not in the position to give him any military assistance. Abdullah b Sa'ad accordingly failed to recapture power in Egypt. He was warned by Muhammad b Abu Hudhaifa not to enter Fustat. Failing to muster sufficient support, Abdullah b Sa'ad retired to Ramlah where he died two years later.

1. *History*: Tabari.

Revolt Against Hadrat Othman[1]

With the capture of power by Muhammad b Abu Hudhaifa in Egypt the stage was set for an open revolt against the caliphate of Hadrat Othman. In Kufa though Abu Musa Ash'ari, as Governor, paid nominal allegiance to Hadrat Othman, he was really a nominee of the rebels and could not go against their wishes. In Basra the Governor Abdullah b 'Aamir left for Hajj and in his absence the affairs of the province fell into a state of confusion. Thus the three main provinces of Egypt, Kufa and Basra came to be cut off from the caliphate of Hadrat Othman and became the centres of revolt.

In the month of Shawwal, a contingent of about 1,000 persons was sent from Egypt to Madinah. These persons travelled in four separate groups and gave out that they were going to perform the Hajj. They were fully armed and their instructions were to overthrow the government of Hadrat Othman and to murder him. The contingent was led by Amir Ghafqi b Harb. Ibn Saba accompanied the contingent as their general adviser.

Similar contingents marched from Kufa and Basra to Madinah. The Kufa contingent was led by Ashtar Nakh'i while the contingent from Basra was led by Hakim b Jabala.

All these contingents converged on Madinah according to a pre-arranged plan. Reaching the neighbourhood of Madinah the contingent from Egypt encamped at Dhil Marwah. The contingent from Basra encamped at Dukhshab, while the contingent from Kufa encamped at Ahwas. From these camps the contingent sent their representatives to one another for mutual consultation. They also sent their representatives to Madinah to contact the leaders of public opinion. The representatives of the contingent from Egypt waited on Hadrat Ali and offered him the caliphate in succession to Hadrat Othman. Hadrat Ali turned down their offer. The representatives of the contingent from Kufa waited on Zubair, while the representatives of the contingent from Basra waited on Talha and offered them their allegiance as the next Caliph. These offers were turned down. This move on the part of the rebels neutralised the bulk of public opinion in Madinah. Madinah could no longer offer a united front; it became a divided house. Hadrat Othman could enjoy the active support of the Umayyads and a few other persons in Madinah. The rest of the

---

1. *Othman b Affan*: Raza Misri.

people of Madinah chose to be neutral and help neither side. That was a big gain for the rebels. After surveying the situation in Madinah, the rebels felt satisfied that the circumstances were favourable to the launching of their campaign for overthrowing the government of Hadrat Othman.

The Campaign Against Hadrat Othman[1]

The accounts that have come down to us about the activities of the rebels are very much distorted and confused. The usual version is that Hadrat Othman appealed to Hadrat Ali to intervene and use his influence with the rebels to prevail upon them to withdraw from Madinah. It is related that Hadrat Ali was critical of the conduct of Hadrat Othman and Hadrat Othman gave a solemn undertaking that in future he would be guided by the counsels of Hadrat Ali. It is said that Hadrat Ali met the rebels and prevailed upon them to retire from Madinah. They agreed to do so, in case formal orders were passed by the Caliph for the deposition of Abdullah b Sa'ad from the governorship of Egypt. Hadrat Othman passed the orders for the deposition of Abdullah b Sa'ad and the appointment of Muhammad b Abu Bakr as the Governor of Egypt.

It is stated that on the demand of Hadrat Ali, Hadrat Othman addressed the people in the Prophet's mosque; admitted his mistakes; prayed for the forgiveness of Allah and the people; and undertook to make amends within three days. It is said that on this occasion Hadrat Othman wept and the audience wept with him. The accounts continue that under the influence of Marwan b Hakam Hadrat Othman retracted from his repentance and did not make any amends. Hadrat Othman and Hadrat Ali had another meeting at which Hadrat Ali accused Hadrat Othman of breach of faith. Hadrat Ali felt deeply annoyed and said that that was the parting of ways between them.

The accounts that have come down to us continue that when the rebels from Egypt proceeded a few stages from Madinah they came across a slave of Hadrat Othman who was carrying a letter of Hadrat Othman to the Governor of Egypt commanding him not to give effect to the orders regarding his deposition, arrest the rebels and execute them. That made the rebels return to Madinah. The rebels from Kufa and Basra returned likewise. It is stated that the rebels brought this

1. Ibid.

breach of faith on the part of Hadrat Othman to the notice of the leaders of public opinion in Madinah and invoked their assistance. Hadrat Othman admitted that the letter bore his official seal but he denied all knowledge about the contents of the letter. It was contended that the letter was in the handwriting of Marwan. Marwan was, however, never confronted with the letter and the accounts recorded in histories leave the matter about the contents of the letter unresolved.

Analysis of the Accounts Embodied in Histories

If the accounts contained in the histories are analysed we arrive at the conclusion that such accounts do not bear the test of subjective scrutiny. These accounts paint Hadrat Othman as a fickle old man with no will of his own, who is apt to be led by other persons. This does not appear to be a true picture of the character and personality of Hadrat Othman and the accounts are obviously biased and prejudiced. Hadrat Othman was a man of great intelligence. He was one of the richest persons in Arabia and he could not have amassed such riches if he were not a good judge of men and matters around him.

The accounts that Hadrat Othman asked Hadrat Ali to intervene and he did so on Hadrat Othman giving the assurance that he would make amends and would in future be guided by the advice of Hadrat Ali do not appear to be correct. We have an alternative version in Tabari that the rebels met Hadrat Othman himself in a village outside Madinah and after hearing him they felt satisfied and returned to Egypt.

The story that Hadrat Othman offered repentance, admitted his faults and promised to make amends does not make sense. In his speech at Makkah on the occasion of the pilgrimage and thereafter in his speech at Madinah, Hadrat Othman had offered full defence and had justified his conduct. It is plain common sense that in the face of such defence wherein he had categorically refuted all charges against him he could not turn a somersault and admit his faults. It has also to be borne in mind that in case Hadrat Othman admitted that he had made mistakes he forfeited the right to the caliphate. It is plain common sense that if a person in high office admits his mistake the only honourable course for him is to resign, for a man who has made mistakes cannot be allowed another lease of life in office to make more mistakes. The irresistible conclusion to which we are forced is that the story that Hadrat Othman admitted his mistakes is an invention of partisan writers whose aim was to present Hadrat Othman in false colours.

The story that Hadrat Othman had repented and that he turned a somersault at the instance of Marwan is too crude to be correct. The story was given currency by the enemies of Hadrat Othman whose aim was to present Hadrat Othman as a man unfit to hold the high office of the caliphate for he had no will of his own and was apt to play in the hands of others. Nothing could be farther from the truth. History has done great injustice to Hadrat Othman by suppressing the true facts and narrating only such distorted facts that suited the enemies of Hadrat Othman.

Again the story of the forged letter that the Egyptians are said to have intercepted has no legs to stand upon. It may be recalled that at that time Muhammad b Abi Hudhaifa was in control of Egypt and Hadrat Othman could not write to him who was hostile to him to arrest the persons who were his own men.

It has also to be borne in mind that the rebels had been commissioned to prevail on Hadrat Othman to abdicate or to murder him in the event of refusal. These rebels could, therefore, not return to Egypt merely by securing an order for the deposition of Abdullah b Sa'ad, particularly when he was no longer in office and had retired to Ramlah.

The truth of the matter appears to be that there was no intervention on the part of Hadrat Ali, there was no repentance on the part of Hadrat Othman, the Egyptians did not return to Egypt and there was no interception of any letter, forged or otherwise. What happened actually was merely this that the rebels studied the position in Madinah and when they felt satisfied that the people of Madinah would not offer them any resistance, they entered the city of Madinah and laid siege to the house of Hadrat Othman. The rebels declared that no harm from them would come to any person who did not choose to resist them. They advised the people of Madinah to remain in their homes. Most of the people of Madinah left for their gardens in the suburbs. Those who did not leave Madinah remained confined to their houses. Only some persons, mostly the Umayyads gathered in the house of Hadrat Othman but they were instructed by Hadrat Othman to refrain from violence.

SIEGE OF THE HOUSE OF HADRAT OTHMAN

Wary Stages of the Siege

When the rebels besieged the house of Hadrat Othman, the siege was not severe at the early stage. The rebels merely hovered around the house of Hadrat Othman and did not place any restrictions on the movements of Hadrat Othman. Hadrat Othman went to the Prophet's mosque as usual and led the prayers. The rebels offered prayers under the leadership of Hadrat Othman.

Hadrat Othman's Address in the Prophet's Mosque

On the first Friday after the siege, Hadrat Othman addressed the congregation in the mosque. After offering praises to Allah and the Holy Prophet, Hadrat Othman invited the attention of the people to the commandment in the Holy Qur'ān requiring the people to obey Allah, His Apostle and those in authority among them. He observed that the Muslims had been enjoined to settle all matters by mutual consultation. He said that he had kept the doors of consultation wide open. All the allegations that had been levelled against him had been duly explained by him and shown to be false. He had expressed his readiness to solve the legitimate grievances of the people, if any. He observed that under the circumstances it was uncharitable on the part of some persons to create disturbances in the city of the Holy Prophet. He said that he was not afraid of death but he did not want the Muslims to be guilty of bloodshed. To him the solidarity of the Muslim community was very dear and in order to prevent dissensions among the Muslims he had instructed his supporters to refrain from violence. He wanted the people to be afraid of Allah and not to indulge in activities subversive of Islam. He pointed out that the foreign powers smarting under their defeat inflicted by the Muslim arms had sponsored some conspiracies to subvert Islam. He warned the people not to play in the hands of the enemies of Islam. He appealed to the rebels to retire from Madinah. He wanted the people of Madinah to support the cause of truth and justice and withhold their support from the rebels bent on mischief.

Rowdyism in the Mosque

Some two or three persons from among the congregation stood up to assure Hadrat Othman of their support. They were manhandled by the rebels and were forced to sit down. The rebels including 'Amr b Al 'Aas, 'Ammar b Yasir and Muhammad b Abu Bakr raised their voices against Hadrat Othman. One Jabala b 'Amr Saahadi addressing Hadrat Othman said, "Beware you foolish old man, that unless you abdicate we will strangle you to death". When Hadrat Othman was addressing the congregation from the pulpit, one Jamjah Ghaffari seized the staff from the hands of Hadrat Othman and broke it on his knees. Addressing Hadrat Othman, Jamjah Ghaffari insolently said that he had brought a dirty apparel and an old camel for Hadrat Othman to wear and ride, for he was no longer worthy of wearing the robes of the caliphate. Hadrat Othman merely dismissed him with remarks, "May Allah curse you and all that you have brought."

Some of the supporters of Hadrat Othman took up cudgels on behalf of Hadrat Othman. Hot words were exchanged between the parties. Tempers flared up on both the sides and that led to the pelting of stones at one another. The state of complete rowdyism came to prevail in the mosque. One of the stones hit Hadrat Othman and he fell unconscious. The gathering dissolved in a state of great disorder and Hadrat Othman was carried to his house in a state of unconsciousness.

Intensification of the Siege[1]

The proceedings in the mosque showed to the rebels that Hadrat Othman did not enjoy the full support of the people of Madinah. Apart from the Umayyads and a few other persons, most of the people of Madinah preferred to be neutral and watch developments. When the rebels felt that the people of Madinah were not likely to offer active support to Hadrat Othman, they changed their strategy and tightened the siege of the house of Hadrat Othman. Hadrat Othman was denied the freedom to move about. He was not allowed to go to the mosque. Prayers in the mosque were now led by Amir Ghafiqi, the leader of the rebels. Madinah thus came to be in the full control of the rebels.

As days passed on and no one came forward to oppose the rebels, they felt bold and intensified their pressure against Hadrat Othman. They forbade the entry of any food or provisions into the house of Hadrat Othman. Then they placed an embargo even on the

---

1. Ibid.

entry of water into the house of Hadrat Othman. Hadrat Othman had purchased a well with his money and dedicated it to the use of the Muslims and now he was denied water from the well which belonged to him. Hadrat Umm Habiba, a widow of the Holy Prophet and a sister of Muawiyah came to see Hadrat Othman and brought some water and provisions for Hadrat Othman. She was not allowed to enter the house of Hadrat Othman. Hadrat Ayesha made a simiiar attempt and she was also prevailed upon by the rebels to go back.

HADRAT OTHMAN'S LETTER TO THE PILGRIMS

Hadrat Othman and the Hajj

Hadrat Othman remained the Caliph for twelve years. During these twelve years, Hadrat Othman presided at the Hajj ceremonies personally for ten years. He could not perform the pilgrimage during the first year of his caliphate, as he was suffering from the oozing of blood from the nose. That year Abdur Rahman b Auf led the Muslims in Hajj on behalf of Hadrat Othman. Hadrat Othman could not perform the pilgrimage during the last year of his life, as he was besieged in his house by the rebels. On that occasion, Hadrat Othman appointed Abdullah b Abbas as the "Amir-ul-Hajj".

Hadrat Othman's Letter to the Pilgrims[1]

Hadrat Othman addressed a letter to the pilgrims assembled at Makkah. This letter was entrusted to Abdullah b Abbas and he was required to read the letter at the gathering of the pilgrims at Makkah. This letter is contained in Zia Misri's book *Othman b Affan* and Taha Hussain's book *Othman*. The letter reads:

"In the name of Allah, the most merciful, the beneficent. From Amirul Mominin Othman to all Muslims. Salutations.

After offering praise and glory to Allah, I wish you to turn to Allah Who had favoured you and chose Islam for you as your religion. Instead of waywardness, He gave you guidance. He released you from the bondage of *Kufr*. He armed you with guidance. He released your sustenance. He made you victorious against your enemies. He showered His favours on you.

---

1. Othman: Taha Hussain.

Allah says, "If you take the favours of Allah into account, you will find them too numerous to be counted. But man is rebellious and ungrateful by nature."

O believers, have the fear of Allah in your hearts. Pray that when you die you die in Islam. Be united and hold fast to the cord of Allah".

Allah also says, "O believers, recall the favours of Allah. Keep in mind the covenant that you have made with Him of your obedience and faithfulness."

Allah says, "O ye believers, if any miscreant brings to you a news, fully verify it before accepting it as the truth."

Allah says that those who purchase this world are the losers and they will have nothing to their credit in the hereafter.

Fear Allah and do not violate the pledges that you have taken.

Allah has enjoined you to obey Him, obey His Prophet and obey those in authority among you.

Those who believe and do good deeds, Allah has promised them the inheritance of the earth. Those who rebel against authority incur the wrath of Allah.

Allah said, "They who pledge allegiance to you pledge allegiance to Me. On them is My Hand."

In the light of these verses from the Holy Qur'ān bear in mind that Allah is pleased with those who obey authority and who stand for unity and solidarity. Allah has condemned dissension and discord. He has brought home this point to us by narrating the stories of previous communities. Therefore act according to the injunctions of Allah and be afraid of His punishment. If you ponder over history, it will be revealed to you that the previous communities were destroyed because they became victims of dissension. For the good of people, there is no way other than this that they should have a head, in whose obedience they should be united. If you follow the way of discord and dissension, your community would disintegrate and the enemy would come to dominate over you.

If all this comes to pass, then the religion of Allah would receive a setback and the community would disintegrate into a number of sects. Allah told the Holy Prophet, "Have no concern with the people who have broken their unity and disintegrated into sects. Leave them to Allah. Allah will take them to task for their misdeeds."

I offer you the same advice as Allah has offered. I ask you to fear his punishment. Hadrat Shuaib had told his people, "O people beware lest my opposition would lead you to the same end as befell the communities of Noah, Hud or Salih." Since sometime past, some people from amongst us have tried to present themselves as the apostles of truth, who are not interested in the affairs of the world and who have no axe to grind. But when they were presented with reality, some of them accepted the truth but some of them disputed the truth. Some of them stood for falsehood but they posed as if the truth lay with them. Such persons feel upset at my longevity. They covet power. They long for an immediate revolution. Such persons have written to you that they are waging the struggle against me to get their rights. I do not know of which rights I have divested them, which they now demand from me. They demanded that no one should be above the law. I told them that I fully agreed with them. I asked them to bring all cases to my notice and I assured them that the law would be enforced against all, high or low without any, distinction. But they could bring no case to my notice where any person had defied the law and proper action had not been taken against him. They said that the injunctions of the Qur'ãn should be followed. I said that I wholeheartedly agreed with the demand but would not permit any innovation or deviation. The people demanded that the poor should get bread, the labourer should get his wages. I said that I was at one with them and it is open to them to make their suggestions in the matter. They demanded that, in the matter of *Sadaqa* and *Khums* the right of early one should be protected. I said that I agreed with the demand and they were welcome to make their suggestions in that behalf. I saw the wives of the Holy Prophet and agreed to act according to their advice. I have accepted all legitimate demands but in spite of that I am being oppressed and harassed. I have been prevented from leading the prayers in the Prophet's mosque. The rioters have established their full control over Madinah.

The rioters have put three alternatives before me. They demand *Qasaas* from me for all grievances that any person may have suffered because of any verdict passed by me as Caliph. Their other alternative is that I should abdicate so that they might choose another Caliph. The third alternative is that they should assemble the people who support them and then repudiate the allegiance to my caliphate.

All these demands are preposterous. There have been rulers and Caliphs in history who had been vested with the authority to pass judgements. The judgements might be right or wrong but nobody has the right to sit over such judgement and demand compensation. Such a demand is against all principles of jurisprudence. As regards the demand for abdication I hold myself responsible to Allah and I cannot abandon my post at the behest of anyone. The third alternative is ridiculous. No ruler in his senses would provide facilities to the rioters to rebel against him.

These people are apparently after my life and their sole object appears to be to murder me. I have advised my supporters not to use any force. I do not want that the Muslim community should fall a victim to civil war. I will watch developments with due patience and would await the decision of Allah. If I have to give my life in the way of Allah I would have no hesitation in making the sacrifice. I know that as Caliph I have done nothing wrong. Nevertheless I seek the forgiveness of Allah. May Allah forgive us all. May Allah have mercy on the Muslims.

Analysis of the Letter[1]

If this somewhat lengthy letter is studied analytically it will be seen that Hadrat Othman did not appeal to the Muslims to come to his aid. There is nothing in the letter to incite the Muslims to violence against the rioter. Hadrat Othman merely apprised the people of the situation. He was averse to civil war and did not want any blood to be shed. He resigned himself to the will of Allah and prepared himself to meet eventualities with a smiling face. It appears that the object of the letter was merely to exhort the Muslims to do their duty to Islam. The Muslims were required to fear Allah, to hold fast to the cord of Allah, to maintain unity in their ranks, to take lesson from history, to obey Allah, His Messenger and those in authority and to suppress evils, discord and dissensions. It appears that Hadrat Othman was concerned more with the welfare of the Islamic community than with his personal safety. The letter was read by Abdullah b Abbas at the time of the pilgrimage. It is not known what was the reaction of the people to the letter. It seems that as no attempt was made to rally any support for Hadrat Othman, the people dispersed after hearing the letter. By the time Hadrat Abbas

1. This is based on my original analysis.

returned from the pilgrimage to Madinah, all was over and Hadrat Othman was assassinated.

HELP FROM THE PROVINCES

In his book *Othman*, Taha Hussain has raised the issue why no help came from the provinces in time, when Hadrat Othman had made a formal appeal for help. Taha Hussain is inclined to the view that the people were tired of the long rule of Hadrat Othman and they wanted a change. Taha Hussain has dropped hints that even Governors like Muawiyah who were devoted to Hadrat Othman deliberately delayed such help for political consideration.

Hadrat Othman's Appeal for Help[1]

The letter which Hadrat Othman is reported to have sent to the provincial Governors for help is to the following effect:

> "All praise and glory is for Allah and His Prophet who showed us the right path. We were fortunate to be favoured with Islam. Islam welded us into a single community. Islam gave us the message of unity. The Holy Prophet passed away after fulfilling his mission. After him his mission was carried by Hadrat Abu Bakr and then by Hadrat Umar. After Hadrat Umar, I was chosen as the Caliph. I never coveted the office but when the people took the oath of allegiance to me, I felt myself under an obligation to administer the affairs of the State to the best of my ability. I performed the duties of my office conscientiously and during the earlier part of my rule, the people were satisfied. I allowed the people greater freedom and more privileges. That was done in the best interests of the people. During my caliphate the people have become more prosperous. Instead of being grateful to me for my services to the cause of Islam, some people for some unknown reason have resorted to false propaganda and poisoned the atmosphere. I have made every possible effort to redress the legitimate grievances of the people. It is unfortunate that the malcontents do not come forward with any specific grievance. They make one demand today and make a contrary demand the following day without advancing any reason or argument. I have dealt with these people with due patience and forbearance but their aim appears to be to subvert Islam by promoting disunity.

1. *Othman*: Taha Hussain.

I warn the Muslims in general against the activities of these persons who wish to weaken Islam as a social and political force. In this crisis in the affairs of the Muslims I seek the cooperation of all who are devoted to Islam. He who can side with us may do so."

Analytic Study of the Letter[1]

If this letter is studied analytically, it will be seen that the letter is coached in general terms. There is nothing therein calling upon the supporters of government to muster in strength and come to Madinah for relief. In the accounts that have come down to us it appears that the Governors of Syria and Basra sent some relief forces but that when they were a few stages from Madinah they came to know that Hadrat Othman had been assassinated and on coming to know of this tragedy they returned to their provinces. If these forces had come to fight for Hadrat Othman, there is no reason why they should have returned on coming to know of the tragedy. On the other hand such tragedy should have spurred them to violent action against the rioters. Apparently they had come in aid of maintaining law and order. When the Caliph had been killed it implied that the law and order situation had become grave. In such context the responsibility of these forces was to rush to Madinah to preserve law and order and take the law breakers to task. The truth of the matter is that no force came from any of the provinces because Hadrat Othman wanted to avoid a civil war. It may be recalled that when Muawiyah had offered to send a contingent from Syria to act as a guard, Hadrat Othman had not accepted the offer, because he did not want any blood to be shed in the city of the Holy Prophet. It may also be recalled that when the slaves of Hadrat Othman volunteered to take up arms he restrained them from such action and said, "He who does not take up arms is free". When Imam Hasan and some other persons sought the permission of Hadrat Othman to fight against the rebels, Hadrat Othman did not permit them to do so and asked them to retire to their houses. In this crisis, Hadrat Othman set the noble example of resignation to the will of Allah. He preferred to sacrifice his own life rather than lead the people to civil war. The story that the provincial forces came late and returned when they came to know of the assassination of Hadrat Othman appears to have been invented by the party opposed to Hadrat

1. This is based on my own assessment.

Othman to create the impression that Hadrat Othman had become unpopular even in provinces where his relatives were the Governors. The memory of Hadrat Othman deserves to be cherished as a great soul who sacrificed his life in vindication of the principles for which he stood. May Allah have mercy on the soul of Hadrat Othman.

MARTYRDOM OF HADRAT OTHMAN

Deepening of the Crisis

With the departure of the pilgrims from Madinah to Makkah, the hands of the rebels were further strengthened and as a consequence the crisis deepened further. The rebels apprehended that after the Hajj, the Muslims gathered at the Makkah from all parts of the Muslim world might march to Madinah to the relief of the Caliph. They, therefore, decided to take action against Hadrat Othman before the pilgrimage was over.

Mugheera b Shu'ba[1]

It is related that during the course of the siege, Mugheera b Shu'ba went to Hadrat Othman and placed three courses of action before him, firstly to go forth and fight against the rebels, secondly to mount a camel and go to Makkah; and thirdly to betake himself to Syria. Hadrat Othman rejected all the three proposals. He rejected the first proposal saying that he did not want to be the first Caliph during whose time blood in shed. He turned down the second proposal to escape to Makkah on the ground that he had heard from the Holy Prophet that a man of the Quraish would be buried in Makkah on whom would be half the chastisement of the world and he did not want to be that person. He rejected the third proposal on the ground that he could not forsake the city of the Holy Prophet.

Ten Distinctions[2]

It is recorded on the authority of Abu Thaur al Fahami that he visited Hadrat Othman when he was besieged and Hadrat Othman referred to his ten distinctions *vis-a-vis* Islam, namely:

(1) He was one of the first four converts to Islam.
(2) He had the distinction of marrying two daughters of the Holy Prophet.

1. *History of the Caliphs*: Suyuti.
2. Ibid.

(3) He had not applied his hand to worldly use since he had offered allegiance to the Holy Prophet.
(4) He liberated a slave every week.
(5) He never committed fornication.
(6) He never committed a sin.
(7) He preserved the text of the Holy Qur'ān.
(8) He was one of the ten persons who were given the tidings of paradise during their lifetime.
(9) He freely spent his wealth in the way of Allah.
(10) The Holy Prophet, Hadrat Abu Bakr and Hadrat Umar were happy with him.

Abdullah b Salam[1]

Abdullah b Salam, a companion visited the house of Hadrat Othman and he is reported to have addressed the besiegers as follows:

"Slay him not, for by Allah not a man among you shall slay him but he shall meet the Lord mutilated without a hand and verily the sword of Allah has continued sheathed but surely by Allah if you slay him the Lord will indeed draw it and will never sheath it from you. Never was a Prophet slain but there were slain on account of him, 70,000 persons and never was a Caliph slain but 35,000 persons were killed on his account."

Nayyar b Ayyad[2]

A companion Nayyar b Ayyad Aslami who joined the rebels exhorted them to enter the house and assassinate Hadrat Othman. When the rebels under the leadership of Nayyar b Ayyad advanced to rush into the house, Kathir b Salat Kundi, a supporter of Hadrat Othman, shot an arrow which killed Nayyar. That infuriated the rebels. They demanded that Kathir b Salat Kundi, the man who had killed Nayyar, should be handed over to them. Hadrat Othman said that he could not thus betray a person who had shot an arrow in his defence. That precipitated the matters. Hadrat Othman had the gates of the house shut. The gate was guarded by Hadrat Hasan, Hadrat Hussain, Abdullah b Zubair, Marwan and a few other persons. Open fighting now began between the rebels and the supporters of Hadrat Othman. There were some casualties among

1. *Othman b Affan*: Raza Misri.
2. *History of the Caliphs*: Suyuti.

the rebels. Among the supporters of Hadrat Othman Hadrat Hasan, Marwan and some other persons were wounded.

Assassination of Hadrat Othman[1]

The rebels increased their pressure and reaching the door of the house of Hadrat Othman set it on fire. Some rebels led by Muhammad b Abu Bakr climbed the houses of the neighbours and then jumped into the house of Hadrat Othman. It was the seventeenth day of July in the year 856 C.E. Hadrat Othman was keeping the fast that day. The previous night he had seen the Holy Prophet in a dream. The Holy Prophet had said, "Othman, break your fast with us this evening. We will welcome you". That made Hadrat Othman feel that it was his last day of life. He prepared himself for death. He sat reading the Holy Qur'ãn and his wife Naila sat by his side. Some rebels entered the room of Hadrat Othman but they could not dare murder the Caliph. Then Muhammad b Abu Bakr entered the room and held the beard of Hadrat Othman. Hadrat Othman said that he was like a nephew to him and he would be false to the memory of his father Hadrat Abu Bakr if he contemplated any violence against him. That made Muhammad b Abu Bakr waver in his resolve and he walked out of the room. Seeing this some of the rebels entered the room and struck blows at the head of Hadrat Othman. Hadrat Naila threw herself on the body of Hadrat Othman to protect him. She was pushed aside and further blows were struck on Hadrat Othman till he was dead. From Allah he had come and to Allah he returned. He died while keeping the fast and true to his dream he broke the fast in the company of the Holy Prophet that evening.

Some slaves of Hadrat Othman fell on the person whose blows had killed Hadrat Othman and killed him. There was some fighting between the rebels and the supporters of Hadrat Othman. There were casualties on both the sides. Rowdyism prevailed for sometime and the rebels looted the house. When the women raised loud lamentations over the dead body of Hadrat Othman, the rebels left the house.

---

1. Ibid.

THE FUNERAL OF HADRAT OTHMAN

The Vengeance of the Rioters

Even after the gruesome murder of Hadrat Othman, the rioters did not feel satisfied that they had taken the full revenge. They wanted to mutilate the dead body of Hadrat Othman. They were also keen that the dead body was denied burial. When some of the rioters came forward to mutilate the dead body of Hadrat Othman, his two widows covered the dead body and raised loud lamentations which deterred the rioters from pursuing their nefarious design. Thereafter the rioters hovered round the house with a view to preventing the dead body being carried to the graveyard.

The Funeral[1]

The dead body of Hadrat Othman lay in the house for three days. Hadrat Naila, the wife of Hadrat Othman, approached some of the supporters of Hadrat Othman to help in the burial of Hadrat Othman. Only about a dozen persons responded to the call. These included Marwan b Hakam, Zaid b Thabit, Huwatib b Alfarah, Jabir b Muta'am, Abu Jahm b Hudaifa, Hakim b Hazam and Niyar b Mukarram. The dead body was lifted at dusk. In view of the blockade no coffin could be procured. The dead body was not washed as water was not available. Hadrat Othman was carried to the graveyard in the clothes that he was wearing at the time of his assassination. According to one account permission was obtained from Hadrat Ali to bury the dead body. According to another account, no permission was obtained and the dead body was carried to the graveyard in secret. According to another account when the rioters came to know that the dead body was being carried to the graveyard they gathered to stone the funeral but Hadrat Ali borbade them to resort to any such act and they withdrew. According to one account Hadrat Ali attended the funeral, There is, however, overwhelming evidence to the effect that Hadrat Ali did not attend the funeral. Hadrat Naila, the widow of Hadrat Othman, followed the funeral with a lamp but in order to maintain secrecy the lamp had to be extinguished. Hadrat Naila was accompanied by some women including Ayesha, a daughter of Hadrat Othman.

---

1. *Othman b Affan*: Raza Misri.

The Burial

The dead body was carried to "Baqi' al Farqad", the graveyard of Muslims. It appears that some persons gathered there and they resisted the burial of Hadrat Othman in the graveyard of the Muslims. The supporters of Hadrat Othman insisted that the dead body would be buried in the graveyard of the Muslims. Those who were opposed to such burial grew in strength and fearing lest such opposition might take a more ominous turn, the dead body of Hadrat Othman was taken to the neighbouring graveyard of the Jews "Hush Kaukab" and buried there in a hurry. The funeral prayers were led by Jabir b Muta'am and the dead body was lowered in the grave without much of ceremony. After burial, Hadrat Naila, the widow of Hadrat Othman and Ayesha, the daughter of Hadrat Othman, wanted to speak but they were advised to remain quiet as danger was apprehended from the rioters.

Assessment of the Accounts about the Burial of Hadrat Othman[1]

When we reflect at the accounts that have come down to us about the funeral of Hadrat Othman we cannot help but grieve at the helpless state of affairs to which the Muslim polity had become a victim. What a pity that the Caliph of the Muslims could not be given even a decent burial. No tragedy could be more tragic than that. It is not understood why the people of Madinah had become so callous that they could not attend the funeral of the Caliph who had looked after their interests for twelve years and who had done so much for the promotion of their interests. It is most ironical that he who had been the Caliph of the Muslims was denied burial in the graveyard of the Muslims and had to find a resting place in the graveyard of the Jews who had worked for the subversion of Islam. When Muawiyah came to power he had the wall between the Muslim graveyard and "Hush Kaukab" demolished. More Muslims were buried around the grave of Hadrat Othman and this part of "Hush Kaukab" became a part of "Baqi' al Farqad", the graveyard of the Muslims.

---

1. This is based on my own assessment.

FUNERAL ORATIONS

Funeral Orations of Ayesha b Othman[1]

When the dead body of Hadrat Othman left the house, Ayesha, the daughter of Hadrat Othman, gave a funeral address in the following terms:

> "I bitterly mourn the death of my father Hadrat Othman. He was not a father to me alone, he was a father to the entire Muslim community. Alas, those whom he regarded as his sons have murdered him.
>
> O ye murderers of Othman bear in mind that we all are the creatures of Allah and all of us have to return to Him. How deplorable that in the sacred city of the Holy Prophet, a person so close and dear to the Holy Prophet was murdered in cold blood. Even after his assassination, the murderers created difficulties in the burial of his dead body.
>
> O Allah if the murdered Caliph had chosen to exercise his authority many persons would have arisen to defend him. Truth and justice were on his side and Allah fearing people would have certainly taken up cudgels on his behalf. In that case the rioters would have been shot at, their heads would have been cut off and there would have been lot of bloodshed. But that was not the way of Hadrat Othman. What you considered right he held it to be wrong. He was against any bloodshed. He preferred to give up his own life rather than resort to measures which were likely to promote civil war.
>
> O ye murderers, as Muslims you had to be loyal and faithful to your Caliph at whose hands you had taken the oath of allegiance. By murdering your Caliph you have betrayed Islam; you have proved false even to yourself. You let loose a flood of false propaganda against him and made allegations against him which were groundless. He refuted all such allegations in categorical terms but you persisted in your evil design. You have murdered an innocent man and his blood cries for vengeance.
>
> Father, may Allah have mercy on you. You resigned yourself to the will of Allah as a true Muslim. In the midst of trials and

1. *Othman b Affan*: Raza Misri.

tribulations you exhibited patience and bore all hardships without complaint. You met your death with a smiling face. You are martyr in the cause of Allah. In the heavens your place is now in the company of the Holy Prophet.

Now dissensions have broken up among your enemies and they are quarrelling among themselves. Mischief is abroad and tyrannies of your enemies are now becoming manifest. Now the veil of their hypocrisy is being turned and they have begun to indulge in conspiracies against one another.

O the murderers of Hadrat Othman, how cruel and unjust you have been. You were actuated by extraneous considerations and you raised preposterous demands. Hadrat Othman merely followed in the footsteps of his predecessor. Why did you not raise any demand in the time of Hadrat Umar. He was harsh and you did not raise a voice against him as you were afraid of him. On the contrary Hadrat Othman treated you kindly. You took undue advantage of his kindness and instead of appreciating his kindness and mildness you indulged in a vilification campaign against him. That was ingratitude of the worst type. Ingratitude is a great crime before man and Allah. Ungrateful persons have never prospered. Know that history would never forgive you for your betrayal and ingratitude. Also know that in the world to come severe punishment awaits those who are unjust. Hell will be their abode.

You may recall that the caliphate of Hadrat Umar was a period of great trial for you. You lived in an atmosphere of awe and fear. He imposed restrictions on your movements. He curtailed your liberties. You submitted to him without raising any protest. You could not dare speak before him, you could not criticise him. He was the Caliph who always carried a whip in his hand. He treated you as dumb cattle and you submitted to this fate. Hadrat Othman treated you as men. He allowed you full liberties. He removed all the restrictions on your movements. He increased your stipends and looked after your welfare in every way. You have recompensed him by murdering him. That is very strange. You have falsified all Islamic values. You have repaid good with evil. Today the Grace of Allah has been estranged from you. You have been guilty of a great crime. Know that evil cannot hold for long. Ultimately truth will triumph, you will be called to account for your misdeeds. I have perfect faith in Allah and I am sure Allah will duly avenge the murder of Hadrat Othman. May the soul of Hadrat Othman rest in eternal peace in the heaven! He has been the victim of grave injustice in this world, I am sure Allah will duly compensate him in the next world."

Funeral Oration of Hadrat Naila, the Widow of Hadrat Othman[1]

On the occasion of the funeral of Hadrat Othman, Hadrat Naila, the widow of Hadrat Othman, addressed the people of Madinah in the following terms:

"O brethren of Islam do not be surprise at my standing before you and giving expression to what is in my heart. Do not regard my talk as vain or superfluous. I am most aggrieved and distressed. The shock of the assassination of my dear husband before me is too deep to be expressed in words. I have wept bitterly and now the tears have frozen in my eyes. A great calamity has befallen. I have suffered irreparable bereavement. But in such matters we human beings are helpless. What cannot be cured has to be endured. From Allah he came and to Allah he has returned. I mourn his death. His death is not a personal tragedy for me, his assassination is a great tragedy for the entire Muslim community.

Hadrat Othman was a close companion of the Holy Prophet. Hadrat Othman had the unique honour of marrying two daughters of the Holy Prophet, one after the other. For this he won the title of "Dhun Nurain"—the possessor of two luminaries. He was a counseller of the Holy Prophet. After the Holy Prophet, Hadrat Abu Bakr and Hadrat Umar held him in great esteem and consulted him in important affairs of the State. In qualities of head and heart he was second to none. He was most noble, most modest, most generous, most magnanimous, most gentle and most kind. He promoted good and suppressed evil. His generosity knew no bounds. He supported many orphans and widows. He was always active in affording relief to those in distress. His beneficent acts are fully known and too numerous to be cited.

He ruled as Caliph for twelve years. His period of caliphate was

1. *Othman b Affan*: Raza Misri.

longer than the period of the caliphate of his predecessors. His rule was historically memorable. In his rule extensive conquests were made. Under him the Muslims became the masters of the sea for the first time.

Hadrat Othman was a beneficent ruler. He increased your stipends. Under his rule the country became prosperous. When he became the Caliph Madinah was not a large town, under him Madinah grew into metropolitan dimensions. He embellished Madinah with many works of public character. He enlarged and embellished the Prophet's mosque. He constructed numerous wells to provide adequate supply of water to you. In the time of famines he distributed large stocks of grain purchased by him out of his own money in the way of Allah.

Hadrat Othman was the first citizen of your city. He did much for you but you did little for him. He was assassinated by rioters in front of you but you remained confined to your houses. Every murder is heinous but the murder of Hadrat Othman is the most heinous and most grievous of all murders in history. The murder of their Caliph by the people is a betrayal of Islam. He was assassinated in the sacred city of Madinah and that was a great sacrilege. He was murdered during the sacred month of the Hajj and thereby the sanctity of the sacred month was violated.

Islam came as a great blessing to mankind. Islam stood for a complete break with the age of ignorance. The brutal murder of Hadrat Othman amounts to the revival of the age of ignorance. His murder has opened the door of dissensions among the Muslims. With his death the process of our conquests will come to standstill. Henceforward the Muslims instead of fighting against the non-Muslims will fight among themselves. I see dark days ahead for the Muslims. May Allah have mercy on us! May He have mercy in Hadrat Othman and assign him a fitting abode in the paradise!"

ELEGIES ON THE DEATH OF HADRAT OTHMAN

The tragedy of the assassination of Hadrat Othman was a great tragic event in the history of Islam. It inspired some of the poets of Arabia to give vent to their grief in some heart-rending verses.

Hassan b Thabit[1]

In his elegy Hassan b Thabit said:

"O ye miscreants, instead of going to the frontiers to undertake Jihad,
You have come here to fight against the Muslims.
How regrettable and deplorable is your action?
You have assassinated the Caliph of the Muslims.
Evil was your intention;
And heinous is the crime you have committed.
I grieve for Othman who suffered from trials and tribulations.
He fell a victim to your high-handedness.
The house of Othman is today empty;
Some doors have been broken and some burnt.
At one time people in need called on him,
And he administered relief to them.
Today this place is desolate,
Othman the Ghani is no more.
O people of Madinah give vent to your grief.
You have lost who was the first citizen of this city.
Mourn his death who was like a father to his people.
Curse the people whose hands are stained with his blood.
His blood will not go unavenged.
The people of Syria will rise to demand vengeance.
O the murderers of Othman, beware that Allah is most powerful.
He will not forgive you for the murder of Othman.
Great punishment awaits you both in this world and the hereafter.

Ka'ab b Malik Ansari[2]

In his elegy Ka'ab b Malik Ansari said:

"O Ka'ab b Malik what has happened to the people,
Why have they been bereft of their senses,
Why have they been guilty of the murder of their Caliph.
My eyes are flooded with tears
I am overwhelmed with grief at the death of Othman.
It appears as if the earth has been rent asunder by an earthquake.
On the death of the Caliph
Even the stars have lost their lustre and gone into mourning;

---

1. Ibid.
2. Ibid.

The sun stands eclipsed,
The earth has been enveloped in complete darkness.
Verily Othman is a martyr.
He died defending the Truth;
His reward is with his Allah.
How generous and magnanimous was he?
What large bounties did he give to the people?
What a large number of orphans did he support?
How many widows were cared for by him?
He met every one with a smiling face;
He shared the distress of every one;
His heart flowed with the milk of human kindness.
Alas such a man is now no more!"
He has fallen a victim to the blows of misguided persons.
His murderers have forfeited the right to be called Muslims.
Grievous penalty awaits them both here and in the hereafter.
They will roast in the fire of hell.
O Othman, Ka'ab grieves for you,
You were so good, so kind and so noble,
I bear witness to your generosity, your magnanimity and your large heartedness."

Hatab b Yazid Mujashe[1]

In his elegy Hatab b Yazid Mujashe said:
"With the death of Othman, the age of good has passed away,
Now evil will stalk the earth.
The people have become estranged to their religion.
Everyone is now treading the path of evil and destruction.
O Allah have mercy on Othman,
He was so good and noble.
He stood firm in the cause of Truth,
He welcomed death and did not compromise with the principles for which he stood;
Those who murdered him stand cursed
They are traitors to Islam.

Qasim b Umayya b Abi Al Salat[2]

In his elegy Qasim b Umayya b Abi Al Salat said:

1. Ibid.
2. Ibid.

"I swear by Allah that the murder of Othman is the most heinous crime.

By assassinating a person who was so dear to the Holy Prophet.
You have incurred the wrath of the Holy Prophet.
By murdering the Caliph you have betrayed your faith in Islam.

You are traitors to Islam;
And grievous will be your punishment both in this world and the next.

Zainab bint Al Awaam[1]

In her elegy the poetess Zainab bint Al Awaam said:

"You kept Othman thirsty in his house,
You deprived him of the use of water from the well
Which he had purchased and dedicated to the public use.
In hell you will have to drink hot boiling water,
Which will burn every limb of yours.
None can be more accursed than you;
You are guilty of the worst crime in history."

Laila Akhaylya[2]

In her elegy the poetess Laila Akhaylya said:

"Othman the Caliph, the son of Affan has been assassinated.
All affairs of the Muslims have fallen in the state of disorder.
The good stands suppressed and evil predominates.
The blood of Othman cries for vengeance.
O Muawiyah demand the *Qasaas* for the murder of Othman;
We will not rest content until his death is avenged."

Ibn Khazima[3]

In his elegy the poet Ibn Khazima said:

"Hadrat Othman has been killed in the sacred month,
What a heinous crime have the miscreants committed?
They have the dishonour of killing the Caliph of the Muslims;
They have opened the door to mischief and disunity.
May Allah curse them;
And may Allah have mercy on the soul of Othman!"

---

1. Ibid.
2. Ibid.
3. Ibid.

Walid b Uqba[1]

Walid b Uqba, a step brother of Hadrat Othman, mourned on the death of Hadrat Othman in the following verses:

"What happened to this night,
It is so long and dreary.
The stars have dimmed in their lustre.
O miscreants do not plunder the house of Othman
O Banu Hashim do not be in a hurry about assuming the caliphate!
Before us those who killed Othman;
And those whom they elevate to the caliphate
Are both guilty.
A river of blood flows between you and us,
By Allah I can never forget the tragedy of the assassination of Othman;
How can a thirsty man be indifferent to the well?
They have killed Othman so that they may succeed him;

We will fight against you.
O Muslims rise up to take revenge for the murder of Othman.
If you hesitate you will not be your mother's son
The blood of Othman cries for vengeance
And you must respond to the call.

Aiman b Hazim b Fatik Asadi[2]

In his elegy Aiman b Hazim said:

"The people conspired to murder Othman.
They shed the blood of the Caliph in the sacred city of the Holy Prophet.
They have betrayed Islam.
His murderers have forfeited the right to be called Muslims
They stand condemned before man and Allah;
The murderers of Othman stand cursed;
And grievous will be their end."

1. Ibid.
2. Ibid.

HADRAT NAILA'S LETTER TO AMIR MUAWIYAH

Hadrat Naila

Hadrat Naila b Farafsa was the wife of Hadrat Othman. She belonged to a Christian tribe. She accepted Islam at the time of her marriage. She was married to Hadrat Othman in 649 C.E. The marriage lasted for seven years only. During these years she remained a close companion of Hadrat Othman. She was with Hadrat Othman at the time of his assassination. She was wounded in her attempt to ward off the blows of the murderers on Hadrat Othman. During his lifetime, Hadrat Othman had authorised Amir Muawiyah to demand the *Oasaas* for his murder. After the assassination of Hadrat Othman, Hadrat Naila addressed a letter to Amir Muawiyah.

Hadrat Naila's Letter[1]

In her letter, Hadrat Naila wrote:

"From Naila bint Farafsa to Amir Muawiyah b Abi Sufyan.

By this letter I call you to Allah Who showered His bounties on you, made you Muslim, showed you the light and liberated you from *Kufr.*,

In the name of Allah I appeal to you to rise in the cause of Hadrat Othman who has been butchered mercilessly. By way of your relationship with him, the responsibility to avenge his blood devolves on you. It is the command of Allah that if there is bloodshed between two groups of Muslims you should strive for peace among them but if any group transgresses, take action against the rebels and kill them.

Some people rebelled against Hadrat Othman without just cause. You know what high position Hadrat Othman commanded in Islam. He was very close and dear to the Holy Prophet. He never coveted the caliphate. He was chosen as the Caliph by the people. During the twelve years of his office he worked day and night for the welfare of the people. During his caliphate extensive conquests were made. Immense wealth flowed into the public treasury. The stipends of the people were increased. The people became more prosperous. Instead of appreciating the benefits of his rule some

1. Ibid.

miscreants because of ulterior considerations conspired against him. Hadrat Othman could have suppressed such agitation with force but he refrained from using force against his people. As a true Muslim he resigned himself to the decree of Allah.

He satisfactorily explained all the allegations that were levelled against him. During the twelve years of his caliphate he did not charge anything for his emoluments from the public treasury. He spent large amounts from his own resources for public benefit. He was the richest man in Arabia at the time of becoming the caliph; after becoming the caliph his assets steadily diminished. False and frivolous charges of nepotism were levelled against him, he was a good judge of men and matters and he appointed only such persons who enjoyed his confidence and who could be expected to carry forward his policies.

The revolt against Hadrat Othman was the result of some antinational conspiracy. Some extraneous forces pulled the wires. Jealous of the triumphs of Islam they conspired to subvert Islam from within. What is regrettable is that even some eminent companions played into the hands of these conspirators and lent them their indirect support.

The rioters besieged the house of Hadrat Othman. They stood at the door fully armed. They did not allow any food or water to enter the house. We were denied the use of water from the well which Hadrat Othman had purchased with his own money. The rebels accepted the lead of Ali, Muhammad b Abu Bakr, Talha and Zubair in all matters. Among the rioters were the tribes of Khuza'ah, Sa'ad b Bakr, Hudhail, Jahina and the Muzina. They also included contingents from Basra and Kufa. In the siege the rioters wounded Hadrat Othman with arrows. These persons killed some persons who wanted to fight against them in defence of the Caliph. The Caliph looked around him but he could see no person in Madinah from whom he could expect justice.

The rioters penetrated into the house. They burnt the gate, broke the windows and looted property. Muhammad b Abu Bakr pulled the beard of the Caliph. Then one of the rioters struck Hadrat Othman on the head and he fell down unconscious. The rioters wanted to cut off his head. I and Bint Shiba threw ourselves on the body of Hadrat Othman. They pulled us away and robbed us of our ornaments.

I am sending you along with this letter the blood stained clothes of the Caliph. Please see that his blood does not go unavenged. May Allah have mercy on the soul of Hadrat Othman! May the curse of Allah be on his murderers!"

CONSEQUENCES OF THE MARTYRDOM OF HADRAT OTHMAN

Ifs and Buts of History[1]

There are many ifs and buts in history. In the history of mankind we come across events which cast their shadow across the corridor of time and change the very course of history. The assassination of Hadrat Othman is one of such events in the annals of mankind which cast its fateful shadow on the coming events. The tragedy of the assassination of Hadrat Othman does not merely excite feelings of pathos and grief; it provides ample material to ponder and reflect. The assassination of Hadrat Othman was not merely the death of one man, it was as a matter of fact the assassination of values for which Islam stood. It was not merely the murder of a Caliph, it amounted to the assassination of the institution of the caliph itself. Again the assassination of Hadrat Othman was a tragedy which did not end with his death; it set the stage for other tragedies.

Chain Reaction of the Assassination of Hadrat Othman

Hadrat Othman was succeeded as Caliph by Hadrat Ali and Hadrat Ali was assassinated merely five years after his assumption of office as Caliph. If Hadrat Othman had not been assassinated there would have been no occasion for the battle of the Camel or the battle of Siffin. There could likewise be no occasion for the revolt of the Kharijis. And if there had been no revolt of the Kharijis, there would have been no assassination of Hadrat Ali. Over ten thousand persons were killed in the battle of the Camel. There was a large scale massacre of the Kharijis at the battle of Nahrawan. The battle of Siffin also claimed a heavy toll. In these battles something like twenty to thirty thousand Muslims were killed. All this valuable loss of Muslim life would not have occurred, if Hadrat Othman had not been assassinated. Thus those who assassinated Hadrat Othman

---

1. Ibid.

were not merely guilty of the murder of one old man; they were guilty of the massacre of the Muslims at large.

Object of the Revolt Against Hadrat Othman

The revolt against Hadrat Othman was prompted ostensibly because of the growing influence of the Umayyads. Surprisingly enough the revolt did not merely fail to achieve its object; it led to the result which was the very antithesis the purpose for which the revolt was undertaken. Within five years of the death of Hadrat Othman, power was captured by the Umayyads and they established a monarchical order which lasted for well-nigh a century. The assassination of Hadrat Othman instead of ousting the Umayyads from power paved the way for the consolidation of their power. The Umayyads established the monarchical order in order to avoid the conflict and bloodshed which were likely to engulf the Muslim community on the occasion of every new succession. The assassination of Hadrat Othman thus proved to be the assassination of the institution of the caliphate and that was a great disservice to the Muslim community.

The Tragedy of Karbala

In 680 C.E., the Muslim world shook to its foundations by the tragedy of Karbala. The tragedy of Karbala would not have taken place if Hadrat Othman had not been assassinated. If Hadrat Othman had not been assassinated and he had died a natural death, he was likely to be succeeded by Hadrat Ali. In that case there would have been no Ali-Muawiyah conflict for the conflict merely arose because of the demand for the vengeance for the blood of Hadrat Othman. In the absence of such a conflict, Hadrat Ali would not have been assassinated and the Umayyads would not have come into power. As such there would have been no occasion for the tragedy of Karbala.

The Tragedy of the Assassination of Hadrat Othman and the Tragedy of Karbala

If the events leading to the tragedy of the assassination of Hadrat Othman and the events culminating in the tragedy of Karbala are studied dispassionately we find much therein which provides food for thought and reflection. The revolts in both the cases were anti-Umayyad in character. In the revolt against Hadrat Othman, the main point of the agitation against him was that he had appointed the

Umayyads to high offices. In the case of the Karbala tragedy the stand of Imam Hussain was that the Umayyads had converted the caliphate into hereditary monarchy and that Yazid in view of his notorious character was not fit to be the Caliph.

In the case of Hadrat Othman the authority vested in him and the rioters demanded his deposition. Hadrat Othman refused to abdicate because he held that he could not resign from an office which he held on behalf of Allah on account of any pressure from the public. He gave his life but did not agree to abdicate. According to his way of thinking that was the only way to resolve the deadlock. Thus he preferred the cause of Islam to his life and he died as a martyr. In this case the truth and justice were on the side of Hadrat Othman, while the rioters had no just cause to agitate.

Hadrat Hussain stood for the integrity of the caliphate. His objection was against the transformation of the caliphate into royalty. There was also much force in his objection against the character of Yazid. In this case truth and justice were on the side of Hadrat Hussain. Both Hadrat Othman and Hadrat Hussain defended the cause of truth and justice and both have high rank as the martyrs of Islam.

Consequences of the Tragedies

The consequences of both the tragedies were fatal but the consequences of the tragedy of the assassination of Hadrat Othman were more grimful. The tragedy of Karbala did not have much of political repurcussions. The Umayyads instead of being dislodged came to be further entrenched in power. The Alids did not succeed in their bid to capture power. Even when the Umayyads were overthrown in 750 C.E., power was captured by the Abbasids and not the Alids. The tragedy of Karbala thus did not have any repurcussions on Islamic polity. The tragedy of the assassination of Hadrat Othman had, on the other hand, immense repurcussions on the Islamic polity. With the assassination of Hadrat Othman the process of the expansion of Islam came to a grinding halt. Hadrat Othman was assassinated when the Muslims were poised for further advance against the Christian powers in Asia Minor and Europe. But for the assassination of Hadrat Othman, the Muslims would not have been involved in civil war and the resources that were wasted on civil war could have been used with advantage in winning further conquests against non-Muslims.

It is strange that the memory of the tragedy of Karbala is kept alive by Moharrum celebrations every year but the memory of the tragedy of the assassination of Hadrat Othman is not kept alive in the way it should have been kept commensurate to the historical importance of the event.

WHAT THE COMPANIONS SAID ABOUT THE ASSASSINATION OF HADRAT OTHMAN

Hadrat Ali[1]

When Hadrat Ali came to know of the assassination of Hadrat Othman, he raised his hands to the heavens and said repeatedly: "By Allah, I never wished for his murder, nor did I abet his murder. O Allah be my witness that I am not to be blamed for this catastrophe. Those who have done the heinous deed have done a great disservice to Islam".

Ibn Abbas[2]

Ibn Abbas is reported to have said that the assassination of Hadrat Othman was the work of some misguided persons. The Muslims could not agree to the murder of their Caliph. Ibn Abbas added that if the Muslims had agreed to the murder of Hadrat Othman, the Muslims would have been stoned to death by the heavens as had been done in the case of the people of Lut.

Hadrat Ayesha[3]

Hadrat Ayesha said that the way in which Hadrat Othman had stood the siege and met his death was comparable to the cleansing of a utensil or the washing of a soiled cloth. By his steadfastness, determination and faith, Hadrat Othman had purified himself and his reward lay with Allah.

Abdullah b Hakim[4]

Abdullah b Hakim was critical of the people of Madinah in whose midst their Caliph had been murdered in cold blood. He held that even those persons who criticised Hadrat Othman unjustly were guilty of abetting his murder.

1. Ibid.
2. Ibid.
3. Ibid.
4. Ibid.

Hadrat Hudhaifa[1]

Hadrat Hudhaifa was very bitter that with the assassination of Hadrat Othman, a great fissure had occurred in the ranks of the Muslims and this gap was too wide to be filled even by a mountain.

Samama b Adi[2]

When Samama b Adi who was the Governor of Yemen heard of the assassination of Hadrat Othman he wept bitterly and said that with the assassination of Hadrat Othman all was over with the caliphate and the caliphate would give place to hereditary monarchy.

Abu Hamid Al Saadi Ansari[3]

Abu Hamid Al Saadi Ansari, a companion of the Holy Prophet and who had fought at the battle of Badr, mourned the death of Hadrat Othman. He said that those who had murdered their Caliph had violated the right to be called as Muslims. He took the oath that after the death of Hadrat Othman he would never laugh and would continue to mourn his death. He fulfilled this oath and never laughed again in life.

Abu Huraria[4]

Abu Huraria condemned the assassination of Hadrat Othman in very strong terms. He said that it was a great tragedy for the Muslim community. He would often beat his breast and lament at the death of Hadrat Othman. He said that those who had killed Hadrat Othman would have their punishment with the Lord.

Abdullah b Salam[5]

Abdullah b Salam said that those who had shed the blood of Hadrat Othman were guilty of revolt against Allah. He said that when a Prophet is killed unjustly, 70,000 persons are killed in sequel and when a Caliph is killed unjustly, 35,000 persons are apt to suffer death in sequel. He added that after Hadrat Othman there would be great bloodshed among the Muslims and the toll of death may be as heavy as 35,000.

---

1. Ibid.
2. Ibid.
3. Ibid.
4. Ibid.
5. Ibid.

Abi Qalaba[1]

Abi Qalaba said that those who had assassinated Hadrat Othman were guilty of a great crime. He added that he had seen in a dream that on the Judgement Day, Hadrat Othman would sit as a Judge to try his murderers for their crime.

Hudhaifa b Alyaman[2]

Hudhaifa b Alyaman said that there could be no element of good in the assassination of Hadrat Othman. It was an evil act fraught with evil consequences for the Muslim community.

Samurah[3]

Samurah said:

"Verily Islam was in a strong fortress and they have made in Islam a breach by their slaying of Othman, which will not be closed till the day of resurrection. Verily the caliphate was with the people of Madinah but they have cast it forth and it shall not return to them."

Muhammad b Sirin[4]

Muhammad b Sirin held that the piebald horses on which the angels fought for the Muslims were never missing until Othman was slain and never were there variations in the appearance of the new moons until Othman was slain.

HADRAT ALI B ABU TALIB

Early Life

Hadrat Ali was the son of Abu Talib, the uncle of the Holy Prophet. Hadrat Ali was younger than the Holy Prophet by some thirty years. The Holy Prophet brought up Hadrat Ali as a son. When the Holy Prophet left Makkah for Madinah, Hadrat Ali slept on the bed of the Holy Prophet to give the Quraish the impression that the Holy Prophet was still there. Hadrat Ali fought in all the battles of Islam. He was a prodigy of valour. He was the victor of the Khyber. The Holy Prophet married his daughter Hadrat Fatima to Hadrat Ali. The Holy

---

1. Ibid.
2. *History of the Caliphs*: Suyuti.
3. Ibid.
4. Ibid.

Prophet was much attached to Hadrat Hasan and Hadrat Hussain, the sons of Hadrat Ali from Hadrat Fatima.

Hadrat Ali and the Caliphate Issue

The Holy Prophet did not nominated a successor. On the death of the Holy Prophet, Hadrat Abu Bakr was elected as the Caliph. According to some accounts it appears that Hadrat Ali did not offer allegiance to Hadrat Abu Bakr and that he offered such allegiance after six months when Hadrat Fatima had died. According to other accounts, Hadrat Ali offered allegiance to Hadrat Abu Bakr soon after his election.

After Hadrat Abu Bakr, Hadrat Umar became the Caliph. During the caliphate of Hadrat Umar, Hadrat Ali was a member of the Majlis-i-Shura and he fully cooperated with Hadrat Umar.

Hadrat Ali and Hadrat Othman

On the death of Hadrat Umar, there was again a crisis in the matter of the election of the Caliph. In the matter of the election of Caliph there was a tie between Hadrat Ali and Hadrat Othman. Abdur Rahman b Auf who was virtually acting as the chairman of the Board of Electors gave his verdict in favour of Hadrat Othman and Hadrat Othman accordingly became the Caliph. Hadrat Ali did not feel happy at being passed over. Hadrat Ali continued to be a member of Majlis-i-Shura but it appears the Majlis-i-Shura was not very active in the time of Hadrat Othman. During his caliphate Hadrat Othman had to depend on advice from other sources as well.

From the accounts that have come down to us, it appears that Hadrat Ali played no conspicuous role in the early years of the caliphate of Hadrat Othman. During the early years of his caliphate, Hadrat Othman enjoyed considerable popularity with the people and Hadrat Ali had practically no part to play. In the later part of the caliphate of Hadrat Othman, when agitation began against Hadrat Othman, Hadrat Ali came into the picture.

Unfortunately the accounts which have come down to us in this respect are coloured and prompted by partisan interests. Hadrat Ali played the role of a mediator but it is not clear what exactly was the nature of the part that Hadrat Ali played. According to the most common account it appears that Hadrat Ali arrived at some terms with the rioters, which Hadrat Othman undertook to fulfil but Hadrat

Othman went back on such undertaking. Thereupon Hadrat Ali is reported to have parted company with Hadrat Othman for his breach of faith. These accounts are obviously the work of such persons who somehow or the other justify the assassination of Hadrat Othman. According to my research, there was no understanding between the rioters and Hadrat Ali. Hadrat Othman gave no undertaking and as such there was no breach of faith on the part of Hadrat Othman.

Hadrat Ali commanded respect with the rioters but it is not correct that they were under his command or they obeyed him in all matters. Hadrat Ali posted his sons Hadrat Hasan and Hadrat Hussain to stand guard at the house of Hadrat Othman. That shows that there was no straining of relationship between Hadrat Ali and Hadrat Othman because of an alleged breach of faith on the part of Hadrat Othman. As a matter of fact it was when Hadrat Hasan was wounded in the defence of Hadrat Othman that the rioters decided to hurry up with the murder of Hadrat Othman, lest the Hashimites might come to fight to help the cause of Hadrat Hasan. It appears that Hadrat Ali had no control over the rioters. What happens in such cases of mob revolt when scenes of perfect rowdyism prevailed and this was something beyond the control of Hadrat Ali. Both Hadrat Ali and Hadrat Othman were great souls. They were most eminent Muslims and may Allah bless their souls. It is unfortunate that some writers, because of partisan considerations, have tried to create the impression that there were strained relations between Hadrat Ali and Hadrat Othman and they worked in opposite camps. That is far from the truth. There was no love lost between Hadrat Othman and Hadrat Ali but unfortunately things got out of control and neither Hadrat Othman nor Hadrat Ali could avert the crisis. It may be recalled that Hadrat Ali had no political power; he could exercise moral pressure only and in a crisis when a mob is a victim of rowdyism, moral pressure cannot go a long way in making the people see the light of reason.

My analysis of the situation is that in this crisis, Hadrat Ali did not play any active role. His role was of peripheral character. The version that Hadrat Ali commanded any influence with the rioters is not correct. The rioters were in no mood to follow reason and as such they could not be under the influence of a man like Hadrat Ali.

7

ASSESSMENT

DISTINCTIONS OF HADRAT OTHMAN[1]

Hadrat Othman was a man of many distinctions. He had the honour of being the first and foremost in many things.

Unique Distinction

Hadrat Othman had the unique distinction of having married two daughters of the Holy Prophet, one after the other. On account of this honour he came to be known as "Dhun Nurain"—the possessor of two luminaries.

The First Umayyads

Hadrat Othman was the first among the Umayyads to become a Muslim. The Umayyads and the Hashimites were rival sections of the Quraish. Hadrat Othman was the first to rise above such rivalry by offering allegiance to the Holy Prophet who was a Hashimite.

Tidings of Paradise

The Holy Prophet gave the tidings of paradise to ten persons in their lifetime. Hadrat Othman was one of these ten persons called *Ashra Mubashshara*. Over and above this, Hadrat Othman was given the tidings of paradise on three other occasions; when he purchased the "Beer Rauma" well and dedicated it to the use of the Muslims; when he financed the project for the extension of the Prophet's mosque at Madinah and when he made a liberal contribution for the financing of the expedition to Tabuk.

Resemblance to Abraham and the Holy Prophet

The Holy Prophet declared on several occasions that among the Muslims, Hadrat Othman resembled Abraham and the Holy Prophet himself most.

Embellishment of Mosques and the Holy Ka'aba

Hadrat Othman was the first Caliph to extend and embellish the Prophet's mosque at Madinah and the Holy Ka'aba at Makkah.

Khyber Campaign

In the Khyber campaign, Hadrat Othman was the first to climb the castle of the Jews.

Baiyat-ur-Ridwan

On the occasion of the Hudaibiya campaign, the Holy Prophet chose Hadrat Othman as his emissary to the Quraish. On the occasion of Baiyat-ur-Ridwan, the Holy Prophet took the pledge on behalf of Hadrat Othman and this was a unique honour not shared by anyone else.

Uniform Text of the Holy Qur'ãn

Hadrat Othman had the unique distinction of uniting the Muslim community on a uniform dialect of the Holy Qur'ãn.

The First to Learn the Holy Qur'ãn By Heart

He was the first person among the Muslims to learn the Holy Qur'ãn by heart.

The First to Divorce Non-Muslim Wives

He was the first person among the Muslims to divorce his wives who did not accept Islam.

The First to Migrate

Hadrat Othman was the first person among the Muslims to migrate in the way of Allah.

The First to Command the First Call to Prayer

Hadrat Othman was the first to command the first call to prayer.

Pronouncement of the Takbir

Hadrat Othman was the first to lower his voice in pronouncing the Takbir.

Eid Prayer

Hadrat Othman was the first who made the discourse precede the Eid prayer.

Lifetime of His Mother

Hadrat Othman was the first person among the Muslims to become the Caliph during the lifetime of his mother.

Meals During the Ramadhan

Hadrat Othman was the first Caliph who provided meals for all persons during the month of fasting.

Stipends for the Muadhdhins

Hadrat Othman was the first Caliph who allowed stipends for the Muadhdhins.

Ban on the Flying of Pigeons

Hadrat Othman was the first Caliph to impose a ban on the flying of pigeons in the matters of wagers.

Naval Action

Hadrat Othman was the first Caliph under whom the Muslims constructed fleets and undertook naval warfare.

Occupation of Persia

It was under Hadrat Othman that the Sassanian empire was finally overthrown and the whole of Persia was occupied by the Muslims.

Longest Rule

Among the rightly guided Caliphs, Hadrat Othman was the longest lived and his rule was the longest.

The Richest Caliph

Among the rightly guided Caliphs, Hadrat Othman was the richest.

Purchase of Land in Conquered Territories

Hadrat Othman was the first Caliph to permit the purchase of land by the Arabs in conquered territories.

Enclosing of Pastures

Hadrat Othman was the first Caliph to order to enclosing of state pastures.

Liberation of Slaves

Hadrat Othman liberated the largest number of slaves. It is recorded that he used to liberate a slave every week.

The First Caliph to be Assassinated

Hadrat Othman was the first Caliph to be assassinated by the Muslims.

Immunity from Judgement[1]

Hadrat Othman was the only person about whom the Holy Prophet granted general immunity with regard to future judgement. On the occasion of the expedition to Tabuk the Holy Prophet declared that Hadrat Othman was not to be judged for any acts that he did thereafter.

HADRAT OTHMAN AND TRADITIONS

Traditions Reported by Hadrat Othman

Hadrat Othman was very close to the Holy Prophet. Hadrat Othman reported about 150 traditions of the Holy Prophet. Hereunder we refer to some of the traditions reported by Hadrat Othman.

Entry to Paradise[2]

Hadrat Othman reported that Allah's Messenger said, "Whoever dies knowing that there is no God but Allah will enter Paradise".

Grave as the First Stage of the Next World[3]

Hadrat Othman reported that Allah's Messenger said that the grave is the first stage of the next world. If one escapes from it, what follows is easier than it but if one does not escape from it, what follows is more severe than it. The Holy Prophet also said: "I have never seen a sight as horrible as the grave."

Performance of the Ablutions[4]

Hadrat Othman reported Allah's Messenger having said: "If

---

1. The distinctions of Hadrat Othman given in this section are an enlargement of the distinctions of Hadrat Othman contained in Suyuti's "*History of the Caliphate*".
2. Sahih Muslim.
3. Sahih Tirmidhi.
4. Sahih Bukhari and Muslim.

anyone performs the ablutions well, his sins will come out of his body and even from his nails."

Details about the Ablutions[1]

Hadrat Othman reported that the Holy Prophet performed each detail of the ablutions three times and said: "This is how I perform the ablutions. This is how the prophets before me performed it and how Abraham performed it."

Performance of Prayers in Company[2]

Hadrat Othman reported that Allah's Messenger said: "If anyone performs the evening prayer in company, it is as if he had remained awake in prayer half the night but if anyone prays the morning prayer in company, it is as if he had prayed the whole night."

Building a Mosque[3]

Hadrat Othman reported that Allah's Messenger said: "If anyone builds a mosque for Allah, Allah will build a house for him in the paradise."

Who is a Hypocrite[4]

Hadrat Othman reported that Allah's Messenger said: "If the Adhan is called when anyone is in the mosque and he goes out for any other reason than some necessary purpose, not intending to return he is a hypocrite.

The Best Among the Muslims[5]

Hadrat Othman reported that the Holy Prophet said: "The best among the Muslims is one who learns and teaches the Qur'ān."

Recitation of the Surah Aal Imran[9]

Hadrat Othman reported that the Holy Prophet said: "If anyone recites the Surah *Aal Imran* at night the reward of a night spent in prayers is recorded in his favour."

---

1. Sahih Muslim.
2. Sahih Bukhari and Muslim.
3. Ibid.
4. Ibn Majah.
5. Sahih Bukhari.
6. Ibid.

Marriage on the Occasion of the Pilgrimage[1]

Hadrat Othman reported that the Messenger of Allah said: "One who is on pilgrimage may not marry or give someone in marriage or make a betrothal."

Purchase of Neighbour's Property[1]

Hadrat Othman reported that the Messenger of Allah said: "When boundaries have been set up in land, there is no option to buy the neighbour's property. The option does not apply to wells and male palm trees."

A Day on the Frontier[3]

Hadrat Othman reported that the Messenger of Allah said: "A day on the frontier in Allah's path is better than a thousand days in any other place."

Rights of Men[4]

Hadrat Othman reported that the Messenger of Allah said: "The son of Adam has a right only in a house in which he lives, in a garment with which to conceal his private parts, fry bread and water."

Inner Nature[5]

Hadrat Othman reported that the Holy Prophet said: "If anyone has a good or evil inner nature, Allah will make apparent some sign of it by which such nature can be recognised."

Groups Authorised to Make Intercession[6]

Hadrat Othman reported that the Holy Prophet said: "Three groups will make intercession on the day of resurrection; the prophets, next the learned and next the martyrs."

Treachery to the Arabs[7]

Hadrat Othman reported that the Holy Prophet said: "He who is treacherous to the Arabs will not be included in my intercession and will not receive my love."

---

1. Sahih Muslim.
2. Ibid.
3. Sahih Tirmidhi.
4. Sahih Muslim.
5. Sahih Bukhari.
6. Ibn Majah.
7. Sahih Tirmidhi.

WHAT THE HOLY PROPHET SAID ABOUT HADRAT OTHMAN

Traditions about Hadrat Othman

Hadrat Othman was very close to the Holy Prophet. In some of the traditions there are references to Hadrat Othman. These traditions show the affection and regard that the Holy Prophet had for Hadrat Othman. These accounts afford glimpses of the character and personality of Hadrat Othman.

Modesty of Hadrat Othman

In the traditions it is stated on the authority of Hadrat Ayesha that one day the Holy Prophet was reclining in her chamber in an informal mood, Hadrat Abu Bakr and then Hadrat Umar came to see the Holy Prophet and he saw them while reclining in the informal mood. Then Hadrat Othman sought permission to see the Holy Prophet. Before permitting Hadrat Othman to enter the chamber the Holy Prophet gathered his clothes and sat in a formal mood. After the visitors had left, Hadrat Ayesha asked the Holy Prophet as to why he was formal about Hadrat Othman, while he was not so in the case of Hadrat Abu Bakr and Hadrat Umar. The Holy Prophet said: "Othman is very modest and shy and if I had been informal with him, he would not have said that he had wanted to say."

On another occasion the Holy Prophet said: "Why should I not be bashful before whom even the angels stand abashed."

According to another tradition recorded on the authority of Ibn Umar, the Holy Prophet said: "Verily, the angels stand abashed before Othman as they stand abashed before Allah and His Prophet."

Resemblance of Hadrat Othman with the Holy Prophet and Abraham

Ibn Asakir records on the authority of Abu Huraira that the Holy Prophet said: "Othman among the companions resembles me most in disposition."

In the traditions, it is recorded on the authority of Hadrat Umm Kulsum that when she was married to Hadrat Othman, the Holy Prophet said to her: "Verily, your husband resembles most among your forefather Abraham and your father Muhammad".

Ibn Asakir has recorded on the authority of Ibn Umar that the Holy Prophet said, I find a resemblance in Othman to my forefather Abraham".

Hadrat Othman as the Holy Prophet's Son-in-law

At Tabarani records on the authority of Asma b Malik that when Hadrat Umm Kulsum died, the Holy Prophet advised the Muslims: "Give your daughters in marriage to Othman. If I had a third daughter I would assuredly give her in marriage to him and I have never wedded any to him save under inspiration".

Ibn Asakir records on the authority of Hadrat Ali that the Holy Prophet said: "If I had forty daughters, I would wed them with Othman one after the other until not one of them is left".

Baiyat ur Ridwan[1]

On the occasion of Baiyat ur Ridwan when the Holy Prophet took the oath of allegiance on behalf of Hadrat Othman, he said: "Verily, Othman is employed in the requirements of Allah and the needs of the Apostle. May Allah bless him".

Troubles Ahead for Othman[2]

It is recorded on the authority of Zaid b Thabit that he heard the Apostle of Allah say that Othman passed him and there was with him one of the angels who said: "He shall be a martyr; his people will slay him. I am abashed before him".

Al Tirmidhi records on the authority of Murrah b Ka'ab that he said: "I heard the Apostle of Allah speaking of the troubles that he thought to be near at hand when a man passed by muffled in his garments and he said, 'This man today is in the path of salvation." Murrah adds that he went to the man and he was Othman.

It is recorded on the authority of Anas that the Holy Prophet said: "Verily the Lord has a sword sheathed in a scabbard as long as Othman lives and when Othman is slain that sword shall be drawn and it will not be sheathed until the day of resurrection".

Al Tirmidhi records on the authority of Hadrat Ayesha that the Holy Prophet said to Hadrat Othman: "O Othman perchance the Lord may clothe you with a garment and if the hypocrites desire to take it away from you, do not put it off till you meet me in paradise".

---

1. *History of the Caliphate*: Suyuti.
2. Ibid.

WHAT HADRAT OTHMAN SAID

Speeches of Hadrat Othman

As Caliph Hadrat Othman had to deliver frequent addresses. No record of such addresses has been preserved. Only some stray remarks of Hadrat Othman here and there have come down to us. It appears that Hadrat Othman was a man of few words but whenever he spoke his words were surcharged with wisdom. Hereunder we present some of the sayings of Hadrat Othman by way of sample.

Useless Things

Hadrat Othman said that four things were useless and these were:

(1) Knowledge without practice,
(2) Wealth without expenditure in the way of Allah,
(3) Piety for the sake of show prompted by worldliness and
(4) Long life with no stock of good deeds.

The Things He Loved

Hadrat Othman said that he loved three things, namely:

(1) To feed the hungry,
(2) To clothe the naked and
(3) To read and teach the Holy Qur'ān.

Fear Allah

In his addresses, Hadrat Othman tried to inculcate in the people the fear of Allah. He said, "Fear Allah, for to Him you are to be gathered".

Quarrels and Disputes

He always advised the Muslims to avoid quarrels and disputes and maintain unity in their ranks. He said, "Do not quarrel and do not create differences among yourselves. Hold fast to the rope of Allah and maintain unity in your ranks".

Spiritual and Terrestrial Worlds

He distinguished between the spiritual and the terrestrial worlds in the following terms:

"The thought of the spiritual world sheds light on the soul but the thought of the terrestrial world casts darkness thereon".

Patience

Hadrat Othman highlighted the virtues of patience in the following terms:

"Under all circumstances, a person should be patient, otherwise disgrace would be his lot".

Habits to be Acquired

Hadrat Othman exhorted the people to acquire two habits, namely:

(1) The habit to speak the truth and
(2) The habit to do good deeds.

Hadrat Othman's Concept of History

Hadrat Othman conceived history as a means of acquiring wisdom. He said: "Acquire wisdom from the story of the dead".

Pride

Hadrat Othman condemned pride in the following terms:

"The world is proud. Leave it alone lest it entraps by its guises and teaches you pride which will keep you away from Allah".

Essential Things

Hadrat Othman held the following four things as essential, viz:

(1) To associate with the worthy is laudable but to follow them is essential.
(2) To read the Holy Qur'ãn is virtue but to act according to its injunctions is essential.
(3) To visit the sick is meritorious but to cause them to make their behests is essential,
(4) To visit the shrines of holy men is piety but to be prepared for death is essential.

His Surprise at the Conduct of Persons

Hadrat Othman said that he was surprised at the conduct of a Person:

(1) Who knows the world to be transient, yet loves it,
(2) Who knows death to be certain, yet does not take it seriously,
(3) Who believes in hell, yet commits sin,

(4) Who believes in the existence of Allah, yet seeks assistance from others,
(5) Who is aware of paradise, yet is engaged in worldly pleasures,
(6) Who knows Satan to be his enemy, yet obeys its dictates,
(7) Who believes in predestination, yet feels aggrieved with what happens and
(8) Who knows that account is to be rendered on the day of resurrection, yet hoards wealth.

Unity and Faith

Hadrat Othman said:

(1) When the Muslims are disunited they would falter in their faith and would be bereft of their inherent strength
(2) O people, if I give you all the world, that would not suffice as the price for your faith.
(3) You will not be conscious of the reality of faith till love for Allah is held dearer than the passion to acquire wealth.
(4) The highest degree in faith is that you always regard yourself in the presence of Allah.

Fears for a Man of Piety

A man of faith and piety is always subject to the following fears:

(1) The fear of Allah, lest by any disobedience there is any faltering in faith,
(2) The fear of the angels lest they may record anything against you which may be a cause of remorse for you on the day of resurrection,
(3) The fear of the Satan lest he may tempt you to any evil,
(4) The fear of the angel of death, lest your life is taken before you have sought pardon for your sins,
(5) The fear of the world, lest by its temptation it make you oblivious of the next world and
(6) The fear of the family members lest by your attachment to them you become oblivious to your duty to Allah.

Happiness and Grief

Hadrat Othman said, "One should not feel happy at the acquisition of wealth, nor should be feel grieved at its loss".

Delicious Food

Hadrat Othman said, "He who is fond of delicious food, let him bear in mind that ultimately he is to be food for worms"

Justice

Hadrat Othman laid down the criteria for justice in the following terms: "The dictates of justice demand that a proper equation should be maintained between the rights and obligations of the people. Whatever is their right should be conceded to them and steps should be taken to ensure that whatever is their obligation is duly fulfilled".

Backbiting

Hadrat Othman condemned backbiting in the following terms:

"A backbiter harms three persons, firstly himself, secondly the person whom he is addressing and thirdly the person whom he is backbiting".

Heedlessness

Hadrat Othman said:

"O people, do not be heedless of your obligations for Allah is ever heedless. If you are heedless of your obligations, Allah is aware of what you do. He is ever watchful".

Drinking

About drinking, Hadrat Othman said: "Drinking is at the roots of all evils".

Good Deeds and Death

Exhorting the Muslims to good deeds, Hadrat Othman said: "See that during your lifetime you amass a number of good deeds, for after death it would not be possible for you to do any deed".

Guidance from the Holy Qur'ãn

Hadrat Othman said, "He who makes the Book of Allah as his guide would remain safe from sin and he would be counted among the best of men".

Cause of Contempt

Hadrat Othman said, "No one is to be held in contempt on account of poverty. Only he is to be held in contempt who is oblivious of his religious duties".

Rights of the People

Hadrat Othman said: "Allah has created the people to establish the truth and do the right. Allah accepts only what is true and right. Therefore give to the people what is their right and is due to them and see that they perform whatever are their obligations to Islam".

Tyranny

Hadrat Othman said: "See that there is no tyranny against the people particularly the poor and the orphans. If they are aggrieved, bear in mind that Allah Himself would take up their cause".

Distress

Hadrat Othman said: "In the event of distress, a man depends solely on his own plans and relies on the people. When he is disappointed from all sides, then alone he turns to Allah".

Testing People

Hadrat Othman said: "On testing people, I have found some of them more poisonous than poisonous animals".

Anger

Hadrat Othman said: "Silence is the best cure of the malady of anger".

Extravagance

Hadrat Othman said: "Extravagance amounts to thanklessness to Allah for His gifts".

Knowledge

Hadrat Othman said: "That knowledge is of no avail which is not put into practice. There can be no practice without knowledge and any knowledge without putting it to practice is useless. That knowledge is blameworthy which is used solely to acquire wealth".

The Lord

Hadrat Othman said: "It is painful to realise that while an animal recognises its master, human beings do not recognise their Lord".

Distress or Difficulty

Hadrat Othman said: "He who is not put to any distress or difficulty for an year at a stretch let him realise that Allah is displeased with him."

Obedience

Hadrat Othman said: "Obedience to Allah is that one should remain within bounds fixed by Allah, promises made should be fulfilled, one should be satisfied with what he has and should be patient in respect of what he does not have".[1]

HADRAT OTHMAN AND SUFISM

Hadrat Othman as a Sufi

The Sufis regard Hadrat Othman as one of themselves. In his book *Kashful Mahjub*, Hadrat Data Ganj Bakhsh refers to Hadrat Othman as one of the prominent Sufis. The attributes of Sufism which were very conspicuous in Hadrat Othman were his modesty, his piety, his humility, his charity and his resignation.

Hadrat Othman's Modesty

It is recorded in the traditions on the authority of Ibn Umar that the Holy Prophet said that the angels stood abashed before Othman as they stood abashed before Allah and His Apostle. It is recorded on the authority of Hadrat Hasan that about the modesty of Hadrat Othman the Holy Prophet said: "If it were that Othman was in the middle of his house and the door was closed upon him and he were to put aside his clothes to pour water upon himself, modesty would prevent him to straighten his back".

Hadrat Othman's Piety

Hadrat Othman was most virtuous and pious. He spent a greater part of the night in prayers. He would recite the whole of the Qur'ãn during one night.

Hadrat Othman's Humility

Hadrat Data Ganj Bakhsh observes in his book *Kashful Mahjub* that Hadrat Othman possessed four hundred slaves but one day he was found coming forth from his plantation of date-palms carrying a bundle of firewood on his head. He was asked why he was carrying the bundle himself and why he had not allowed any of his slaves to carry the burden, he said that by carrying the load himself he was making a trial of himself.[2]

1. This section is based on "*Hadrat Othman Ne Farmaya*" by Abdul Jalil Quraishi.
2. This section is based on "*Kashful Mahjub*", of Hadrat Data Gunj Bakhsh.

It is also related that during nights he would not disturb any of his servants to help him in making the ablutions or attending to other needs. When asked the reason for that he said that the night was meant for their repose.

Hadrat Othman's Charity

Hadrat Othman spent liberally in the way of Allah. He purchased the Beer Rauma well from a Jew and dedicated it to public use. He financed the project for the extension of the Prophet's mosque. He met a greater part of the expenses for the financing of the expedition to Tabuk. In the event of a famine the traders in Madinah offered to purchase his stock of foodgrains after allowing him considerable profit. He distributed the entire stock among the people free and declared that thereby he would earn a ten times profit from Allah, which no merchant could offer him.

Resignation of Hadrat Othman

It is related by Abdullah b Rabah and Abu Qatada that they were with Hadrat Othman on the day when his house was attacked. His slaves seeing the crowd of rebels gathered at the door took up arms. Hadrat Othman said to them, "Whoever of you does not take up arms is a free man". Hadrat Othman thus forbade his slaves to take up arms on his behalf.

It is also related that Imam Hasan came to Hadrat Othman and wanted his permission to draw sword against the rebels. Hadrat Othman said to him, "O my cousin go back to your house and sit there until Allah brings His decree to pass. I do not wish to shed blood".

Hadrat Data Ganj Bakhsh observes in his book *Kashful Mahjub* that these words betoken resignation and show that Hadrat Othman had attained the rank of a friend of Allah. The Sufis take Hadrat Othman as their exemplar in sacrificing life and in resigning his affairs to Allah in sincere devotion.

POLITICS IN THE TIME OF HADRAT OTHMAN

The Holy Prophet

In the time of the Holy Prophet there was hardly any politics among the Muslims. Whatever the Holy Prophet commanded was obeyed by the Muslims faithfully and there was no occasion for any dissension among the Muslims. In the early days there was some opposition from the Jews and the hypocrites. With the expulsion of the Jews from Madinah and the death of the leader of the hypocrites even this opposition ceased.

Hadrat Abu Bakr

On the death of the Holy Prophet, politics erupted among the Muslims with the demand of the Ansar for the election of the Caliph from among them. The viewpoint of the Quraish was that the Caliph should be chosen from among the Quraish, the tribe to which the Holy Prophet belonged. Wiser counsels prevailed and the Ansar agreed to the election of the Caliph from among the Quraish. Hadrat Abu Bakr was accordingly elected as the Caliph and the Ansars offered their allegiance to him. Soon after the election of Hadrat Abu Bakr, politics took the form of the demand for the non-payment of *Zakat* by the tribes. Hadrat Abu Bakr did not accept the demand and all opposition was suppressed as a result of the apostasy campaigns.

Hadrat Umar

Hadrat Umar suppressed all political activity. He took measures to ensure that political power was not concentrated in any particular group. Although he himself was a Quraish he imposed restrictions on the activities of the Quraish. He did not allow the Arabs to acquire lands in the conquered territories. He imposed restrictions on the movements of the companions and did not allow them to leave Madinah. He even did dot permit them to participated in the wars. He declared that whatever eminence the companions had achieved during lifetime of the Holy Prophet was quite enough for them and it was necessary that henceforward they should lead a retired life; neither the world should see them, nor they should see the world. He deposed most of the Governors not because of any lapse on their part but because he did not want them to become more powerful. He deposed Khalid b Walid from the supreme command of the Muslim army, lest the people should have an impression that all the victories were because of the genius of Khalid b Walid. Hadrat Umar was not only harsh with other people; he was harsh even with himself and his family members. As such even when the people felt bitter at the harshness of Hadrat Umar they could not dare complain. Consequently political activity remained suppressed.

Political Policies of Hadrat Othman

Hadrat Othman was temperamentally democrat, kind liberal and generous. He could not, therefore, maintain the autocratic policies followed by Hadrat Umar. Hadrat Othman relaxed most of the restrictions that had been imposed on the people by Hadrat Umar. He allowed the companions to leave Madinah at their discretion. He allowed the Arabs to acquire lands in conquered territories. Hadrat Othman removed the restrictions on trade. Consequently the Quraish amassed considerable fortune. With such fortune the Quraish acquired large estates in Iraq. That caused some discontentment among the Iraqis. Realising the importance of agricultural lands, the army raised the demand that the lands in the conquered territories should be distributed among them. Hadrat Othman deposed some Governors because of the requirements of the State. Profiting from the kinds nature of Hadrat Othman the deposed functionaries collected groups of people round them and they began to indulge in the criticism of Hadrat Othman. Availing of the freedoms that had been allowed under Hadrat Othman some movements were launched. e.g. the movement of Ibn Saba which aimed at the subversion of Islam from within.

Under Hadrat Othman, the people became economically more prosperous and on the political plane they came to enjoy a larger degree of freedom. No institutions were devised to channelise political activity and in the absence of such institutions, the pre-Islamic tribal jealousies and rivalries which had been suppressed under Islam erupted once again. The people ceased to see things from the higher Islamic point of view; they came to be prompted by personal and parochial considerations. Differences between the Quraish and the Ansar grew sharper. While the older generation among the Ansar preferred to remain quiet, the younger generation among the Ansar became restive and they felt dissatisfied at the dominance of the Quraish. Among the Quraish the differences between the Umayyads and the Hashimites became threatening in character. The Bedouin Arabs chafed at the centralisation of power at Madinah. With the extension in conquests, population grew and the non-Arabs joined the fold of Islam in large numbers. Differences grew between the Muslims and the non-Muslims, the Arabs and the non-Arabs. With the growth of population and economic prosperity cities grew. The unscrupulous elements made the cities the hotbeds of sedition and discontentment. Under Hadrat Othman Fustat, Kufa and Basra became the three principal centres form where revolt was led against Hadrat Othman.

In view of the democratic and liberal policies adopted by Hadrat Othman the liberties allowed to the people soon degenerated into licence and such licence became a headache for the State which culminated in the assassination of Hadrat Othman. Hadrat Othman fell a victim to the tyrannies of his people not because his rule was tyrannical or unjust but because in advance of his time, he aspired to be kind and liberal in an age suited for an autocratic rule alone. When the caliphate later gave place to a hereditary monarchical order that was a confession of the fact that in that age of autocracy the caliphate system based on the principles of democracy and liberalism could not prosper.

Nothing succeeds like success and nothing fails like failure. As the caliphate of Hadrat Othman ended with his assassination we are precluded from concluding that Hadrat Othman's policies were successful. The blame for the failure of such policies, however, does not lie on Hadrat Othman. He was a well meaning noble hearted Muslim and he acted in the best interests of Islam and the State. If in spite of his good intentions he failed as a ruler that was due to the fact that he was in advance of the times and was too democrat, too liberal and too virtuous.

HADRAT OTHMAN IN HISTORY[1]

Hadrat Othman and History

Hadrat Othman was the third Caliph of early Islam. Among the rightly guided Caliphs his rule was the longest. Extensive conquests were made during his period. History has, however, not done full justice to him. He has become a controversial figure in history and different historians have expressed different views about him.

Ameer Ali[2]

In his book *History of the Saracens*, Ameer Ali assesses Hadrat Othman in the following terms:

---

1. This section is based on my own assessment.
2. *History of the Saracens*: Ameer Ali.

"The election of Othman proved in the end to be the ruin of Islam. Othman though virtuous and honest was very old, feeble in character and quite unequal to the task of government. He fell under the influence of his family. He was guided entirely by his Secretary Marwan, one of the most unprincipled of the Umayyads. Othman displaced most of the lieutenants employed by Umar and appointed in their stead incompetent and worthless members of his own family. The weakness of the Caliph and the wickedness of his favourites created a great ferment among the people. Loud complaints of exaction and operation by his Governors began pouring into the capital. Ali expostulated several times with the Caliph on the manner in which he allowed the government to fall into the hands of his unworthy favourites. But Othman, under the influence of his evil genius Marwan, paid no heed to these counsels."

Philip K. Hitti[1]

In his book *History of the Arabs*, Philip K. Hitti observes as follows:

"Othman who committed the words of Allah to an unalterable form and whose reign saw the complete conquest of Iran, Azarbaijan and Armenia was a pious well meaning old man but too weak to resist the importunities of his greedy kinsfolk. His foster brother Abdullah, formerly the Prophet's amanuensis who had tampered with the words of the revelation and who was one of the ten proscribed by Muhammad at the capture of Makkah, was appointed Governor of Egypt. His half brother Walid b Uqbah who had spat in Muhammad's face and had been condemned by the latter, he made Governor of Kufa. His cousin Marwan b al Hakam, a future Umayyad Caliph, was put in charge of the Diwan. Many important offices were filled by the Umayyads, the Caliph's family.

Charges of nepotism became widespread. The feeling of discontentment aroused by his unpopular administration was fanned by the three Quraishite aspirants to the caliphate, Ali, Talha and Zubair."

---

1. *History of the Arabs*: Philip K.Hitti.

Prof. K. Ali[1]

In his book *A Study of Islamic History*, Prof. K. Ali observes:

"Othman was upright, dutiful and generous. In chastity and integrity, Othman was as firm as a mountain. Modesty was the salient feature of his character. The Prophet himself was so much pleased with him that he gave his two daughters in marriage to him. He was very rich but he contented himself with plain dress. His services in the recension of the Holy Qur'ãn were invaluable. He sacrificed his own life rather than wield the sword against the rebels. A man who sacrificed his life for the solidarity of Islam and the good of his subjects can easily be called a true patriot and a benign ruler".

S. A. Salik[2]

In his book *Early Heroes of Islam*, S. A. Salik observes as follows:

"Such was the tragic end of one of the most generous, pious, pure and heroic souls of early Islam. In spite of his opulence he led a simple life but with a magnificent liberality he spent his money in charity. He purchased the well named Beer Rauma and assigned it for the benefit of the public, subscribed liberally for the force which eventually took part in the battle of Tabuk, distributed to the needy a large quantity of grain in a period of famine at his own expense, acquired lands and extended the apostolic mosques of Madinah and Makkah and performed the duties of the caliphate without any remuneration. To his recension of the Qur'ãn we owe the present correct edition of the Book. On account of a verse in the Holy Qur'ãn he considered it a sacred duty to help his relatives. He put them in important public offices and gave them large sums of money out of the public treasury. Taking advantage of his kind and mild nature his unworthy relatives, several of whom were Governors of provinces, committed acts of high-handedness and injustice which caused discontent. Being faced by strong and even armed opposition he would at times consent to their dismissal, though not convinced of the necessity of the step. As soon as such opposition ceased he would withdraw his consent. He was,

1. *A Study of Islamic History*: K.Ali.
2. *Early Heroes of Islam*: G.A.Salik.

however, willing to punish those responsible for specific complaints though he declined to dismiss them wholesale or to deliver them to blind fury. With equal magnanimity he declined to employ force against the malcontents and cause unnecessary bloodshed among Muslims but with awful coolness, uncommon courage and exemplary self-sacrifice he laid down his own life to allay the fury of the rebels. But for his mildness which leaned to the virtue's side, he would have been an ideal ruler of men. As a private individual his character was simply adorable."

Jalaluddin Suyuti

In his book *History of the Caliphs*, Jalaluddin Suyuti observes:

"Othman ruled the caliphate twelve years. For six years, he governed the people without the people having anything to reproach against him and he was more beloved by the Quraish than Umar, for Umar was stern with them and when Othman ruled them, he treated them with leniency and was attached to them. But afterwards he became heedless of their affairs and appointed his kinsmen to high offices during the last six years and bestowed upon Marwan a fifth of the revenues of Africa and lavished on his kindred and family the property of the State and explained it as the assistance to kindred which the Lord had enjoined and said, "Verily Abu Bakr and Umar have neglected in that matter and I have taken it and divided it among my kindred but the people disapproved of it".

Mazharuddin Siddiqi[1]

In his book *Development of Islamic State and Society*, Mazharuddin Siddiqi observes:

"There were too many interests to be reconciled, the Ansar against the Muhajreen; the Hashimites against the Umayyads; the bedouin tribes against the aristocracy of Madinah. In a democratic set-up which did not provide for a regular constitutional machinery with well-defined rights and duties, everything depended on the personal quality of the ruler. Othman would have succeeded if he had been a dictator either temperamentally or constitutionally or if there had been an adequate constitutional machinery behind the social democracy of Islam. But it was

---

1. *Development of Islamic State and Society*. Mazharuddin Siddiqi.

clearly a dangerous solution to have democratic liberties such as the Arabs had without a strong hand like Umar or without a full fledged democratic constitution which was inconceivable in an age like that or in a country like Arabia."

Professor Muhammad Khizri Bek[1]

In his book *History of the Caliphs,* Professor Muhammad Khizri Bek has expressed the view that all the allegations that were levied against Hadrat Othman were frivolous and were with regard to matters which vested in the authority of Hadrat Othman and with regard to which he was competent to act in his discretion. The main charge against him was about the behalf. Islam authorised and those Holy Prophet made no restrictions in that behalf. Islam enjoined equality and Hadrat Othman was free to choose anyone from among his relatives for any appointment if he considered him fit for such appointment. Professor Khizri has expressed the view that in Shariah the demand for the deposition of the Caliph was not authorised and those who raised the demand betrayed Islam.

Raza Misri[2]

In his book *Othman b Affan*, Raza Misri observes that in the caliphate of Hadrat Othman there was great discontentment against Hadrat Othman on account of the appointment of his relatives. In the course of time the discontent multiplied. If Hadrat Othman had wished he could have made amends. What happened was that he would repent and would promise the deposition of his relatives but would do nothing to implement or fulfil his promise. If he wanted to favour his relatives there could have been other ways of doing so. They could have been appointed to less important posts for they were not at all capable of being appointed to higher posts. The times needed the appointment of men of calibre and good record to high office. Many companions of stainless character were available and if Othman had availed of their services history would have taken a different course.

Sir William Muir[3]

In his book *The Caliphate*, Sir William Muir has observed that the history of the period has been coloured by the jealousy and

1. *History of the Caliphs*: Muhammad Khizri Bek.
2. *Othman b Affan*: Raza Misri.
3. *The Caliphate*: Sir William Muir.

animosity between the Umayyads and the Abbasids. When the Abbasids came to power they tried to tarnish the history of the Umayyads. Sir William Muir observes that in these accounts, Marwan, the unpopular cousin of Othman, has received constant abuse as the author of Othman's troubles. Marwan is painted as the evil genius but all this is tinged by the Abbasid and anti-Umayyad prejudices. Sir William Muir holds that the story of large free gifts to Marwan which formed one of the grounds of impeachment against Hadrat Othman reads like a party calumny.

Assessment[1]

Unfortunately, history has not done proper justice to Hadrat Othman. Extensive conquests were made during the caliphate of Hadrat Othman. While sufficient details are available about the conquests made during the caliphate of Hadrat Abu Bakr and Hadrat Umar, no details are available about the conquests made during the caliphate of Hadrat Othman. A greater part of Spain was conquered during the time of Hadrat Othman but surprisingly no details are available in this behalf and even the names of the territories occupied by the Muslims are not known. It appears that most of the history books were written during the Abbasid period and the tendency with the pro-Abbasid writers was to suppress the achievements of the Umayyads and the history of the period of Hadrat Othman was mutilated because Othman was an Umayyad.

Shia writers have been very loud in their criticism of Hadrat Othman. Even a writer like Ameer Ali has condemned Hadrat Othman as an old man, feeble in character and quite unequal to the task of government. The view is obviously biased and therefore unfair.

The Sunni writers were supposed to take a favourable view of the caliphate of Hadrat Othman but as history books were mostly written during the Abbasid period and the Abbasids were opposed to the Umayyads, the tendency with pro-Abbasid writers was to suppress the achievements of the caliphate of Hadrat Othman simply because he was an Umayyad.

The source books that have come down to us are loaded with so much material unfavourable to Hadrat Othman that some of the Sunni writers when writing about Hadrat Othman took the apologetic

---

1. This is based on my own analysis.

way of approach and shifted the blame to Marwan and other Umayyads around Hadrat Othman. These writers have purposely or otherwise projected the view that Hadrat Othman was himself virtuous and honest and the Umayyads who were close to Hadrat Othman were his evil genius. Sir William Muir's view is that such allegations are frivolous and are merely due to party calumny.

We do not have many books about the biography of Hadrat Othman. In Pakistan only two books in Urdu are available on the subject. One is a book by Raza Misri and the other is a book by Taha Hussain. Taha Hussain has not furnished much of biographical details about Hadrat Othman. A greater part of the book is devoted to the justification of the agitation against Hadrat Othman. Raza Misri has given some biographical details but his impressions about the activities of Hadrat Othman are on the whole unfavourable.

Unfortunately I have not come across any publication containing an objective assessment of Hadrat Othman or his caliphate. As I have studied the history of the period and studied the facts as an impartial historian my impression is that much of the criticism that was levelled against Hadrat Othman was misplaced and the agitation against him was the result of a conspiracy sponsored by foreign powers with a view to subverting Islam from within.

Nothing succeeds like success and nothing fails like failure. As the caliphate of Hadrat Othman came to an end in chaos and confusion culminating in his assassination, we cannot regard his rule as a Caliph to be a success. As a man Hadrat Othman was not liable to any reproach; he was an embodiment of all the good qualities that a good Muslim should have. He was, however, not successful as a ruler. That was not so because of any lapse or weakness on his part; that was so because he was ahead of the times. Hadrat Umar, his predecessor, ruled with a strong hand and in this way, he kept the democratic tendencies of the Arabs under control. Hadrat Othman tried to rule as a democrat and in the absence of any safeguards to restrain the people from indulging in false propaganda, the liberties of the people degenerated into licence and brought the Muslim polity to grief. Hadrat Othman did not succeed as the Caliph not because he was weak or he favoured his relatives but because he was kind to the people and the people took undue advantage of his kindness.

HADRAT OTHMAN THE MAN

Paragon of Virtues

As a man, Hadrat Othman was the paragon of virtues. He was a man of stainless character, very pious, very religious and very virtuous. He was an embodiment of all the Islamic values. Even in the days of ignorance he never touched wine, never gambled and never had an intimacy with a woman outside wedlock. According to the Holy Prophet among the Muslims, Hadrat Othman most resembled him (the Holy Prophet) and Hadrat Ibrahim. Hadrat Othman had the look of a patriarch. There was a particular radiance about his personality. He observed all the injunctions of Islam faithfully. He would pray for a greater part of the night. He would recite the whole of the Qur'ān in the course of a single prayer. He specialised in the performance of the Hajj ceremonies.

His Modesty

He was conspicuous for his modesty. According to the Holy Prophet, after the prophets, Hadrat Othman was most conspicuous for his modesty. We have it on the authority of Hadrat Ayesha that when the companions like Hadrat Abu Bakr and Hadrat Umar visited the Holy Prophet, the Holy Prophet would receive them without any formality but when Hadrat Othman visited him he took care to be very formal. That was because of the modesty of Hadrat Othman. The Holy Prophet said that unless he paid due regard to Hadrat Othman, a modest person like him was not likely to say what he wanted to say. The Holy Prophet also used to say that the angels of Allah stood abashed before Hadrat Othman as they stood abashed before the prophets.

His Humility

Hadrat Othman was the richest persons among the Quraish. He had considerable wealth and owned a large number of slaves but in spite of that he was most humble and did not make any show of his wealth or power. It is reported that one day he was seen coming out of his land estate carrying a bundle of logs of wood. He was asked that as he had so many slaves, why he had not asked any of his slaves to carry that burden for him. He said that he did so because he wanted to make a trial of himself. He would keep awake during a greater part of the night and he would never ask any of his slaves or servants to help him in the performance of the ablutions or in any other way. When asked why he did not avail of the services of his servants and slaves he said that the night was meant for them to take rest and he did not want to disturb them in their rest.

His Generosity

He was most generous and for his generosity he was called Othman, the Ghani. He helped his relatives liberally. He was very particular in helping the orphans and the widows. He allowed them liberal stipends. On the occasion of the expedition to Tabuk, the Holy Prophet invited contributions from his followers. Hadrat Othman made the greatest contribution. The Holy Prophet gave Hadrat Othman the tidings of paradise for his unbounded generosity.

His Wisdom and Foresight

Hadrat Othman was a man of great wisdom and foresight. During the time of Hadrat Umar, Amir Muawiyah had sought his permission to invade Cypress. Hadrat Umar refused the permission on the ground that he did not want to expose the Muslims to the perils of the sea. Amir Muawiyah repeated the request when Hadrat Othman became the Caliph. Hadrat Othman gave the permission subject to the condition that in the case of such invasion Muawiyah should take his wife with him. The idea was that if Muawiyah should take his wife with him that would be indicative of the fact that no peril was involved in the sea journey.

Once a person came to Hadrat Othman after he had made love to a woman. Seeing him Hadrat Othman said: "People come to me when their eyes betray their passion." The man said, "Has the revelation not ceased after the Holy Prophet then how is it that you judge of what I have been doing?" Hadrat Othman said, "This is not revelation, this is insight born of faith".

Fear of Allah

Hadrat Othman always had a great fear of Allah. He exhorted the functionaries of the State to fear Allah and do justice to all concerned. In his sermons Hadrat Othman always exhorted the people to do good deeds which could stand them in good stead in the world hereafter. Whenever Hadrat Othman passed a graveyard he would weep bitterly. When asked to explain the reason for his weeping he said that he had heard the Holy Prophet say that the grave was the first stage to the next world and if that stage passed off peacefully, there would be little trouble at the succeeding stages.

His Munificence

Hadrat Othman was known for his munificence. He was very kind hearted. He could not bear to see anyone in distress. He liberally helped those in distress or in straitened circumstances. He cared for widows and orphans. He was very kind and considerate to his relatives. He took pleasure in helping them. He was one of the most kind hearted rulers the world has ever seen. He was, however, in advance of his age. His kindness and generosity was misconstrued as his weakness. It is unfortunate that he was misunderstood and betrayed by the people for whom he was more than a father.

His Beneficent Activities

He was always in the forefront in the undertaking of beneficent activities. When the Muslims came to Madinah there was only one well of sweet water in the city which belonged to a Jew who imposed restrictions on the use of the well by the Muslims. Hadrat Othman purchased the well from the Jew and dedicated it to the use of the Muslims. When after the conquest of Makkah, the people came to accept Islam in large numbers and the need for the extension of the Prophet's mosque was keenly felt Hadrat Othman exclusively financed the project for the extension of the mosque. In the time of Hadrat Umar a severe famine broke out in the country and there was a great scarcity of foodgrains. At that time a caravan arrived in Madinah which brought a large stock of foodgrains belonging to Hadrat Othman. The traders in Madinah rushed to the house of Hadrat Othman and tried to prevail upon him to sell the goods to them at profit. Hadrat Othman asked them to offer their bid about the profit that they would give him. The highest bid offered provided for a cent per cent profit. Hadrat Othman said that he could not accept their offer as the bid was low. The traders said that nobody could give a higher bid than that. Hadrat Othman said that he already had an offer of ten times profit. The traders wanted to know as to who had made such a high offer. Hadrat Othman said that Allah had made such offer to him. Thereupon Hadrat Othman donated the entire stock to the State for free distribution among the poor and the needy.

His Steadfastness

Hadrat Othman was known for the firmness and steadfastness

of his faith. When he was converted to Islam. His uncle Hakam, his mother Urwa and other family members put great pressure on him to recant Islam and revert to the faith of his forefathers. Hadrat Othman did not yield to such pressure and remained firm and steadfast in his faith in Islam. When in his last days, Hadrat Othman was besieged by the rioters in his house at Madinah he was assured that if he abdicated no physical harm would come to him. He refused to abdicate because he held that he could not divest himself of the robe with which Allah had vested him. He preferred to lay down his life rather than compromise with the principles for which he stood.

His Principles

Hadrat Othman was a man of principles. He held fast to his principles through thick and thin. He refused to abdicate because such abdication was against his principles. When he was besieged and some persons devoted to him wanted to fight against the rebels he forbade them to take up arms in his defence, because as a matter of principle he did not want to involve his people in a civil war. When he was asked to escape from his house through the backdoor, he held that such a course was not in conformity with his dignity as the Caliph of the Muslims. When asked to go to Syria, he said that he could not leave the city of the Holy Prophet.

REFLECTIONS ON THE CALIPHATE OF HADRAT OTHMAN

Historiographic Thought

According to the secular historiographic thought, history is primarily a matter of narration and the task of a historian is to narrate facts as they are. According to the Islamic historiographic thought, the task of a historian is not merely to narrate facts but to reflect as well on what happened in history. The caliphate of Hadrat Othman is a crucial period in the history of early Islam and we have to reflect why in spite of the eminence of Hadrat Othman, his caliphate was not as successful as it should have been and why it culminated in the tragedy of the assassination of the Caliph?

Responsibility of Hadrat Othman

In this connection the first point to be considered is, whether Hadrat Othman is to be blamed in any way for the sins of omission or commission that led to the tragedy. In the earlier part of this book I have referred to all the allegations that were levelled against Hadrat Othman. Hadrat Othman in his address delivered on the occasion of the Hajj in 655 C.E. dealt with all such allegations and refuted them with due argument. The explanation offered by Hadrat Othman is most convincing and must be accepted by every person who studies these events objectively. It may also be recalled that when Hadrat Othman made a liberal contribution towards the financing of the expedition to Tabuk, the Holy Prophet said that Hadrat Othman was not to be judged for anything thereafter. This does not mean that Hadrat Othman had been given the licence to indulge in any sins of omission and commission and was to be immune to judgement. This merely meant that whatever Hadrat Othman did later, no blame was to rest on him. In view of this verdict of the Holy Prophet, it does not lie in the mouth of any Muslim writer to pass any judgement on the alleged sins of omission and commission on the part of Hadrat Othman, I am aware of the fact that apart from the Shia writers, even the Sunni writers have found fault with Hadrat Othman in some way or the other. I am of the confirmed view that in view of what the Holy Prophet said, no Muslim writer has the authority to impute any blame to Hadrat Othman for his alleged sins of omission or commission. As such it must be held that in the crisis that overwhelmed the Muslim community during the caliphate of Hadrat Othman, no blame rested on him.

Allegations Against Hadrat Othman

According to the accounts that have come down to us the main allegations against Hadrat Othman were that he had appointed the Umayyads to high offices; that he had allowed liberal grants out of the Baitul Mal to his favourites and that he had played into the hands of unscrupulous persons. I have discussed all these allegations in the earlier part of this book. My conclusion is that there is no force in these allegations. This means that most of the allegations are false and if any allegation is factually correct, Hadrat Othman was justified in doing whatever he did.

Demands of the Agitators

If the allegations against Hadrat Othman were false or frivolous, then the next question is: what exactly were the demands of the agitators. Surprisingly in all the accounts that have come down to us, there is no mention of such demands in specific terms. The agitators made vague, confusing and conflicting demands. If the available accounts are analysed, it appears that the main demand was about the deposition of the Governors. In Egypt the demand was that Abdullah b Sa'ad should be deposed. No specific allegations were made against him. When it was pointed out that under him the revenues of the province had been increased, it was observed that the young ones of the she-camel had been starved, which implies that the process of tax collection had been oppressive. It was, however, never brought out where lay the oppression. When the rule of Abdullah b Sa'ad came to an end in Egypt with the capture of power by Muhammad b Abu Hudhaifa, the agitation did not subside; on the other hand it burst into armed revolt.

In Kufa, the people demanded that Saeed b Al 'Aas should be deposed and Abu Musa Ash'ari be appointed as the Governor. Hadrat Othman accepted the demand. The new Governor secured an undertaking from the people that they would no longer indulge in agitation. In spite of that they continued their agitation. This shows that the real object of the agitators was not to secure the deposition of Governors, their main purpose was to create unrest and confusion.

Disorder in Kufa

When what happened in Kufa is studied analytically we get some idea as to what was at the bottom of the agitation. When Saeed b Al 'Aas was the Governor of Kufa he held a gathering at his house every night which was attended by the principal citizens. At one of the meetings some one expressed the wish that certain lands in Iraq were assigned to Saeed b Al 'Aas so that he could indulge in charity. This was apparently an innocent wish but it led to violence and exchange of blows. This shows that the people of Kufa were very sensitive in the matter of the ownership of land in conquered territories. The background of the matter is that the soldiers demanded that like other booty, lands should also be distributed among the soldiers of the conquering army. Hadrat Umar did not accept the proposal. He laid down that the land left by the non-Muslims should become State property. Hadrat Othman followed the policy laid down by Hadrat Umar. Hadrat Umar had laid down restrictions on the purchase of such property. Hadrat Othman relaxed those restriction and anyone could purchase such land. Most of the land in Iraq had been purchased by the Quraish and that led Saeed b Al 'Aas to observe that Sawad was the garden of the Quraish. That was resented by the people of Kufa and they resorted to agitation. When the matter was reported to Hadrat Othman he directed that the ring leaders be sent to Syria. In his book *Othman*, Taha Hussain has found fault with this order of Hadrat Othman. He has held that the punishment of exile was severer than imprisonment and the cutting of hands and feet. I fail to understand the logic in the argument of Taha Hussain. It is not understood how the sending of certain agitators from one part of the country to another as a corrective measure could be severer than imprisonment and even the cutting of hands and feet. In Syria Amir Muawiyah tried to make these people see the light of reason but he failed. Then they were sent to "Jazira". Abdur Rahman, the ruler of Jazira, dealt with these people harshly and they repented. Ashtar, their leader, next went to Madinah where he repented before Hadrat Othman. Hadrat Othman allowed him to return to Kufa. What these people really wanted was that lands in conquered territories should be distributed among the soldiers of the conquering army. When they repented, this implied that they had withdrawn their demand. Thus when in 656 C.E., the people from Kufa marched to Madinah to put pressure on Hadrat Othman, they had no demand to present; they were merely agitating for the sake of agitation.

Contempt of Authority

In his book on *Othman*, Taha Hussain has quoted a letter addressed by Ashtar, the rebel of Kufa, to Hadrat Othman. On the strength of this letter, Taha Hussain argues that the rebels did not deny the authority of Hadrat Othman; they merely wanted the government to be just and fair.

This letter is quoted hereunder:

> "From Malik b Harith (Ashtar) to the Caliph who is guilty and blameworthy; who has strayed from the path of the Holy Prophet and who has neglected the Holy Qur'ān.
>
> We have read your letter. Your rulers should refrain from being tyrannical. They should not exile the citizens. We agree to be loyal to you. You are under the impression that we have acted unjustly. This is your misconception that has hurled you in the precipice, whereby tyranny appears as justice to you and falsehood looks as the truth to you. Refrain from being unjust

to our people do not exile them from their cities and do not appoint your favourites as our Governors. Repent before Allah and appoint Abdullah b Qais or Abu Musa Ash'ari or Hudhaifa as our Governor. We are happy with these persons. Save us from your Walid, your Saeed and other men of your family."

It is very strange that on the basis of this letter, Taha Hussain supports the stand of the rebels and finds fault with Hadrat Othman. This is most unfair and uncharitable. A mere glance at the letter will show that it is coached in most disrespectful language. At the outset, Ashtar has expressed in very strong terms his want of confidence in Hadrat Othman by referring to him as guilty, blameworthy, one who has strayed from the right path and one who has neglected the Qur'ān. Nothing could be more disrespectful to the authority of the Caliph and after expressing such no-confidence it was preposterous to hold that they were loyal to him. The trend of the letter clearly betrays that the rebels were bent on mischief and they wanted to create disorder on one pretext or the other.

After reading the above letter I have arrived at the conclusion that the rebels had no real grievance against the government; they were merely spearheading a subversive movement, at the instance of powers hostile to Islam. Those who raised the bogey of tyranny and injustice on the part of Hadrat Othman or his government were merely playing in the hands of the enemies of Islam.

Conspiracy against Islam

We have next to ask the question: if the agitation against Hadrat Othman was a conspiracy against Islam why did Hadrat Othman not take steps to crush it with force? No hard and fast answer can be given to this question but some probabilities can be attempted. At that stage of the history of Islam, the State was organised to deal with the enemy from without; it lacked the organisation to deal with the enemy from within. Within the country the State rested on the moral authority of Islam and even no police had been organised. The State had armed forces but the task of the army was to fight the non-Muslims across the border. Hadrat Othman was averse to use the army for the purposes of civil war amongst the Muslims. Hadrat Othman did all he could to use the moral force at his disposal. He explained his position at great length. He categorically refuted all the allegations levelled against him. When in spite of that the agitation persisted, Hadrat Othman willingly offered his own life rather than summon any force to his aid and thereby involve the people in bloodshed and civil war. This is a unique case in history. No other ruler in history ever refused to use force for self-defence. In refusing the use of force for self-defence, Hadrat Othman set up admirable example of self-sacrifice. This trait of the character of Hadrat Othman has not been fully brought out in the accounts that have come down to us. It is necessary that this aspect of the character of Hadrat Othman should be understood in proper perspective and Hadrat Othman should be honoured as one of the greatest heroes of Islam. He sacrificed his life for he did not like to shed the blood of other Muslims merely to protect him. This assures for Hadrat Othman a high ranking place among the great Muslims.

Why Failure?

If it is held that no blame rested on Hadrat Othman and his place is among the great men of history, the question that puzzles us is: why in spite of his greatness, the Caliphate of Hadrat Othman ended in disaster? The Arabs were individualists and highly democratic. Democracy unless effectively controlled is apt to degenerate into licence. That was exactly the position in the pre-Islamic era of ignorance. The Holy Prophet introduced a new order, whereunder the democratic urges of the people were effectively controlled by the moral injunctions of Islam and the exemplary character of the Holy Prophet. After the death of the Holy Prophet, the moral influence of the Holy Prophet was no longer available. The Holy Prophet was succeeded by Hadrat Abu Bakr. Hadrat Abu Bakr was known as a kind hearted man but as Caliph he followed a stern line of action. Even when men like Hadrat Umar advised that the offer of the tribes not to pay Zakat be accepted, Hadrat Abu Bakr took the stand that if Zakat was withheld, he would fight. That saved the situation. The apostasy campaigns were over within a year and the whole of Arabia was won back for Islam. Hadrat Umar who followed Abu Bakr was already known for his hot temper. He kept the people under strict control and as such during his caliphate the democratic urges of the people could not degenerate into a licence. Hadrat Othman was liberal, soft spoken and kind hearted. Under Hadrat Othman there was a relaxation of control and because of such relaxation, the democratic urges of the people degenerated into licence and there was a recrudescence of the values of the days of ignorance which Islam had taken pains to suppress.

Dilemma of Democracy

We have next to ask ourselves the question whether Hadrat Othman is to be blamed in any way for this relaxation of control and the degeneration of the democratic urges of the people into licence? We cannot impute any blame to Hadrat Othman in this behalf for the simple reason that this issue has not been satisfactorily resolved during the last fourteen hundred years and the dilemma of democracy continues to be as serious and grave today as it was in the time of Hadrat Othman.

The dilemma of democracy is that while at individual level the Muslims are the most democratic people in the world, at the collective level democracy has practically failed in almost all the Muslim countries in the world. In the course of Islamic history when there was a strong ruler he maintained law and order and kept the democratic urges of the people under control. This evoked reaction and the people led the struggle for the restoration of liberties. With the restoration of liberties, democratic urges of the people once again degenerated into licence. Things have thus moved in a vicious circle and history has witnessed a succession of dictatorships and loose democratic rule creating problems of law and order.

It is unfortunate that we have so far not evolved a political system whereunder a proper balance could be maintained between the democratic urges of the people and the requirements of law and order. This unsatisfactory state of affairs is not peculiar to Islam; it applies to secular orders as well. As a matter of fact the so-called democracy of the western pattern is a spent force. The need of the day is to evolve a new political system based on the principles of Islam. In the Holy Qur'ãn, Allah has referred to the Muslim community as the best community among mankind. The lesson that is brought out by the life story of Hadrat Othman is that we should create a new political order whereunder proper balance is maintained between liberty and authority, according to the principles of Islam. I visualise that the day is not far when the Muslims would once again assume the leadership of the world and sponsor a political system which is a happy synthesis of liberty and authority. May Allah help us in our mission!

CHRONOLOGY

576 C.E.	Birth of Hadrat Othman.
596	Death of Affan, the father of Hadrat Othman.
610	Conversion to Islam.
611	Marriage to Hadrat Ruqayya, the daughter of the Holy Prophet.
615	Migration to Abyssinia.
616	Birth of Hadrat Othman's son Abdullah.
618	Return from Abyssinia.
622	Migration to Madinah.
624	Death of Hadrat Ruqayya.
625	Battle of Uhud.
626	Marriage to Umm Kulthum, another daughter of the Holy Prophet.
627	Death of Hadrat Othman's son Abdullah.
628	Baiyat ur Ridwan.
630	Conquest of Makkah.
631	Expedition to Tabuk.
632	Farewell Pilgrimage and death of the Holy Prophet. Election of Hadrat Abu Bakr as the first Caliph of Islam.
634	Death of Hadrat Abu Bakr and the election of Hadrat Umar as the second Caliph of Islam.
644	Death of Hadrat Umar and the election of Hadrat Othman as the third Caliph of Islam.
645	Deposition of Mugheera b Shu'ba from the governorship of Kufa. Appointment of Saad b Abi Waqas as the Governor of Kufa. Byzantines invasion of Egypt.
646	Byzantines driven away from Egypt. Deposition of 'Amr b Al 'Aas from the governorship of Egypt. Appointment of Abdullah b Sa'ad as the Governor of Egypt. Conquest of North Africa. Battle of

Sabetula, Deposition of Sa'ad b Abi Waqas from the governorship of Kufa. Appointment of Walid b Uqba as the Governor of Kufa.

647 Re-conquest of Azarbaijan and Armenia.

648 Deposition of Abu Musa Ash'ari from the governorship of Basra. Appointment of Abdullah b 'Aamir as the Governor of Basra. Defeat of the Byzantines in Asia Minor. Hadrat Othman marries Naila b Farafsa.

649 Conquest of the island of Cypress. Re-conquest of Fars. Hadrat Othman leads the Hajj ceremonies, and offers four rakaats of prayers at Mina instead of availing of the concession of offering two rakaats.

650 Recension of the Holy Qur'ān. Hadrat Othman has a well dug at Arees. The Holy Prophet's ring falls from the hand of Hadrat Othman and is lost. Campaigns in Kirman and Seestan. Campaign against Nubia.

651 Deposition of Walid b Uqba from the governorship of Kufa. Appointment of Saeed b 'Aas as the Governor of Kufa. Campaign in Khurasan. Death of Yazdjurd, the emperor of Persia. Re-conquest of Tabaristan. Naval battle in Egypt.

652 Campaigns in Khurasan. The Byzantines defeated in the naval battle of the Masts. Death of Abu Sufyan. Death of Abu Dhar Ghifari.

653 Campaigns in Transoxiana.

654 Saeed b 'Aas is removed form the governorship of Kufa. Abu Musa Ash'ari is appointed as the Governor of Kufa. Agitation against Hadrat Othman.

655 Hadrat Othman presides at the Hajj ceremonies, and refutes all the allegations levelled against him.

656 Armed revolt against Hadrat Othman. Martyrdom of Hadrat Othman.

BIBLIOGRAPHY

1. *Othman bin Affan*: Raza Misri
2. *Othman*: Taha Hussain
3. *Tarikh-ul-Umum al Islamia*: Khizri Bek
4. *Sirat-ul-Khulafa*: Khizri Bek
5. *Kitab-ul-Khulafa al Islamia*: Rashid Rida
6. *Ashab-e-Rasul Ke Karname*: Nabi Ahmad Suha
7. *The Book of the Battles*: Al Waqidi
8. *Tabaqat*: Ibn Saad
9. *The Book of Conquests*: Al Baladhuri
10. *History*: Tabari
11. *History of the Times*: Masudi
12. *Universal History*: Ibn Khaldun
13. *Lions of the Forest*: Ibn al Athir
14. *Demise of the Prominent People*: Ibn Khallikan
15. *History*: Yakubi
16. *Heroes of Early Islam*: G.A. Salik
17. *Hundred Great Muslims*: Khawaja Jameel Ahmad
18. *Digest of the Holy Qur'ān*: Prof. Masudul Hasan
19. *Hadrat Abu Bakr Sidiq*: Prof. Masudul Hasan
20. *Hadrat Umar Farooq*: Prof. Masudul Hasan
21. *Life of Iqbal (two volumes)*: Prof Masudul Hasan
22. *Life and Thought of Maulana Maududi (two volumes)* Prof. Masudul Hasan
23. *Life of Hadrat Data Ganj Bakhsh*: Prof. Masudul Hasan
24. *History of Islam (three volumes)*: Prof. Masudul Hasan
25. *Short History of the Saracens*: Ameer Ali
26. *A Study of Islamic History*: K.Ali
27. *Cambridge History of Islam*
28. *History of the Arabs*: Philip K. Hitti
29. *History of the Islamic People*: Brockelmann
30. *The Arab Kingdom and its Fall*: Wellhaussen
31. *History of the Caliphs*: Suyuti.

32. *The Glorious Caliphate*: Athar Hussain.
33. *Annals of the Early Caliphate*: Sir William Muir
34. *Successors of Muhammad:* Washington Irving
35. *Muslim Conquest of Persia*: Lt. Gen. A. I. Akram.
36. *Muslim Conquest of Egypt and North Africa*: Lt. Gen. A. L Akram
37. *Muhammad and the Conquests of Islam*: Gabrieli
38. *Life of Muhammad*: Guillamme
39. *The Prophet Muhammad*: Haji Ghulam Sarwar
40. *Muhammad at Makkah*: Montgomery Watt
41. *Muhammad at Madinah*: Montgomery Watt
42. *Muhammad, Prophet and Statesman*: Montgomery Watt
43. *Muhammad, the Prophet*: Iqbal Ali Shah
44. *Short Encyclopædia of Islam*